JOSE~~
THEOLOGI<

Ontology & History:
- 28, 40-42,
- Review: 43
- 39-42

- 29: 2
  IT ↔ ET

- 37, 41, 44

JOSEPH RATZINGER'S
THEOLOGICAL RETRACTATIONS

CONG QUY JOSEPH LAM

PETER LANG

Bern · Berlin · Bruxelles · Frankfurt am Main · New York · Oxford · Wien

Bibliographic information published by die Deutsche Nationalbibliothek
Die Deutsche Nationalbibliothek lists this publication in the Deutsche National-
bibliografie; detailed bibliographic data is available on the Internet
at ‹http://dnb.d-nb.de›.

British Library Cataloguing-in-Publication Data: A catalogue record for this book
is available from The British Library, Great Britain

Library of Congress Cataloging-in-Publication Data

Lam, Joseph C. Quy (Joseph Cong Quy)
 Joseph Ratzinger's theological retractations / Cong Quy Joseph Lam. – First edition
  pages cm
 Includes bibliographical references and index.
 ISBN 978-3-0343-1449-7
 1. Benedict XVI, Pope, 1927- 2. Catholic Church–Doctrines–History–
20th century. 3. Catholic Church–Doctrines–History–21st century. I. Title.
 BX1378.6.L35 2013
 230'.2092–dc23
                              2013022823

The print of this book was supported by the Australasian Province of the Order
of Saint Augustine and the Australian Catholic University.

ISBN 978-3-0343-1449-7 pb.   ISBN 978-3-0351-0607-7 eBook

© Peter Lang AG, International Academic Publishers, Bern 2013
Hochfeldstrasse 32, CH-3012 Bern, Switzerland
info@peterlang.com, www.peterlang.com

All rights reserved.
All parts of this publication are protected by copyright.
Any utilisation outside the strict limits of the copyright law, without the permission
of the publisher, is forbidden and liable to prosecution.
This applies in particular to reproductions, translations, microfilming, and storage
and processing in electronic retrieval systems.

Printed in Switzerland

Table of Contents

Foreword
by Archbishop Gerhard Ludwig Müller,
Prefect of the Congregation for the Doctrine of the Faith 9

Preface
by Prosper Cardinal Grech, OSA 11

Abbreviations 13

Introduction 15

Chapter One: *Revelation* 23

1. Introduction 23
2. The Concept of Revelation in Bonaventure 30
    2.1 The *Habilitation* on Bonaventure 30
    2.2 Revelation as God's Self-communication and Action ... 34
    2.3 Metaphysical Foundation of Revelation 39
    2.4 Revelation and Salvation History 42
    2.5 Jesus Christ as the Centre of History 45
    2.6 Conclusion and Prospect for Vatican II 51
    2.7 Ratzinger and the Vatican II Constitution
         "Dei Verbum" 54
    2.8 Ratzinger's Critical Assessment of
         "De fontibus revelationis" 57
    2.9 Ratzinger's Comments on the Achievements of
         "Dei Verbum" 64
    2.10 Ratzinger's Concept of Revelation and
         Contemporary Approaches to Theology 71
3. Summary 86

Chapter Two: *Christology* 89

1. Introduction 89
2. The Church's Remembrance as the Realm
   of Understanding 95
3. The Faith in Jesus Christ 100
4. The God of Jesus Christ 105
5. The Spiritual Christology of Joseph Ratzinger 109
6. Christology and Prayer 113
7. The Lord's Prayer and Gethsemane as Distinguished
   Manifestation of Jesus Christ's Inner Reality 117
8. Christology and Soteriology 120
9. *Excursus*: Christian Worship vs. Roman Cult:
   Charity as Form of Christ's Sacrifice 123
10. Christology in *Dominus Iesus* 127
11. *Jesus of Nazareth* – A Theological-Spiritual Exploration
    into the Real Jesus 135
12. Summary 143

Chapter Three: *Ecclesiology* 147

1. Introduction 147
2. Ratzinger in the School of Augustine 151
   2.1 *Excursus*: The Open System in the Theological
       Methodology of Gottlieb Söhngen 155
   2.2 Ratzinger's Methodological Approach
       to Augustine's Writings 159
3. The Awakening of Ecclesiology in the Post-War
   Germany: *Corpus Christi mysticum* vs. People of God 160
4. Ratzinger and the Empathy for the Faith
   of the Church 164
5. Ratzinger and Augustine's Concept of the Church 167
   5.1 Augustine and the People of God 168
   5.2 Against the Manicheans: The Visible Catholicity
       of the Church 172

    5.3 The Discovery of Neo-Platonism
        and the Anti-Donatist Controversy 174
6. The House or Temple of God 179
    6.1 The New Cult 181
    6.2 The Eucharist as Sacrament of the Body of Christ 186
        6.2.1 The Eucharist as Sacrifice 187
    6.3 Active, Full and Fruitful Participation
        in the Eucharistic Celebration 194
    6.4 Eucharist and Mission 200
    6.5 *Dominus Iesus* and the Universality of the Church 205
7. Summary 210

Conclusion 213

Selective Bibliography 219

Index of Names 227

Foreword[1]

During the Second Vatican Council Joseph Ratzinger was the theological adviser to Joseph Cardinal Frings, Archbishop of Cologne, and at the same time an official *peritus* at the Council. In October 1962 he conceived the initial text for a new schema for the document on divine revelation, which was subsequently expanded into a fuller text, developed in co-operation with Karl Rahner.[2] Yet Joseph Ratzinger's active engagement with the development of the concept of revelation extends back to the time of the authorship of his *Habilitationsschrift*, completed in 1955 and published in 1959 with the title *Saint Bonaventure's Theology of History*, together with a number of shorter studies on Bonaventure.[3]

These publications mark out a path which led directly to the Dogmatic Constitution on Divine Revelation, *Dei Verbum*. God communicates his own self and chooses tradition and Scripture as the forms of his self-communication, which are passed on in the Church in an authentic and authoritative way. Revelation precedes Scripture and is borne witness to within it. This means that revelation always remains greater than what is written in Scripture, and that the Church, as the subject of understanding, accompanies Scripture. The concept of revelation requires the one who receives, who undertakes life's journey in answer to God's promise of salvation given in revelation.

---

1 Translated from German by Robert Gascoigne.
2 Joseph Ratzinger, *Zur Lehre des Konzils. Formulierung – Vermittlung – Deutung* (= JRGS 7), Freiburg 2012, 177–209. *(On the Teaching of the Council. Development – Communication – Interpretation.)*
3 Published in: Joseph Ratzinger, *Offenbarungsverständnis und Geschichtstheologie Bonaventuras. Habilitationsschrift und Bonaventurastudien* (= JRGS 2), Freiburg 2009, 419–647. *(Bonaventure's Concept of Revelation and Theology of History. Habilitationsschrift and Studies on Bonaventure.)*

Even though revelation has its highest and definitive expression in Jesus Christ, this 'divine approach to humanity'[4] is a process which is real even today. The guarantee of this is that the revealing Word of God does not exist as an historically sealed-off archaeological memory, but rather inscribes itself as a living reality in the hearts of the faithful: 'Revelation is something living, something greater and, moreover, the hearing and receiving of revelation is integral to it, otherwise it has not in fact become revelation.'[5]

In his writings, Joseph Ratzinger always had the whole in view. Church, Revelation, Scripture and tradition may not be separated from each other and are 'inseparable from the living God.'[6] Beyond the particularization of Biblical texts as subject to the historical-critical method, his perspectives are building blocks for a deeper understanding of the complexity of meaning in the work of salvation. His syntheses will continue to challenge theology and to provide fresh resources for responding to the questions of our time.

In view of all this, I am glad that the author of this study has set a new stone in the mosaic of interpretation of the theology of Joseph Ratzinger/Benedict XVI, for the benefit of scholarly discussion and for all who are interested in and engaged with this subject.

I wish this scholarly work broad dissemination and a good reception.

Gerhard Ludwig Müller
Archbishop
Prefect of the Congregation for the Doctrine of the Faith

Rome, on the Feast of the Presentation of the Lord, 2013.

---

[4] Joseph Ratzinger, *Aus meinem Leben. Erinnerungen (1927–1977)*, Stuttgart 1998, 129. (Joseph Ratzinger, Milestones: Memoirs, 1927–1977)

[5] Joseph Ratzinger, *Aus meinem Leben. Erinnerungen (1927–1977)*, Stuttgart 1998, 129.

[6] Joseph Ratzinger, *Aus meinem Leben. Erinnerungen (1927–1977)*, Stuttgart 1998, 129.

Preface

Benedict XVI is not the first pope-theologian, he follows Leo the Great, Gregory the Great, and a number of other pontiffs. As professor of theology he published books and articles, he contributed to the discussions and documents of Vatican II. As prefect of the Congregation for the Doctrine of the Faith he guided many important documents. His activities as pope have not hindered his research, the three volumes *Jesus of Nazareth* are bestsellers, as are many of his minor publications, with a broad spectrum of subjects. Ratzinger is much more flexible and open to critique than some people think, his recent exposure to *twitter* is the best proof of his breadth of vision.

As Supreme Pontiff, Pope Benedict is bound to defend the traditional dogmatic teaching of the Church. As a theologian, he is freer to express his personal considerations and make public the outcome of his research. Theologians do change their stance, however; they can leave behind earlier convictions, progress in other fields of study or alter their opinions regarding certain subjects of which they had no longer convinced. They would not be true theologians if they do not enter into discussion with other thinkers, be they Catholic or not, to enrich their own ideas. When St. Augustine, later in life, wrote his *Retractationes*, he pinpointed various changes of opinion, admitted to progress of thought and corrected some errors. It is therefore no wonder that both Ratzinger himself as well as his colleagues can trace the development of his theologizing; he too would be entitled to compose his own *Retractationes*. What Joseph Ratzinger did not do Joseph Lam has done for him. The present volume traces the various stages of Pope Benedict's theology and seeks to detect changes of opinion, withdrawals and fresh openings. It is not inconceivable that if Pope Benedict reads this book he might discover something about himself of which he was not aware, this happens to all of us

11

when we hear or read other peoples' comments on our writings, but whether Lam's observations are just or not it is only for Ratzinger to decide.

Prosper Cardinal Grech, OSA
Rome

Abbreviations

Documents of the Church

CCC	*Compendium of the Catechism of the Catholic Church.*
GS	*Gaudium et Spes.*
SC	*Sacrosanctum Concilium.*
SCar	*Sacramentum Caritatis.*

Works by Joseph Ratzinger / Pope Benedict XVI

CDV	*Commentary on the Documents of Vatican II.*
DC	*Deus Caritas Est.*
DoS	*Dialectics of Secularization. One Reason and Religion.*
ET	*The End of Time.*
EV	*Ecclesiology of Vatican II.*
FoC	*Fathers of the Church. From Clement of Rome to Augustine.*
GChr	*The God of Jesus Christ. Meditations on God in the Trinity.*
GnU	*God is near us.*
GW	*God and the World. Believing and Living in Our Time. A Conversation with Peter Seewald.*
JRGS	*Joseph Ratzingers Gesammelte Schriften.*
JoN	*Jesus of Nazareth.*
LoChr	*To Look on Christ. Exercises in Faith, Hope, and Love.*
IC	*Introduction to Christianity.*
LW	*Licht der Welt.*
Mi	*Milestones. Memoirs 1927–1977.*
NSL	*A New Song for the Lord.*
NTM	*The Nature and Mission of Theology. Approaches to Understanding Its Role in the Light of Present Controversy.*
OGB	*Offenbarungs- und Geschichtstheologie Bonaventuras.*
OWC	*On the Way to Jesus Christ.*

PFF	*Pilgrim Fellowship of Faith.*
PO	*The Pierced One. An Approach to a Spiritual Christology.*
PCT	*Principles of Catholic Theology.*
RREP	*The Ratzinger Report: An Exclusive Interview of the State of the Church.*
RT	*Revelation and Tradition.*
SE	*Salt of the Earth: Christianity and the Catholic Church at the end of the Millennium. An Interview with Peter Seewald.*
SL	*Spirit of Liturgy.*
SpS	*Spe salvi.*
THV	*Theological Highlights of Vatican II.*
UChr	*Unterwegs zu Jesus Christus.*
VHG	*Volk und Haus Gottes in Augustins Lehre von der Kirche.*

Journals

EphTL	*Ephemerides Theologicae Lovaniensis.*
NV	*Nova et Vetera.*
ZfRG	*Zeitschrift für Religions- und Geistesgeschichte.*

Introduction

Joseph Ratzinger is one of the most prolific and prominent Catholic theologians of our time. His theological career began more than six decades ago and continues to this day, even as Pope. His writings are bestsellers, and have been translated into a number of major languages. While there has always been great interest in his theology, it is only in recent years that theologians have begun to study his writings anew. My book, published in 2009, endeavoured to examine the theological affinity between Augustine of Hippo and Joseph Ratzinger by focussing on the latter's early reflections on the Church and on the theology of the Church Fathers, in particular Augustine.[1] Since 2009 many other publications in German,[2] in

---

1   Joseph Lam Cong Quy, *The theologische Verwandtschaft: Augustinus von Hippo und Joseph Ratzinger/ Papst Benedikt XVI.* (Würzburg: Echter, 2009).
2   To name a few recent publications in German: Hansjürgen Verweyen, *Joseph Ratzinger – Benedikt XVI. Die Entwicklung seines Denkens* (Darmstadt: Primus, 2007); Id., *Ein unbekannter Ratzinger. Die Habilitationsschrift von 1955 als Schlüssel zu seiner Theologie* (Regensburg: Friedrich Pustet, 2010); Maximilian H. Heim, *Joseph Ratzinger – Kirchliche Existenz und existentielle Theologie* (Frankfurt: Peter Lang, 2005); and my own work Joseph Lam Cong Quy, *Theologische Verwandtschaft: Augustinus von Hippo und Joseph Ratzinger/Papst Benedikt XVI.* (Würzburg: Echter, 2009); Rudolf Voderholzer (ed.), *Der Logos-gemäße Gottesdienst. Theologie der Liturgie bei Joseph Ratzinger* (Regensburg: Friedrich Pustet, 2009); Kurt Koch, *Das Geheimnis des Senfkorns. Grundzüge des theologischen Denkens von Papst Benedikt XVI.* (Regenburg: Friedrich Pustet, 2010); Andrei Marga, *Gott heute denken. Zur Philosophie und Theologie Joseph Ratzingers* (Regensburg: Friedrich Pustet, 2010); Marianne Schlosser – Franz-Xaver Heibl (eds.), *Gegenwart der Offenbarung: zu den Bonaventura-Forschungen Joseph Ratzingers* (Regensburg: Friedrich Pustet, 2011); Christian Schaller (ed.), *Kirche – Sakrament und Gemeinschaft. Zu Ekklesiologie und Ökumene bei Joseph Ratzinger* (Regensburg: Friedrich Pustet, 2011); Michaela-Christine Hastetter – Helmut Hoping (eds.), *Ein hörendes Herz. Hinführung zur Theologie und Spiritualität von Joseph Ratzinger/Papst Benedikt XVI.* (Regensburg: Friedrich Pustet, 2012). In

Spanish[3], in Italian[4] and in English[5] have emerged. For example, Maximilian H. Heim considers Ratzinger as an ecclesiologist because the Church forms a central aspect of Ratzinger's theology.[6] Others see in the liturgy a 'prominent and inescapable feature' of his Pontificate.[7] Again some recognize in Christology 'the inner motivation and fulcrum of his theology.'[8] Still another view points to the dominance of an "Augustinian Thomism" in the theology of Ratzinger.[9]

3   Most prominent is Pablo Sarto Blanco, 'La teología de Joseph Ratzinger. Temas centrales', in *Revista Catalana de Teología* 36,1 (2011), 257–281; Id., 'El concilio de Joseph Ratzinger. Notas sobre su actividad durante el Vaticano II', in *Anurario de Historia de la Iglesia* 21 (2012), 245–281; Id., *Joseph Ratzinger: Vida y Teología*, (Madrid: Rialp, 2006); Id., '"Logos". Joseph Ratzinger y la historia de una palabra', in *Revista de filosofía y psicología* 14 (2006), 57–86.
4   Joseph Ratzinger – Benedetto XVI, *Fede, ragione, verità e amore. La teologia di Joseph Ratzinger*, edited by U. Casale (Torino: Lindau), 2009.
5   Aidan Nichols, *The Thought of Pope Benedict XVI: An Introduction to the Theology of Joseph Ratzinger* (London – New York: Burns and Oates, 2007); Maximilian H. Heim, *Joseph Ratzinger: Life in the Church and Living Theology: Fundamentals of Ecclesiology* (San Francisco: Ignatius, 2007); Joseph Murphy, *Christ, Our Joy. The Theological Vision of Pope Benedict XVI* (San Francisco: Ignatius, 2008); Tracey Rowland, *Ratzinger's faith : The Theology of Pope Benedict XVI* (Oxford – Melbourne: University of Oxford, 2008); Id., *Benedict XVI: A Guide For the Perplexed* (London – New York: T & T Clark, 2010); Emery De Gáal, *The Theology of Pope Benedict XVI: The Christocentric Shift* (New York: Palgrave Macmillan, 2010); Anselm J. Gribbin, *Pope Benedict XVI and the Liturgy. Understanding Recent Liturgical Developments* (Herefordshire: Palgrave Macmillan, 2011).
6   Heim, 9.
7   Gribbin, vi.
8   De Gaál, 1.
9   Rowland, 151 f. It is interesting to note that Ratzinger rejects the suggestion by some scholars who depicted Bonaventure as an incomplete Thomist because of his election to the high pastoral office of his order. This election has prevented him from academic progress, and thus from reaching the scholastic maturity. But Ratzinger contests this interpretation by claiming the opposite. According to him, it was precisely this pastoral office which prevented Bonaventure from intellectual narrowness. His concept of revelation was therefore less theoretically instructive. The pastoral awareness takes into account the mystery of God's revelation. Surely the term "Augustinian Thomism" cannot be applied to Bonaventure, and perhaps less to Ratzinger; see *JRGS* 2, 79–80.

These studies are valuable contributions to the many specific aspects of Ratzinger's life and thoughts, such as on liturgy, ecclesiology or Christology.

Why, one could ask, is there a need for another book on Ratzinger? An academic book, of course, is an intellectual exercise aiming to rectify certain deficits. However, this is only possible on the basis of new materials and evidences. Such an event in this case was the release of the critical edition of Ratzinger's *opera omnia* in 2009 by the Herder publishing house in Freiburg, Germany.[10] It was the then Bishop of Regensburg Gerhard Ludwig Müller, now Prefect of the Congregation for the Doctrine of the Faith, who in May 18th 2007 established the Pope Benedict XVI Institute in Regensburg. Its purpose is to promote the publication of the works of Joseph Ratzinger.[11] In cooperation with Herder the Institute of Pope Benedict XVI plans a total of sixteen volumes of which six are now readily available to the theological community. For the first time Ratzinger's early writings on Patristic theology and Augustine (1951–1963) and more importantly his entire post-doctoral thesis *(Habilitationsschrift)* on Bonaventure's conception of revelation, including his studies of medieval theologians, have been published in a complete scholarly edition.[12]

These early works permit a deeper and more comprehensive insight into Ratzinger's theological method and the development of his key ideas, such as Revelation, Christology and ecclesiology. They allow us to examine the genesis of Ratzinger's theological thought. The examination of these early works also shows the theological coherence of Ratzinger's thinking which was instrumental for his later involvement at the Second Vatican Council (1962–1965). These early works are also keys to the understanding of the exercise of his *magisterial* roles, first as Prefect of the CDF and now as Pope. At the

---

10 The critical edition is named as *Joseph Ratzingers Gesammelte Schriften* (abbreviated as *JRGS*).
11 <www.institut-papst-benedikt.de>.
12 Up to this date only the second part of his post-doctoral thesis was edited in German, English and Italian.

same time the early works are also clues which permit us to recognize the methodological impact of his theological teacher Gottlieb Söhngen. This work has not been done so far.

In reviewing *(Retractations)* Ratzinger's own theological works on key issues, such as Revelation, Christology and ecclesiology, I will offer a comprehensive account of Ratzinger's theological *genesis*, bearing in mind the various stages in the life and ministry of Ratzinger. This theological appraisal also explains the choice of the title of this book. The word "Retractations" is the name of one of Augustine's mature works which he completed in the year 426, four years before his death. The Latin word *"Retractationes"* is often translated in English as "Reconsiderations". In his work Augustine offered a retrospective re-lecture and a personal commentary of his own theological writings. In the prologue of his *Retractationes* he writes:

> For a long time I have been thinking about and planning to do something which I, with God's assistance, am now undertaking because I do not think it should be postponed: with a kind of judicial severity, I am reviewing my works – books, letters, and sermons – and, as it were, with the pen of a censor, I am indicating what dissatisfies me.[13]

The reason for this review was his concern that the vast quantity of his writings might serve not only as a source of orthodox theology, but might also be used as sources against Augustine himself. By focussing too selectively on certain statements of Augustine's writings, his opponents had previously accused him of being theologically inconsistent, in particular on the question of grace and free will. With the *Retractationes* the aged Bishop of Hippo reacted against his critics by demonstrating his faithfulness to the teaching of the Church. Thus, the *Retractations* gives an account of the unity of his theology, perhaps comparable to his *Confessiones* which offers a spiritual testimony of his conversion.

---

13   *Retr.*, Prologue (The Fathers of the Church, vol. 60), 3.

Ratzinger endured the same accusation theologically. It has been suggested by some writers that Ratzinger's theological thought should be divided into two chronological-theological phases. According to these persons, in the first phase there was the young progressive Ratzinger before and at Vatican II, and in the other there is a conservative Ratzinger after Vatican II, who, disillusioned with the liberal society, makes efforts to turn back the wheel of time. A comparison of his early writings and with his later magisterial publications as Prefect of the CDF and as Pope clearly shows the consistency of Ratzinger's theological thought. Of course, it is an organic unity of thoughts because nuances in personal thoughts evolve and become clearer during the various stages of life. And yet the constants of his theological thought are planted in his early studies of Augustine and Bonaventure, although their theological perspectives mature systematically only in the dialogue with contemporary authors.

Thus, this present book does not intend to correct or to modify Ratzinger's theological thought, but to appraise it in its whole, highlightening the various stages within the constants of his thinking. In applying this title to my study of Ratzinger's theological works, I would like to re-read his theology from the sources that only so recently have become available. This is a task not without risk. However, it is similar to the risk Ratzinger took on board when he studied the works of Augustine in the early 1950s.

In the preface of his book on Augustine's ecclesiology, Ratzinger acknowledged that his embarking on this doctoral project was not without risk. Post-war Germany in 1950s experienced profound social and political changes, and furthermore, the ecclesiastical post-war situation showed many signs of uncertainties, in spite the fact the Church was awakened in the souls of the people. At the theological faculty in Munich there were only limited resources available. Additionally, the search for a new theological-philosophical methodology was just in its infancy. Amidst these uncertainties Professor Gottlied Söhngen entrusted to his student Ratzinger, who was at this time only 24 years old, a very difficult task to solve: Ratzinger should investigate the ecclesiological concept of Augustine and see whether

Augustine would confirm the then emerging ecclesiology. Amazingly, Ratzinger completed his thesis in just nine months. More than that, his thesis also revised some of the common theological views which had dominated the theological debates of that time.

Any intending author of a book about Ratzinger's theology must accept the reality that much has already been written on this subject. But there is another equally important obstacle. What is the right method to adopt? When I embarked on this project some five years ago, I was confronted with the question of where to start. I had two possibilities. Either I could examine Ratzinger's writing in chronological order or I could study his works from a theological perspective. But a mere historical-chronological approach may be less desirable because it would put Ratzinger in a chain of historical theology. Since faith concerns the mystery of God which goes beyond historical reasoning, it is therefore logical to begin with theology. This approach carries certain risks. Ratzinger not only is a brilliant theologian, but also Pope. He belongs to the few still alive who actively participated in the recent major events of the Church, such as the Second Vatican Council. His theological reflection testifies the ups and downs of philosophical, biblical and theological traditions. It seems impossible to capture the entire richness of Ratzinger's thinking. What I present here are only the *nuclei* of his thinking.

As *scientia dei* theology begins with divine revelation which is the foundation of faith. The first chapter of this book therefore begins with the investigation of Ratzinger's post-doctoral thesis on Bonaventure's idea of revelation which Ratzinger completed in the second half of 1960s. The reason for Ratzinger's choice of Bonaventure lies in the latter's historical and spiritual epistemology. This Franciscan scholar stood at the very beginning of the scholastic era which was not yet entirely imprisoned by an inflexible scholastic system. Furthermore, Bonaventure's greatness lies in his spirituality which he inherited from St. Francis who preserved a great deal of the evangelical heritage. From this theological-spiritual background Bonaventure's conception of revelation differs from the prince of scholasticism Thomas Aquinas whose theology inhaled fully the

Aristotelian philosophical system. For this reason the Thomistic concept of revelation appeals more to intellectual perception. Bonaventure interpreted revelation as divine action which includes creation and illumination. Thus, divine revelation is not a manifestation of a set of divine truths which, however, can remain external to the life of the faithful. For the Franciscan minister general revelation happens through words and deeds. Of course, divine revelation in its fullness comes to us only in the person of Jesus Christ. As the Word of God Christ is not the end, but the centre of human history. This theological insight cannot be completely unveiled by historical-critical exegesis because history is only the witness to, but not the source of God's salvific action.

For this reason Ratzinger maintains that only a spiritual *"vademecum"*, meaning only a Christology from within, can bring about the full insight of the reality of Jesus Christ. This is the topic of the second chapter. From the theological-spiritual perspective Christology logically would end in an ecclesiology because the Church is depending on Christ. The Pope's three volumes on *Jesus of Nazareth*, published between the years 2007–2012, are outcomes of the spiritual Christology which he discovered in 1981, although its seed was already planted in this early works. Thus, the Church is intended by Christ. *Lumen Gentium* clearly points to this Christological ecclesiology when it points to Christ as the 'Light of nations'. Furthermore, it sees the Church in Christ as a sacrament and instrument of a very closely knit union between God and humanity.[14] The Church therefore continues in the true sense the *"missio Dei"*.

The foundation of the sacramental-missionary character of the Church was already laid in the early 1960s when Ratzinger studied the writings of Augustine. For the Bishop of Hippo the Church's centre is the Eucharist. The Eucharistic Church necessarily includes *communio*, albeit this concept was not the principal concept of Vatican II. It is only in the post-Vatican II phase that Ratzinger discovers the full

14 *LG* no. 1.

meaning of the communion-ecclesiology. This is the topic of the third chapter. Throughout the three chapters the theological-spiritual dimension of Ratzinger's theology should become visible. The spiritual dimension of theology grew gradually over many years of Ratzinger's theological career. It is only in 1981 that he became aware the importance of a spiritual Christology which, of course, is a direct result of his insight into divine revelation. This spiritual theology reaches its climax in the recent works of Pope Benedict on Jesus of Nazareth.

I would like to acknowledge the many helpers without whom this "risky" project would remain a less than complete canvas. To my colleagues at the Australian Catholic University I express my deepest and sincere gratitude. In particular I would like to name Prof. Anthony Kelly, CSsR, who is a member of the Pontifical International Theological Commission, and Prof. Robert Gascoigne, the former National Head of the School of Theology. During the years of labour I could always rely on their support and theological insights. I am also grateful to my Augustinian brothers, who patiently offered their best to assist me in bringing this project to fruition. Among them I would like to single out Rev. Dr. Michael Endicott, OSA, who tirelessly has read and re-read the many drafts of this project. Many "angels", whose names I will keep in my heart, have kindly offered their prayers and good wishes. To them I am also indebted.

I would like to dedicate this work as a humble gift to His Eminence Cardinal Prosper Grech, OSA, who *bene meriti pro ecclesia* was created Cardinal-Deacon of Santa Maria Goretti on February 18th 2012 by His Holiness Pope Benedict XVI. I had the privilege to learn from his wisdom and work with him at the *Institutum Patristicum Augustinianum* in Rome. As well as the Cardinal, I would like to include also the Augustinian Province in Australia, which commemorates in 2013 the 175th Anniversary of the arrival in Australia of its first member Fr. James Alypius Goold, OSA, who ten years later on October 4th 1848 was appointed the first Bishop of Melbourne.

Chapter One: *Revelation*

1. Introduction

Since the early Church, theology is often understood as a process whereby faith is seeking understanding.[1] In our modern times, the emergence of new philosophical and social ideas has challenged the previous understanding of divine revelation. In his book *Revelation Theology* Avery Dulles presents a total of six models of revelation. They were past and contemporary concepts which attempt to engage with the difficulties arising from divine revelation. With regard to their validity Dulles predicts that,

> the widespread crisis of faith in all the Churches suggests that Christianity is presently passing through an important epochal change, the exact shape of which is not yet clear. What seems certain is that many of the classical positions are being challenged.[2]

Dulles continues to give reasons for the crisis of faith,

> Our contemporaries find difficulty in the idea of supposedly infallible, sacred sources; many are unwilling to be tied to a body of beliefs which allegedly reached completion in the first century of the Christian era; they shy away from giving unconditional credence to agencies that claim to speak decisively in the name of God; nor do they see the meaning or importance of many doctrines which their fathers and forefathers accepted as matters of faith.[3]

---

1 Daniel L. Migliore, *Faith Seeking Understanding* (Grand Rapids, Mich.: Eerdman, 2004).
2 Avery Dulles, *Revelation Theology. A History* (New York: Herder and Herder, 1969), 176.
3 Ibid.

As solution Dulles suggests that,

> the theology of the future will probably be more critical of past tradition and present doctrinal standards. It may also be more pragmatically oriented and more concerned with establishing human community on earth.[4]

In short, Dulles insinuates that theology should be contextual and praxis oriented; otherwise it 'would be dead or moribund.'[5] Reflecting on his *Habilitation* project[6] on Bonaventure's concept of revelation and salvation history[7] in 1953, Joseph Ratzinger observed in post-war Germany a similar difficulty. According to him neo-scholastic theology has become too abstract and so it was perhaps detached from daily life experience and struggle. He recalled in his *Memoirs*,

> at this time the idea of salvation history had moved to the focus of inquiry posed by Catholic theology, and this had cast new light on the notion of revelation, which neo-scholasticism had kept too confined to the intellectual realm. Revelation now appeared no longer simply as a communication of truths to the intellect but as a historical action of God in which truth becomes gradually unveiled.[8]

This quotation at the same time indicates the theological direction of Ratzinger's *Habilitation* project. He wanted to go beyond the confinement of neo-scholastic theology and reached out ecumenically to other Christian denominations, in particular to the Lutherans. In order to comprehend fully Ratzinger's criticism against the narrow neo-scholastic concept of revelation, we ought first to look at the Lutheran view of revelation. In the preface to the English translation

---

4   Ibid., 177.
5   Ibid.
6   In the German system of universities only those who have completed the so-called "Habilitationsschrift" are qualified to hold a university chair.
7   The German title is *Das Offenbarungsverständnis und die Geschichtstheologie Bonaventuras*.
8   *Mi*, 104.

of his *Habilitationsschrift* published in 1971[9] Ratzinger summarized the Lutheran concept of theology with the following words,

> This was a problem which arose above all from contacts with Protestant theology which, since the time of Luther, has tended to see in metaphysical thought a departure from specific claim of the Christian faith which directs man not simply to the Eternal but to the God who acts in history.[10]

In contrast to the neo-scholastic understanding of revelation which had a tendency to perceive revelation as a communication of objective propositional truths, the Lutheran theology interpreted revelation primarily as a personal encounter of the faithful with the living God, 'who makes Himself actively present to man in order to save him and enter into communion of life with him.'[11] Martin Luther, traumatized by the experience of human sins and his subsequent struggle with the question of the justification of a sinful person by God, was convinced that a *theologia gloriae*, by which he 'meant a natural knowledge of

---

9   *The Theology of History in St. Bonaventure*, translated by Zachary Hayes (Chicago: Franciscan Herald, 1971). This work contains only the second part of his original post-doctoral thesis which was accepted and approved by the faculty of theology at the University of Munich. The first part was returned for further revisions and is published by Herder in Freiburg under the title "The Concept of Revelation and the Salvation History in the Writings of Bonaventure" (2009). On the problem of the submission of his *Habilitation* thesis, see *Mi*, 111: 'An idea then came to the rescue. What I had said about Bonaventure's theology of history was certainly interwoven with the whole of my book, and yet it could largely stand on its own. Without much difficulty, it could be detached from the work and reshaped to form a whole ... And so, already in October, I was able to put the rejected opus back on the table in abridged form, much to the faculty's astonishment.'

10 *Theology of History*, Foreword to the American Edition, xi; see also *JRGS* 2 (Freiburg: Herder, 2009), 421: 'Die Problemstellung ergab sich in erster Linie aus einer Auseinandersetzung mit der protestantischen Theologie, die seit der Zeit Luthers dazu tendierte, im metaphysischen Denken einen Abfall zu sehen – vom spezifischen Anspruch des christlichen Glaubens, den Menschen nicht einfach nur mit dem Ewigen in Beziehung zu setzen, sondern zu dem Gott, der in Zeit und Geschichte handelt.'

11 Rene Latourelle, *Theology of Revelation, including a Commentary on the Constitution "dei verbum" of Vatican II* (New York: Alba House, 1966), 214.

God, the knowledge of God's power and glory obtained from the creation,'[12] would not save human souls in thrall to sin. In opposition to this type of theology which attempts to penetrate rationally the mystery of God and which only contributes to puff up human pride, the reformer, in his commentaries on the Psalms, advised his audience to rely only on the saving works of Jesus Christ the crucified.[13] Thus Luther's internal struggle was transformed into a theological controversy which opposes the *theologia gloriae* to the *theologia crucis*. For him the nature of theology is manifest in the cross of Jesus which is associated with humility, suffering and shame, and which

> are completely opposed to inadequate human pictures and conceptions of God. Here the concealment of God is revealed. This does not refer to the – invisible – being and nature of God, but is meant to describe the action of God in Jesus Christ, the event of Christ, which became visible in the world concealed under its contrary and in paradox.[14]

In the Protestant-Lutheran perspective theology is not about the metaphysical speculation of God's being.[15] Rather it is about the interpretation of the meaning of divine salvation in concrete situations of human history. Protestant theologians, such as Emil Brunner and Karl Barth argued therefore that the manifestation of divine salvation in human history which is shattered by our sinful revolt against God, can only be met by faith and trust in the divine mercy through which humans gain unmeritedly the justification by God.[16]

It is evident that the root of the above noted theological disagreement between Catholics and Protestants lies in a different ap-

12 Heinrich Fries, *Revelation* (New York: Herder and Herder, 1969), 29.
13 See Hubert Blaumeister, *Martin Luthers Kreuzestheologie. Schüssel zu seiner Deutung von Mensch und Wirklichkeit. Eine Untersuchung anhand der Operationes in Psalmos (1519–1521)* (Paderborn: Bonifatius, 1995).
14 Fries, 29.
15 Preface to the English translation of *The Theology of History in St. Bonaventure* (1971).
16 Dulles, 99: 'Barth and Brunner, especially the former, restored to modern Protestant theology a sense of the divine transcendence and of the total commitment demanded by faith.'

proach to revelation. From the neo-scholastic perspective revelation is seen as a communication of propositional truths entrusted definitively to the Church and made known to human mind.[17] In following Thomas Aquinas's theological method, Pope Leo XIII considered faith and reason not as opposition, but rather as a harmonious complementation. According to the Encyclical *"Aeterni Patris"*, issued on August 4th 1879, the Pope stated that philosophical reason, if used in a proper manner ("si rite usurpetur"), can pave the way to true faith ("ad veram fidem") which is a prerequisite for the reception of divine revelation.[18] The same document declares further that God has manifested certain truths ("nonnullas manifestavit") in such a way that human reason can penetrate and see in them the proofs of God's government. As a consequence, philosophical reason serves also as the defender of divine truth.[19] Hence human reason is positively valued. From the Lutheran point of view, however, revelation is perceived as God's communication of his upper case word incarnated in human history; it is precisely through the presence and acts of God's Word that the sinful human state is saved and challenged. For Emil Brunner this crisis brought out by God's judgement demands of us a radical commitment, not through the dedication of *gnosis*, but through the imitation of the cross.[20] Revelation expresses essentially a salvific relational reality between God and the believer.

---

17 *Dei Filius*, 136: 'For the doctrine of faith which God has revealed has not been proposed like a philosophical system to be perfected by human genuity, but has been committed to the spouse of Christ as a divine trust to be faithfully kept and infallibly declared. Hence also that meaning of the sacred dogmas is perpetually to be retained which our Holy Mother Church has once declared, and there must never be a deviation from that meaning on the specious ground and title of a more profound understanding'; see *The Christian Faith in the Doctrinal Documents of the Catholic Church*, edited by J. Neuner & J. Dupuis (Dublin: Mercier, 1973), 49.
18 Heinrich Denzinger, *Enchiridion Symbolorum definitiorum et declarationum de rebus fidei et morum*, edited by Peter Hünermann (Freiburg: Herder, 1991), 3136.
19 Denzinger, 3138: 'veritas divinitus tradita religiose tueri, et iis qui oppugnare audeant resistere.'
20 Emil Brunner, *Truth as Encounter* (London: SCM, 1964).

What emerges from this debate is a duality which is centred in the opposition between '"Wort-offenbarung" (Word-revelation) and "Tat-offenbarung" (revelation through act). Ratzinger explains this dichotomy with the following words,

> It is striking that Catholic theology interprets revelation more from the perspective of the sacred doctrine. Thus revelation is a divine communication through which the supernatural truth, which surpasses all human minds, is made known. In contrast, the evangelical theology recognizes revelation as "actio divina", and thus as an action of God as Person. As such it can never be a human possession.[21]

Thus Catholic theology associates the sacred teachings with revelation, while the Protestant-Lutheran view emphasizes the performative relational dimension of the divine revelation which is seen as a moment of grace.

Ratzinger's *Habilitation* project aims at the mediation between the Protestant and Catholic concepts of revelation. In doing so, Ratzinger showed already in this early stage of his academic career a sense for ecumenical dialogue. Thus the goal of his theological enterprise is to reconcile metaphysics with salvation history.

Here he touches the heart of debate initiated by the Protestant theologian and historian Adolf von Harnack, who maintained that early Christians had "hellenized" the message of Jesus into body of doctrine, aliened to the Gospel itself.[22] In this context Ratzinger asked,

> How can that which has taken place historically become present? How can the unique und unrepeatable have a universal significance? But then, on the other

---

21 *JRGS* 2, 59: 'Zunächst fällt in die Augen, dass die katholische Theologie an der Offenbarung mehr das Moment der "sacra doctrina" betont, dies also, dass in der Offenbarung als einem Reden Gottes dem Menschen verstehbare, wenn auch "übernatürliche", d. h. seinem eigenen Forschen nicht erreichbare Wahrheit erschlossen wird. Demgegenüber legt die evangelische Theologie allen Nachdruck darauf, dass Offenbarung "actio divina" ist, ein Tun Gottes, das sich niemals von der Person Gottes ablösen lässt, also dem Menschen niemals als solches "verfügbar" wird.'

22 Adolf von Harnack, *History of Dogma*, trans. by Neil Buchanan (New York: Dover, 1961).

hand: Has not the "Hellenization" of Christianity, which attempted to overcome the scandal of the particular by a blending of faith and metaphysics, led to a development in a false direction? Has it not created a static style of thought which cannot do justice to the dynamism of the biblical style?'[23]

Though he agreed with the Protestant view of revelation as "Tat-offenbarung", Ratzinger argued, none the less, that revelation is also "Wort-offenbarung" which reveals the very inner being of God. Thus salvation history explains not only what God does, but also who He is. Being and acting are together one reality in God: 'Just as action originates in being, so does it return to being in the end.'[24] The divine actions in history are mirrors of God's nature.

In his efforts to mediate between the Protestant-Lutheran and the Catholic concept of revelation, Ratzinger saw in the neo-scholastic Franciscan Bonaventure a theologian whose life and thought could mediate between the two opposite views. Here Ratzinger wanted to achieve a twofold purpose. Firstly, Bonaventure, who belonged to the early beginning of the scholastic theology, can serve as the demonstration of the neo-scholastic narrowness. Secondly, the Seraphic Doctor, whose theology was still much inspired by the Scriptures, was for Ratzinger an appropriate middle-man to mediate between the Protestant and Catholic theology, because he was not yet caught up in theological polemics and controversies which have contributed to widening the gap between Lutherans and Catholics.[25]

23   *Theology of History*, xi; see also *JRGS* 2, 421: 'Wie kann das, was sich in der Geschichte ereignet hat, gegenwärtig werden? Wie kann Einmaliges und Unwiederholbares universal Bedeutung gewinnen? Und auf der anderen Seite: Hat nicht die Hellenisierung des Christentums, die Skadalon des Partikulären durch eine Harmonisierung von Glaube und Metaphysik zu überwinden trachtete, überhaupt in die falsche Richtung geführt? Hat nicht genau dieses Unterfangen die starre Denkart hervor gebracht, die dem Dynamismus biblischen Denkens völlig unangemessen bleibt?'
24   *JRGS* 2, 62: 'So wie das Tun vorher schon von einem Sein kommt, so wirkt es am Ende auch auf das Sein zurück.'
25   Ibid., 58: 'Dieses Vorgehen schien um so mehr gefordert, als der heilige Bonaventura, mit dem sich diese Untersuchung beschäftigt, einerseits als Gipfelpunkt der *katholischen* Scholastik gilt, anderseits als "Klassiker der analogia fidei"

2. The Concept of Revelation in Bonaventure

2.1 The Habilitation on Bonaventure

In the foreword to the American edition of his *Habilationsschrift* Ratzinger gave the impression of a smooth transition from his doctoral thesis on Augustine's ecclesiology to Bonaventure's concept of revelation and salvation history. He wrote:

> Since I had devoted my first study to Augustine, and thus had become somewhat familiar with the world of the Fathers, it seemed natural now to approach the Middle Ages. For the questions with which I was concerned, Bonaventure was naturally a more likely subject for study than Aquinas. The questions which I had hoped to direct to this partner were sketched in general terms in the concepts of: revelation – history – metaphysics.[26]

Ratzinger's preference for Bonaventure against Thomas Aquinas[27] was based upon the experience of his earlier studies in the seminary at Freising as he wrote in his autobiography,

> By contrast, I had difficulties in penetrating the thought of Thomas Aquinas, whose crystal-clear logic seemed to me to be too closed in on itself, too impersonal and ready-made. This may also have had something to do with the fact that Arnold Wilmsen, the philosopher who taught us Thomas, presented us with a rigid, neoscholastic Thomism that was simply too far afield from my own question.[28]

---

bezeichnet wurde und damit als Zeuge einer katholischen Theologie, die sich ihres *evangelischen* Erbes noch nachdrücklicher bewusst war als so manche spätere Theologien, die mehr gegenreformatorisch als katholisch zu sein schienen.'

26 *Theology of History*, xii; *SE*, 61: 'Since my dissertation had dealt with the ancient Church, my teacher, Professor Söhngen, remarked that my postdoctoral work should treat the Middle Ages or the modern period ... Söhngen knew that the Augustinian school appealed to me more than the Thomistic, so he sent me to work on Bonaventure, whom he himself knew quite well and venerated.'

27 Thomism was sanctioned by Pope Leo XIII as the method for Catholic theology; see Denzinger, 845, no. 3139: 'Inter scholasticos Doctores omnium princeps et magister longe eminet Thomas Aquinas.'

28 *Mi*, 44.

From this quotation it is quite evident that it was not so much the theology of Thomas Aquinas that caused this problem, but rather the manner with which his philosophy teacher introduced Thomas to him. Here I ought to say that over time Ratzinger frequently referred to the thoughts of Thomas whose search for truth was as sincere as it was for Augustine whom Ratzinger admired and venerated.[29] Likewise one must with caution evaluate the well-known statement about the 'stormy clouds'[30] which hung over Ratzinger's *Habilitation* project. According to Tracey Rowland, the dispute between Ratzinger's teacher Söhngen and Schmaus, the second reader of Ratzinger's postdoctoral thesis, was a matter of theological disagreement. Rowland wrote,

> Here Ratzinger's criticism of the 'theoretical propositions' account of Revelation, derived from the thought of the Spanish Jesuit Francisco Suárez (1548–1617), drew opposition from one of his examiners – Michael Schmaus-who regarded Ratzinger's thinking as Modernist ... It is said that at the oral defence of his thesis Ratzinger sat mute while his two professors – Michael Schmaus and Gottlieb Söhngen – argued about the Suárezian understanding of Revelation.'[31]

To endorse her point Rowland refers to Läpple who was the prefect of studies at the seminary in Freising at that time,

> Läpple distinguishes their positions by saying that 'according to Schmaus the faith of the Church was to be communicated through definitive and unchanging

---

29   *LW*, 32: 'Ich bin mit Augustinus, mit Bonaventura, mit Thomas von Aquin befreundet'; see also Grzegorz Bachanek, 'St. Thomas Aquinas in the Reflections of J. Ratzinger (Benedict XVI)', in *Logos-Vilnius* (2010) 65, 29–40; with regard to the influence of Augustine see my book Joseph Lam Cong Quy, *Theologische Verwandtschaft: Augustinus von Hippo and Joseph Ratzinger / Papst Benedikt XVI* (Würzburg: Echter Verlag, 2009).
30   *Mi*, 106.
31   Tracey Rowland, *Ratzinger's Faith. The Theology of Pope Benedict XVI* (Oxford: University, 2008), 8. With regard to Rowland's view on Vatican II see also the critical article by Joseph A. Komonchack, 'A Postmodern Augustinian Thomism?' in *Augustine and Postmodern Thought: A New Alliance against Modernity?*, edited by Lieven Boeve, Matthijs Lamberigts, and Martin Wisse (Bibliotheca Ephemeridum Theologicarum Lovaniensium, 219; Leuven: Peeters, 2009), 123–46.

concepts that set out perennial truth; [whereas] for Söhngen the faith was mystery, and was communicated through a history.'[32]

It is striking, however, that Schmaus did not mention the name Suarez in this work on "revelation"[33] nor did Läpple suggested this in his interview to which Rowland referred earlier. Furthermore, a look at official Catholic doctrinal statements attests that Suarez is mentioned only around six times,[34] – most importantly in the letter "Dum praeterito" of Benedict XIV to the Spanish inquisitor who had accused the "sectatores Molinae et Suaresii" to be semi-pelagians. The Pope intervened by saying that a judgement against this accusation was not made yet by the Holy Office, and that they, the supporters of Molina and Suarez should enjoy the protection of the Church.[35] Thus Suarez did not always enjoy the prominence among Catholic theologians. Besides, Suarez exercised his influence not only on Catholic theology, but his was likewise influential on Protestant thinkers.[36] In the light of this historical background, it is difficult to conceive that Suarez was the principal figure in the dispute between Söhngen and Schmaus. In fact, an attentive reading of the later version of *Katholische Dogmatik* does not lead one to the conclusion that the theological gap between Ratzinger and Schmaus was unbridgeable, as the later wrote about the method of a revelation theology,

> As far as the existential element is concerned, the Christian faith, as man's response to divine revelation, must be shown to have genuine meaning for him, and therefore power to bring him fulfilment. With regard to its dynamic character, revelation is to be presented both in its own history and in the history of its effects – that is, in its character as an act. Otherwise we would have merely a description of static essence.[37]

32 Rowland, 8.
33 Michael Schmaus, *Dogma*, vol. 1: God in Revelation (New York: Sheed and Ward, 1968).
34 Denzinger, 1695.
35 Ibid., 701 (2564).
36 See John P. Donnelly, *Calvinism and Scholasticism in Vermigli's Doctrine of Man and Grace* (Leiden: Brill, 1976).
37 Schmaus, *Dogma*, 14 f.

Ratzinger's study of Bonaventure resulted in an understanding of revelation which is not far from Schmaus' concept of revelation, as the latter states: 'Revelation means God's whole speech and action with man.'[38] The same is expressed in Ratzinger's *Memoirs*, 'revelation is always a concept denoting an act.'[39] In my view the 'stormy clouds' over Ratzinger's *Habilitation* had more to do with the personal-political conflict between Söhngen and Schmaus whose works were downplayed by the former as

> only a series of quotations taken from the sources on the various issues of theology, without a vision that took into account the developments in modern philosophy and the questions they posed.[40]

Ratzinger himself recognized explicitly in the preface of his doctoral thesis the helpful dogmatic insights he had gained through the lectures by Michael Schmaus.[41] This impression of personal and political resentment between his principal supervisor and his second reader is endorsed by Ratzinger himself who gave reasons for the return of his thesis. He said that his work 'was not rejected, but given back for revision' due to technical academic insufficiencies.[42] Schmaus' reaction can be seen together with the hurt he felt on an academic level, as Ratzinger wrote in his biography,

> I criticized the superseded positions, and this was apparently too much for Schmaus, especially since it was unthinkable to him that I could have worked on a medieval theme without entrusting myself to his direction.[43]

38 *RT*, 35.
39 *Mi*, 108.
40 'That new beginning that bloomed among the ruins' – an Interview with Alfred Läpple by Gianni Valente and Pierluca Azzaro, in *30Giorni* (2006) 1/2.
41 *VHG*, IX: '…nenne ich doch mit besonderem Dank die fundamentaltheologischen Vorlesungen von Herrn Prof. Söhngen, besonders jene über die Offenbarung, theologische Wissenschaftslehre und Religionsphilosophie, sowie die Dogmatikvorlesung von Herrn Prof. Schmaus. Ohne das systematische Apriori, das mir in diesen Vorlesungen zugewachsen ist, wäre diese Arbeit undenkbar.'
42 *Mi*, 109.
43 *Mi*, 108.

This would suggest that Schmaus did indeed agree with the foundational ideas of Ratzinger,[44] but out of personal resentment, against Söhngen he imposed strict conditions on Ratzinger. However, more revealing is the suggestion by Ratzinger that Schmaus' verdict was based upon 'rumours from some people in Freising concerning the modernity of my theology,'[45] and Schmaus could count on friends and colleagues within the faculty, while Söhngen was somehow isolated, perhaps because of his philosophical premises. After this clarification, let us now proceed to the thoughts of Bonaventure as seen by Ratzinger.

2.2 *Revelation as God's Self-communication and Action*

From the discussion above it should be evident that Ratzinger's choice of Bonaventure was a deliberate decision. There were various reasons for his theological preference, despite the fact that Ratzinger knew only little about Bonaventure's theology and writings when he embarked on his project. Firstly, Söhngen personally preferred the Augustinian school which he understood as a 'counterweight to Thomas Aquinas'.[46] Bonaventure whom Söhngen 'knew quite well and venerated'[47] is known to be a good student of Augustine.[48] Ratzinger

---

44 This was the reason why Schmaus also accepted unreservedly the second part of Ratzinger's thesis.
45 *Mi*, 109.
46 *SE*, 60.
47 Ibid., 61.
48 Christopher M. Cullen, *Bonaventure* (Oxford: Oxford Scholarship online, 2007), 20f.: 'Bonaventure is usually described as being one of the most important Augustinians in the thirteenth century … It is largely accurate to say that Bonaventure became the leading spokesman for the Augustinian tradition in the thirteenth century.' Nevertheless, Bonaventure also took his freedom to depart for Augustine if it was necessary. As an example Ilia Delio pointed to the Trinitarian question, 'Although the Seraphic Doctor studied theology at European university, he did not adhere to the trinitarian theology of Augustine which was influential in the west. Rather, he described a model of the Trinity that had its roots in the Greek patristic tradition, similar to the one described by the fourth century

saw in Bonaventure a theologian who fits well in the ecumenical purpose of his postdoctoral thesis.[49] Ratzinger's theological intention was to reconcile the Lutheran view with the Catholic understanding of revelation through the theology of Bonaventure. Secondly, Bonaventure's spirituality and theology would appeal more to Ratzinger's interest in the philosophy of personalism, which he probably had learned from Theodor Steinbüchel's work *Umbruch des Denkens* (The Revolution in Thought),[50] 'in which he [Steinbüchel] recounted with great verve the revolutionary shift from the dominance of neo-Kantianism to the personalistic phase.'[51] Ratzinger's personalist approach was met by Söhngen's existential theology which is 'a theology for the faith.'[52] Likewise Bonaventure's theology is also known as a theology, 'which is at the same time already proclamation.'[53] Thus the impact of Bonaventure's theological method on Ratzinger did not come only from the former's capacity to construct a theological system based upon scholasticism;[54] but the greatness of Bonaventure lies in his personalist spiritual reading of Christ' message. According to Ilia Delio,

> the theologian-turned-administrator[55] now revealed himself as a passionate lover of Christ. Affectivity marked his writings in a way that not even the Cistercians

---

Cappadocian fathers.'; see Ilia Delio, *Simply Bonaventure. An Introduction to His Life, Thought, and Writings* (New York: New City, 2006), 40.
49 *JRGS* 2, 58; the ecumenical character of Bonaventure is also shown in the fact that he at the fourth session of the Council in Lyon has successfully mediated between the Orthodox churches and Catholic church on issues such as the Papacy, sacraments etc.; see Mullen, 14.
50 Theodor Steinbüchel, *Der Umbruch des Denkens. Die Frage nach der christlichen Existenz erläutert an Ferdinand Ebners Menschdeutung* (Darmstadt: Wissenschaftliche Buchgesellschaft, 1966).
51 *SE*, 60.
52 Interview with Alfred Läpple, in *30Giorni* (2006) 1/2.
53 *JRGS* 2, 80: 'die zugleich auch schon Verkündigung ist.'
54 Bonaventure still belonged to the early phase of scholasticism which was less rigid and far from being polemical.
55 In 1257 Bonaventure was elected to the office of Minister General of his Order.

achieved ... Bonaventure's spiritual writings, which heightened the humanity of Christ, contributed to a new medieval *Zeitgeist*, a new current in spirituality in which a personal relationship with Christ, nurtured by the use of the senses and imagination, could lead one to union with God.[56]

Bonaventure was for Ratzinger no doubt an ecclesiastic whose theology and spirituality may lead the past-war German theology out of an ecumenical gridlock.

With this Bonaventurian background Ratzinger entered into the debate about the revelation which, as he said, had captured the attention of German theologians in post-war period. Of course, in its response to the threat of modernism the ecclesiastic *magisterium* always taught the 'necessity of interior divine grace for the salutary acceptance by faith of that revelation,'[57] but as Karl Rahner continued to underline, 'the intrinsic connection between the grace of faith and historical revelation was not seen.'[58]

According to Ratzinger this problem can be resolved by examining the writings of Bonaventure, in particular his concept of revelation and understanding of salvation history. This means that a clarification of the meaning of revelation is indispensable. Bonaventure, in Ratzinger's view, acknowledged that revelation can have various levels of meaning ("Bedeutungsstufung"). However, apart from its general use or abuse, revelation in the theological sense must first of all be applied to God,

> Revelation in its strictest sense designates that revelation through which the soul is enlightened by grace ... Thus Bonaventure did not use the noun revelation in a theologically neutral way. For him this word is a theological jargon.[59]

56 Delio, *Simply Bonaventure*, 26.
57 Karl Rahner, 'Observation on the Concept of Revelation', in Karl Rahner – Joseph Ratzinger, *Revelation and Tradition*, 10.
58 Ibid.
59 *JRGS* 2, 91: 'Als "revelatio" im strengsten Sinn wird jene "Offenbarung" bezeichnet, "in der die Seele erleuchtet wird von der Gnade" ... dass wir mit dem Wort "revelatio" bei Bonaventura nicht auf theologisch neutrales oder noch unbebautes Gelände treten, sondern dass dieses Wort für ihn ein theologischer Fachausdruck ist...'

This quotation makes plain the theological meaning and function of revelation. It is first and foremost a divine action which illumines human minds. Without this divine enlightenment human intellects cannot understand God's self-revelation. Therefore revelation is not to be understood primarily as a communication of objective truths. Revelation is strictly theological because it describes the way God acts in human minds. In this sense revelation is a mode of God's ongoing action in history. As a specific theological term revelation is grounded in the inner-Trinitarian communication. Firstly, it describes the interior act of God's communication which is identified as an inward act of speaking by which the Word is begotten ("Zeugung des Wortes"). According to Ratzinger this act of the divine inward dialogue is an act of self-attentiveness ("Akt der Selbstbegreifung"). Secondly, God, of course, does not communicate only inwardly, but he also expresses himself externally. The reason for the external expression of God's Word ("Ausdruck") lies at the very core of God's being as *"bonum diffusivum sui"* which Bonaventure probably inherited from Pseudo-Dionysius, and which he complemented with the Trinitarian speculation of Richard St. Victor. This synthesis is best explained by Delio,

> He develops his doctrine of the Trinity by relying on the work of the Pseudo-Dionysius and Richard of St. Victor. From the Pseudo-Dionysius he indicates that the good is self-diffusive *(bonum diffusivum sui)*, and from Richard he identifies the highest good as love which by its very nature seeks to share itself with another. In the Dionysian view, goodness is the preeminent attribute of God; it is the very definition of the superessential Godhead and the deepest basis for God's creative activity. In the Divine Names, the Pseudo-Dionysius writes that goodness gives rise to being: 'The first gift of the absolutely transcendent goodness is the gift of being, and that goodness is praised from those that first and principally have a share of being. From it and in it are being itself, the source of beings, all beings and whatever else has a portion of existence.' The good by nature is self-diffusive, that is, it gives of itself freely to another. Since God is good and since the good is by nature self-diffusive, it follows that God is necessarily self-communicative.[60]

60   Ilia Delio, 'Bonaventure's Metaphysics of Good', in *Theological Studies* 60.2 (1999), 231 f.; Bonaventure might also have read this in Thomas Aquinas' works;

If God is ontologically the source of goodness, then the communication of himself is a logical consequence.

What matters here for Bonaventure is the effect of the divine external communication. The *Seraphic Doctor* interpreted it as an act of divine grace which enlightens the human minds: 'This effect is called "revelatio". God does not "talk" because of his insights; but rather his "speech" produces enlightenment in us.'[61] In this context revelation is seen as the light of human minds.

The light is an important motif in the history of religion whose significance is fully elaborated only in the medieval ages. In following Augustine's metaphysics of light Bonaventure perceived light as a perpetual movement operating in human minds. As such the light is always sparkling from a source of its own. Thus light is both "substance" and a "process of becoming" as well. Here Bonaventure saw parallels to the effects caused by the divine grace,

> which is not perceived as *something* in the soul, but as a continuous lively rays of divine light in us. It is a spiritual light from the primordial light. It is not light in a figurative sense, but in a quite realistic understanding.[62]

It is now evident that grace of revelation in the form of enlightenment is a divine act which removes and unveils to human minds those things which were once hidden. For that reason, the "Word" and the "Light" form a unity through which God illumines the human mind. In Ratzinger's reading of Bonaventure revelation is then

---

see Geoff Deegan, 'On the Goodness of Being According to Thomas Aquinas', in *Universitas* 12 (2005) retrieved from the website of the Centre for Thomistic Studies Australia <http://www.cts.org.au/articles.htm> on Dec 7th 2011.

61 JRGS 2, 99: 'Diese Wirkung des Wortes heißt "revelatio" – Offenbarung. Denn "Rede" schreiben wir Gott nicht zu, weil ihm Einsicht zukommt, sondern auch, weil er durch sein offenbarendes Tun in uns eine gewisse Erleuchtung "bewirkt".'

62 JRGS 2, 720: 'die nicht als ein starres Etwas in der Seele, sondern als die stets lebendige Einstrahlung des göttlichen Lichtes in den Menschen gefasst wird. Sie ist also geistiges Licht aus dem Urlicht Gott, Licht nicht bloß in einem übertragenen, sondern in einem durchaus realistischen Sinn;' this contribution is first published as Joseph Ratzinger, 'Licht und Erleuchtung', in *StGen* 13 (1960), 368–378.

a direct effect, which God causes in human minds.⁶³ This effect, however, should not be understood in an analogical or symbolic sense; rather it is real, because the Word of God and the light, which enlightens human mind so that it understands the Word of God, flow from the one source which is God. This light motif therefore opens the way to the metaphysical dimension of revelation.

2.3 Metaphysical Foundation of Revelation

In Bonaventure's view the metaphysical foundation of revelation is manifested in its Trinitarian cosmological event,

> according to Bonaventure revelation goes much deeper: it is for him an almost metaphysical, rather, a cosmological event. Therefore Bonaventure's theological reflection on the revelation penetrates deeply into the centre of his Trinitarian concept and finds there its foundation.⁶⁴

In Ratzinger's view this metaphysical foundation has been somehow shattered by the Augustinian turn to subjective psychological speculation of the Trinity which had dominated the middle Ages.⁶⁵ In order to rectify this shortcoming and to restore the metaphysical foundation of revelation Bonaventure turned to the Trinitarian speculation of the Cappadocian fathers.⁶⁶ For the Franciscan saint divine revelation, of course, achieves its climax in the person of Jesus Christ⁶⁷ who – within the speculation of the nature and function of the *Logos* –

---

63 *JRGS*, 2, 100: '"Offenbarung" ist nach dem bisher Gesagten von Gott her gesehen eine Wirkung, die er im Menschen hervorbringt.'
64 *JRGS* 2, 131: 'Indes reicht der Rang dieser Offenbarung bei Bonaventura sehr viel tiefer: Sie ist für ihn geradezu ein metaphysisches, besser gesagt: ein kosmisches Ereignis. So greift die Offenbarungspekulation des Heiligen bis mitten in seine Trinitätslehre hinein und findet dort ihre eigentliche Grundlegung.'
65 See also Michael Schmaus, *Die psychologische Trinitätslehre des hl. Augustinus* (Tübingen, 1927).
66 Delio, *Simply Bonaventure*, 40.
67 *RT*, 40f.

is identified as the *verbum medium*. However, the Christological events are not isolated accomplishments. They are always integral parts of the Trinitarian communication ("operationes Trinitatis"). In this context Bonaventure suggested a tripartite nature of the Word: a) the *verbum intelligible*; b) the *verbum sensible*; and finally c) the *verbum medium*. It is evident that the last form is to be understood as the result of the mediation of the two preceding types which are rooted in the inner dialogue of God. The most interesting point in Bonaventure's speculation of the Word is the way he interpreted the *verbum sensibile*. In order to see the theological quality of Bonaventure's hermeneutics of the *verbum sensibile*, one must read it against the background of contemporary thinkers.

In this regard Marsilio Ficino (1433–1499) can offer some insights, despite the fact that he lived almost 200 years later than Bonaventure. However, Ficino's context was not too far from that of Bonaventure. As a person of the Renaissance Ficino represented a system of thoughts which attempted to reintegrate the platonic ideas into the Christian thoughts.[68] As a Christian thinker the person of Jesus Christ is the focus of his thoughts, although Christ does not seem to occupy a central position in his writings.[69] Yet, and different to Bonaventure, Ficino in his cosmological speculation immediately identified the *verbum sensible* with the incarnate Word. In this con-

---

[68] Christopher S. Celenza, 'Marsilio Ficino', in *The Stanford Encyclopedia of Philosophy (Summer 2011 Edition)*, Edward N. Zalta (ed.), URL = <http://plato.stanford.edu/archives/sum2011/entries/ficino/>: 'Ficino regarded himself as a Platonist, but this did not mean that he was interested in finding Plato's intentions in a historicist manner. Instead, he saw himself as one member of a venerable sequence of interpreters who added to a store of wisdom that God allowed progressively to unfold. Each of these "prisci theologi," or "ancient theologians," had his part to play in discovering, documenting, and elaborating the truth contained in the writings of Plato and other ancient sages, a truth to which these sages may not have been fully privy, acting as they were as vessels of divine truth.' (Accessed on 17/11/2011).

[69] Jorg Lauster, 'Marsilio Ficino as Christian Thinker', in *Marsilio Ficino: His Theology, His Philosophy, His Legacy*, edited by Michael J.B. Allen, Valery Rees, Martin Davies (Leiden: Brill, 2001), 54.

text the adjective *sensible* is taken literally when he discussed the redemptive role of the Word, 'ita per quodammodo iam sensible factum sensibilia reformare.'[70] The incarnate Word took sensible form in order to reform those who are bound to the sensible world. In doing so, Ficino confused the sensible with the immutable. The mystery which qualifies the nature of God's being and self-communication is therefore somehow lost in this identification between the *verbum sensible* and the sensible world. In contrast to Ficino, Bonaventure interpreted the *verbum sensible* in the first place within his *Logos*-speculation as he ascribed to it the function of being, the *archetypus mundi* which Ratzinger interpreted as the divine "Weltgedanke" (the primordial idea of creation).[71] Thus the *verbum intelligibile* refers to God's intellectual nature of speaking, while the *verbum sensibile* also contains his creative will. Hence the verbum *intelligibile* and *sensible* are united in the *verbum medium* as their external expression. God therefore communicates and creates through his *verbum medium*. The external expression is rooted in the inner communicative being of God; in other words, the divine always seeks to express itself towards others: 'It is one of Bonaventure's principle ideas that truth is essentially expression, i.e. self-expression towards the other.'[72] The incarnation is then the manifestation ("Kundsein") of the inner-Trinitarian aperture of the intelligible towards the sensible. According to Bonaventure the essence of the Trinitarian communion includes an inward openness towards the creation.[73] Thus in the incarnation God's will *(verbum sensibile)* and being *(verbum intelligibile)* are manifested. Revelation as self-communion of God's being and act has its cause in the immanent Trinity. As such revelation cannot be completely objectified as humans cannot master the immanence of the Trinity which remains always a mystery. Revelation therefore is

70 *Opera omnia*, p. 29; cited according to Lauster, *Marsilio Ficino*, 56.
71 Delio, *Simply Bonaventure*, 84: 'the sum total of the infinite divine ideas.'
72 *JRGS* 2, 134: 'Es ist einer der durch alle Werke hindurch gleichbleibend festgehaltenen Grundgedanken Bonaventuras, dass jeder Wahrheit der Ausdruck, das Sich-Selbst-Ausdrücken auf andere hin, wesentlich ist.'
73 *JRGS* 2, 134: 'von Wesen her [ist es] auf Menschwerdung, auf Öffnung hin.'

a free act of grace. In this point the Franciscan minister general perhaps may have already anticipated Karl Rahner's theological axiom 'Die ökonomische Trinität ist die immanente Trinität.' ("The economic Trinity is the immanent Trinity.")[74] Hence the Trinitarian reflection in Bonaventure's writings is done from the perspective of salvation history as well.

2.4 Revelation and Salvation History

The antecedent section has made plain that revelation has its metaphysical basis in the immanence of the Trinitarian communication which, however, is always a mystery. According to Bonaventure, the Trinitarian communion is the foundation of the divine openness towards history, as creation is intrinsically the operation of the entire Trinity. Here, Bonaventure was more in agreement with Augustine than with the Greek fathers for creation is the image not of the *Logos*, but rather essentially that of the Trinity.[75] This is simply the outcome of God's being as the fountain of goodness and love which is self diffusive. Therefore, salvation is more or less interchangeable with revelation.[76] This fundamental link between salvation and revelation is explained in the papal post-synodal apostolic exhortation *"Verbum Domini"* published in 2010 as a

> reality, ... [which] is born of the word, as *creatura Verbi*, and everything is called to serve the word. Creation is the setting in which the entire history of the love between God and his creation develops; hence human salvation is the reason underlying everything.[77]

---

74 Karl Rahner, 'De Trinitate', in Id., *Schriften zur Theologie*, vol. 4 (Freiburg: Herder, 1964), 115.
75 Basil Studer, *Augustinus: De Trinitate. Eine Einführung* (Paderborn: Ferdinand Schöningh, 2005), 95 f.
76 Gerald O'Collins, *Jesus Our Redeemer. A Christian Approach to Salvation* (Oxford: Oxford University, 2007), 232.
77 *Verbum Domini. The Word of God in the Life and Mission of the Church. Post-synodal apostolic exhortation* (Strathfield: St. Pauls, 2010), 22.

Ultimately salvation, which reaches its turning point in Jesus Christ, is the definitive Word, with which God speaks to humanity, who is always embedded in history and time. In this sense the document continues,

> This condescension of God is accomplished surpassingly in the incarnation of the Word. The eternal Word, expressed in creation and communicated in salvation history, in Christ became a man, "born of woman" (Gal 4:4).[78]

Therefore, revelation in Jesus Christ cannot be interpreted merely as a symbolic action. In contrast to this view, Catholic theology perceives salvation a real action because it comes from God who is the cause of all beings.[79] For Ratzinger, the biblical faith is not an idea which is open to speculations. The events found in the Scripture occurred in the concrete history of this world. For this reason, 'biblical faith does not recount stories as symbols of meta-historical truths.'[80] Nonetheless, Ratzinger recognised that there is a difficulty which is inherent to this concept and which needs to be solved as well. In particular, the relationship between faith and history is problematic. Ratzinger observed that if salvation comes through faith, then logically faith must be the same over time; otherwise salvation is not an unmerited grace, but a result of human merits as faith can increase or decrease according to human efforts and capacity. However, if faith is qualitatively unchanged in the sense that through it all can have equal access to salvation, then it seems that faith is also independent from historical developments and from the quality of human response to the gifts of faith. If it is true that the quality of faith is immutable, then it would mean at the same time that historically there is no distinction in terms of the quality of salvation between the Old Testament and the Christological events reported in the New Testament.

---

78 Ibid., 24.
79 O'Collins, 232: 'Here the revealing and saving activity of God belong inseparably together in constituting the one history of divine self-communication.'
80 *JoN*, vol. 2 103 f.

And yet the difference of the two testaments is undeniable,

> The only crucial difference between Christians and Jews lies simply in the fact that Christians consider the incarnation as an historical event, while the Jews regard it as an event to come.[81]

It is the conviction of the authors of the New Testament that the messianic saviour has indeed appeared in the person Jesus Christ, while the Jews are still waiting for his coming. In this case, it is obvious that the character of the New Testament faith differs substantially from that of the First Testament. According to Ratzinger, the New Testament is not to be understood as a merely *fides explicita* of the *fides implicita* which is hidden in the Old Testament. Salvation history is not simply a positive transition from the Old Testament to the New Testament. Rather, history finds its central point in Jesus Christ, who endows history with a new and definitive meaning,

> In the man Jesus, God has once and for all uttered himself: he *is* his Word and, his Word, himself. Revelation does not end here because God deliberately puts an end to it, but because it has reached its goal … The fact that God's final decision for man has already been made [in Jesus Christ] means … that there is such a thing as finality in history, even if this finality is of such a kind that it does not exclude a future but inaugurates it. This has further consequence that there is and must be such a thing as the final, irrevocable in the life of man too…[82]

It becomes clear that in Bonaventure's concept of salvation history Jesus Christ was not thought of as the end or as the final apocalypse, but rather as the centre of history.

---

81 *JRGS* 2, 163: 'Der Unterschied zwischen Christen und Juden – der einzig entscheidende, den es überhaupt gibt – besteht hier einfach darin, dass die Christen die Inkarnation also schon geschehen, die Juden hingegen sie noch bevorstehend bezeichnen.'
82 *IC*, 199.

2.5 Jesus Christ as the Centre of History

Bonaventure's understanding of salvation history was the outcome of various factors which were interconnected. Firstly, the emergence of the Franciscan order challenged the scholastic concept of tradition and scriptural interpretation inherited from the patristic exegesis. The new mode of Christian existence, exemplified in the Franciscan order, necessitates a theological justification, not only for the new order, but also for the lifestyle of St. Francis who 'dared to make the unheard of attempt to translate the word of the Sermon on the Mount into the living work of his life.'[83] In this context, Bonaventure endeavoured to demonstrate that St. Francis' lifestyle and spirituality were indeed in accordance with the apostolic evangelical teaching. Thus, the main difficulty Bonaventure had to explicate concerned the relationship between the letter and Spirit. At stake was the foundational question whether tradition can still progress in the present time. The *Seraphic Doctor* argued that the decisive norm for Christian living was the spirit of Jesus Christ which is above the letters,

> All tradition is of no avail against the immediate word of the Lord; this is the bold wisdom of the word with which Bonaventure discovered the breakthrough to the immediate encounter with Scripture, following in the footsteps of his master, Francis.[84]

According to Bonaventure, tradition is progressive, and in this context the lifestyle of St. Francis can be seen as the progressive typological unfolding of the spirit of Jesus Christ. However, another difficulty arises here. It is the question of the authentic interpretation of the spirit of Jesus Christ. For Bonaventure, authenticity can be guaranteed only by the Church, who receives her authority not from the Evangelists or the writers of the New Testament, but rather from the Apostles themselves whose faith stories are narrated by the biblical authors. For that reason, the Church in the Holy Spirit trans-

---

83   *Theology of History*, 80.
84   Ibid., 81.

mits and interprets authentically the spirit of Jesus Christ. The fact that the Church in Pope Honorius III approved the Rule St. Francis can be read as recognition of a progressive concept of tradition which is typologically manifested in the emergence of that mendicant order. As a consequence, a pure retrospective interpretation is 'limited by a principle of interpretation which shows a decidedly progressive character.'[85] Secondly, Bonaventure challenged also the traditional scholastic concept of eschatology which is inclined to spiritualize time. According to the scholastic theology, Christ is seen as the inaugurator of the end of all ages which is followed by a new spiritual time initiated by the presence of the Holy Spirit. As a consequence of the spiritualization of history, the time of the Church is reduced to be only a transient period within the chain of spiritual progress which leads ultimately to the time of the Spirit. As a result the historical periods were perceived as 'forms of the unfolding of the one Spirit.'[86] Hand in hand with the spiritualization of history was reluctance to value in an appropriate manner the visible historical dimension of the Church. She was seen only "*sub specie aeternitatis*",

> Church history then becomes simply one period of time that takes its place among the other periods of history; it is no longer the final age. Instead, it is simply the second age which comes after the first age of the Old Testament history. At the same time, the unity of the time of Christ ... is destroyed.[87]

It appears that there was a discrepancy between the scholastic theology and that of the mendicant orders which predicated the Church closer to the suffering and crucified humanity of Jesus Christ.[88] This connection was radicalized later on in the theology of Martin Luther who opposed

---

85 Ibid., 82.
86 *Theology of History*, 101.
87 Ibid.
88 Claudio Leonardi, 'Christ', in *Encyclopedia of the Middle Ages*, vol. 2, edited by A. Vauchez in association with R.B. Dobson (Cambridge: James Clark & Co, 2000), 295 f.

the *theologia crucis* in favour of the *theologia gloriae*.⁸⁹ Within this debate, Bonaventure's theology can mediate between both positions as he saw in St. Francis a Christocentric lifestyle which is also oriented towards this world. Therefore, the mendicants added an historical to the eschatological dimension of the Church. Thirdly, it was the millenarianist hermeneutics of Joachim of Fiore's eschatology which captures mainly the thoughts of Bonaventure, in particular in his work *"Collationes in Haxameron"* which were held as lectures at the University of Paris in 1273. Bonaventure's work reacted against the millenarianist radicalization of Joachim's spiritualism by members of his Franciscan order who in the age of the Spirit expected the emergence of a new order consisting only of the just people (Franciscans) to which the Church is submitted to. In this environment, Bonaventure sought to mediate in the

> struggle for an understanding of its own proper nature somewhere between the extremes of a radically eschatological and purely spiritual self-consciousness on the one hand and an all-too complacent formulation according to the already existing forms of the older Orders on the other hand.⁹⁰

In doing so, he accepted the eschatological concept of Joachim de Fiore who 'foresaw a third age, the Age of the Holy Spirit, as a new period of revelation.'⁹¹ And this new age is projected into the future, although its beginning coincides with the life of St. Francis. Nevertheless, Bonaventure also modified Joachim de Fiore's eschatological concept at a decisive point. For the minister general of the Franciscans, the New Age has already been inaugurated by Jesus Christ. Indeed the time and life of Jesus Christ is the Age of the Holy Spirit,

---

89 Blaumeister, 553: 'Träte die außergewöhnliche Gabe der Teilhabe an Gott ohne alle Verborgenheit und ohne Anfechtung der menschlichen Selbstsuche auf, so würde sie der Mensch freilich liebend gern annehmen, alsbald aber zum Eigenbesitz machen und sie missbrauchen, indem er sich, den Geber vergessend, seiner eigenen Größe und Herrlichkeit rühmt. Eben darum ist Luthers Theologie Theologie des Nein oder besser: Theologie des unter dem Gegenteil verborgenen Ja und nicht Theologie des bloßen Ja: theologia crucis und nicht theologia gloriae.'
90 *Theology of History*, 1f.
91 *SE*, 62.

> Bonaventure's answer ... was to underscore forcefully the connection between Christ and the Holy Spirit according to the Gospel of John. The word revealed in history is definitive, but inexhaustible, and it unceasingly discloses new depths. In this sense, the Holy Spirit, as the interpreter of Christ, speaks with his word to every age and shows that this word always has something new to say ... Bonaventure does not project the Holy Spirit into a future, but it will always be the age of the Holy Spirit. The age of Christ is the age of the Holy Spirit.[92]

Bonaventure's position was also in between the radical apocalyptic view and the total identification with the world. Fourthly, Bonaventure was also opposed to various errors which derived from an inappropriate interpretation of Aristotle's philosophy. To the triad of errors, namely the *aeternitas mundi*, the *unitas intellectus* and the *necessitas fatalis*, Bonaventure argued convincingly,

> There is a violation of the *causa essendi* in the doctrine of the *aeternitas mundi*; there is a violation against the *ratio intellegendi* in the thesis of *unitas intellectus*; finally, there is a violation against the *ordo vivendi* in the affirmation of the *necessitas fatalis*. Thus, the triad of errors violates the three basic forms of truth to which the three primary philosophical disciplines – physics, logic and ethics- are ordered.[93]

What unites all aforementioned factors, namely spiritualization of history inherited from the Fathers of the Church, the millenarianist apocalyptic radicalization of Joachim of Fiore's eschatology within the Franciscan movement and finally the Aristotelian errors, was the

---

92   Ibid., 62 f. I am grateful for the comment of my colleague Prof. Robert Gascoigne who pointed out that Thomas Aquinas (see *Summa Theologiae* art. 4, q. 106, *prima secundae*) likewise had criticized Joachim and had emphasized that the whole *saeculum* is the age of Christ and the Spirit; see Robert Gascoigne, *The Church and Secularity. Two Stories of Liberal Society* (Washington D.C.: Georgetown University Press, 2009), 41 f.: 'Thomas emphasized the centrality of Christ for salvation until the end of time, rejecting the notion of a third age of the Spirit. The point particularly criticized by Aquinas was that Joachim's notion of the third age of the Spirit posited a differentiation in the history of the world, and of the Church, between Pentecost and Parousia, a differentiation that appeared to relativize the definitive character of Christ for all time.'

93   *SE*, 134.

overemphasis on the Holy Spirit which diminished the significance of Jesus Christ and which led to a disregard for a proper understanding of history. In correcting this a-historical tendency of scholastic theology, Bonaventure interpreted the 'fullness of time' neither in the sense of an apocalyptic disappearance of this world in favour of a new aeon nor as a turning point of history which would lead history to the next higher level, but rather the 'fullness of time' is simultaneously understood as 'the centre of time'. As such, Christ is the beginning and end of time and history. At this point, Bonaventure also modified Joachim of Fiore's concept of salvation history: 'The concept is here understood not simply in the sense of mediating salvation, but in the sense of standing in the centre of time.'[94] In fact, Jesus Christ is mediator because he is the centre of time,

> It is precisely the figure of Jesus Christ, the middle person of the Trinity as well as the mediator and middle between God and man, who gradually becomes the synthesis of everything that is expressed for Bonaventure in the concept of centre. Christ becomes the centre. And as a consequence of this general interpretation of Christ from the notion of centre, He becomes also the centre of time ... With the elimination of an independent time of the Spirit, this schema offered a vivid description of Christ's central position in time.[95]

Thus the participation in God, which is the eschatological goal, can only be achieved via Jesus Christ who as God assumes human flesh in order to facilitate the return of the sinners to God, as Paul wrote to the *Philippians* 2:5–8,

> Let the same mind be in you that was in Christ Jesus, who, though he was in the form of God, ... but emptied himself, taking the form of a slave, being born in human likeness. And being found in human form, he humbled himself and became obedient to the point of death – even death on a cross.

In referring to Paul Bonaventure's aim was to exhibit a Christological syllogism which takes together the substantial-metaphysical divine

---

94   Ibid., 110.
95   Ibid., 110.

reality of Christ and his active historical nature.[96] In this Christological context, history or *saeculum* is understood as saving time as it comes from God in Jesus Christ who lives in time, and which in its end returns to Jesus Christ who is the Word of God,

> Time, therefore, is understood right from the start to be saving time ... For Bonaventure, history consists of two corresponding movements from the very beginning – *egressus* and *regressus*. Christ stands as the turning point of these movements and as the centre who both divides and unites.[97]

As the centre of time, Jesus Christ is its beginning (historical Jesus) and its end (Jesus the Christ). After him there will be no other time, be it the time of a new Aeon or be it the time of the Holy Spirit. There will be only the beatific vision of God. Yet, another problem comes to the fore at this point. In Platonic philosophy, time is seen as a fall from unity into multiplicity which constitutes a distance from the divinity. Therefore, the return can only mean an interruption of time by turning to the origin which has no time. Thus redemption means bypassing time. In contrast to Platonic view, Ratzinger argued that in a Christian context the beginning of time is not to be understood as an exit from the unity, but rather the

> *exitus* is to begin with something completely positive: the free act of God whose positive will is that there be created beings as something good ... it is not rooted in a fall but in the positing of God who is good and who creates what is good. The act of being on the part of God that effects created being is an *act of freedom*.[98]

Consequently, the return *(reditus)* is not a revocation or the annulment of the fall and time, but rather

> it means that the coming-into-its-own of the creature as an autonomous creature answers back in freedom to the love of God, accepts its creation as a command of love, so that a dialogue of love begins – that entirely new unity that only love can

---

96   *JRGS* 2, 242–245.
97   *Theology of History*, 142 f.
98   *ET*, 20.

create ... This *reditus* is a "homecoming," but it does not cancel out creation but fully gives it its ultimate validity.[99]

In this sense, the saving turning point which arrives with Jesus Christ is not to dissolve (*"Aufhebung"*) history and time, but to bring it to its proper integrity: 'Its end is not suspension but a way of continuing in existence an illuminated freedom that finds its definitive state in the fusion of truth and love.'[100]

2.6 Conclusion and Prospect for Vatican II

Ratzinger commenced his *Habilitation* project in 1953 with the goal to contribute to the debate at that time on the understanding of revelation and with it to clarify the theological dispute which had divided Catholic scholastic theology from the Protestant Lutheran approach on the meaning of salvation history. In this ecumenical endeavour, Ratzinger might have been encouraged by his principal supervisor Gottfried Söhngen who, 'being a child of a mixed marriage and deeply concerned with the ecumenical question on account of his origins ... took up the debate with Karl Barth and Emil Brunner' – the two giants of Lutheran theology at that time.[101] It was probably the same Söhngen who encouraged his student to study the theology of Bonaventure. The choice for the *Seraphic Doctor*, however, overlaps with Ratzinger's theological preference as Bonaventure stood in the line of the Augustinian personalist-existential approach to theology. None the less, Ratzinger was aware of the risk of submitting the original thoughts of Bonaventure to his own way of thinking.[102] And yet a presentation of a classic of the history of

---

99   Ibid., 20f.
100 Ibid., 22.
101 *Mi*, 55.
102 In the examination of Ratzinger's Habilitation Schmaus accused Ratzinger precisely of this "crime", namely that the latter interpreted Bonaventure from modernist angle.

theology cannot stand in itself, but must also give answers to fundamental questions of faith which are not confined to historical context. In studying Bonaventure's theology, Ratzinger sought to answer the following fundamental questions:

> In summary, one can identify four distinct areas that result from our questioning: 1) The essence of revelation? Fact or Dogma? 2) Ontology of revelation? Revelation and history? 3) Revelation and natural theology? 4) The problem of the contemporaneity of revelation: revelation and tradition, revelation and the Church? These are our problems, and since, as we believe, not only ours, but problems of the Christian "revelation" itself, we must also demand from a medieval theologian answers to them.[103]

We have not allocated much space for the discussion of point four, namely the relationship between revelation and tradition. We will return to this subject in detail later. However, concerning the nature of revelation, Ratzinger states that revelation for Bonaventure should not be understood as what revelation was perceived in contemporary theology of the 1950s in terms of propositional truths, but rather it should be seen in the first place as divine self-communication by which God speaks into the human hearts and minds. In this sense, revelation is at the same time a gracious act with which God illumines the human mind so that it can have faith in him. This enlightenment is necessary as many people saw the works of Jesus, but they did not believe in him. For this reason, vision can become faith through the light coming from God speaking into the heart and minds of human beings. It is now evident that the receiving person is already included in the act of revelation. Hence, revelation is a gracious act from God

---

[103] *JRGS* 2, 70f.: 'Zusammenfassend kann man wohl vier große Problemkreise unterscheiden, die sich aus unserer Frage ergeben: 1. Das Wesen der Offenbarung: Tat oder Lehre? 2. Ontologie der Offenbarung? Offenbarung und Geschichte. 3. Offenbarung und "natürliche Theologie". 4. Das Problem der Offenbarungsgegenwart: Offenbarung und Überlieferung, Offenbarung und Kirche. Dies sind unsere Probleme und da es, wie wir glauben, nicht nur unsere, sondern Probleme der christlichen "Offenbarung" selbst sind, dürfen wir auch von einem mittelalterlichen Theologen Anwort für sie fordern.'

who in his goodness unveils himself to human beings. Consequently, revelation as God's external expression has its root in God's being who is always communicable, simply because he is good. God communicates to human beings who He is and how He cares for his people. From this point of view, revelation aims at salvation which in the fullness of time appeared in Jesus Christ. However, the fullness of time does not mean the suspension of time but rather in Jesus Christ, time and history are endowed with a definitive meaning which comes forth with the act of creation. This meaning culminates in the freedom, with which human beings are created, and which moves towards its perfection through Jesus Christ. Salvation history is in this sense a history in which human freedom can develop and be perfected. From this point of view, history is progressive because the spirit of Jesus Christ unfolds and directs history towards its fullness. In Jesus Christ, who is the centre of time, history is unrepeatable and irreversible. Thus, history can serve as the *analogia fidei*. History is understood as saving time which manifests God's presence and continual care in this world. This concept of revelation which Ratzinger found in the writings of Bonaventure leads to various consequences. With regard to point four, namely the relationship between revelation and tradition, revelation, understood as a gracious act of God, should be interpreted as the mode of God's continual communication which goes beyond scripture and tradition because it conveys a reality which forms the source of scripture and tradition. This reality cannot be completely confined to the scripture alone or to tradition. This concept of revelation therefore, can help to avoid the rigid interpretation of scripture and tradition. With this understanding, Scripture and tradition become more dynamic.

In his biography, Ratzinger told its readers that

> these insights, gained through my reading of Bonaventure, were later on very important for me at the time of the conciliar discussion on revelation, Scripture, and tradition. Because, if Bonaventure is right, then revelation precedes Scripture and becomes deposited in Scripture but is not simply identical with it. This in turn means that revelation is always something greater than what is merely written down. And this again means that there can be such things as pure sola scriptura...,

because an essential element of Scripture is the Church as understanding subject, and with this the fundamental sense of tradition is already given.[104]

2.7 Ratzinger and the Vatican II Constitution "Dei Verbum"

In an earlier stage, we have said that Ratzinger approached Bonaventure's theology with a set of foundational questions of faith to which he hoped to find answers through a historical and theological examination of the Franciscan's writings. The insights which Ratzinger had gained through the study of Bonaventure's theology proved to be useful for his task as a conciliar adviser (*"peritus"*). As such, Ratzinger participated in various conciliar commission gatherings and discussions,

> (1) He helped on the Doctrinal Commission's revisions of *De ecclesia* and from March 7th, 1964 onwards he was appointed to the special Sub-commission for *De revelatione*;[105] (2) he assisted the Council's commission on Missions in its early 1965 creation of what became Chapter I of *Ad gentes*; and (3) he proposed in October 1965 a revision leading to new material in an important paragraph of the schema *De ecclesia in mundo huius temporis* later promulgated as *Gaudium et spes*, no. 10.[106]

While the debate about the role of Ratzinger at Vatican II is still being engaged,[107] he himself downplayed his contribution,

> You should never, as Karl Rahner often said, overestimate the role of an individual pointing to the general atmosphere of the Council's participants who de-

---

104 *Mi*, 109.
105 *CDV*, 162.
106 Jared Wicks, 'Six texts by Prof. Joseph Ratzinger as *peritus* before and during Vatican Council II', in *Gregorianum* 89 (2008) 2, 233–311.
107 Thomas Weiler, *Volk Gottes – Leib Christ. Die Ekklesiologie Joseph Ratzinger und ihr Einfluß auf das Zweite Vatikanische Konzil* (Mainz: Grünwald, 1997); Maximilian H. Heim, *Joseph Ratzinger – Kirchliche Existenz und existentielle Theologie unter dem Einspruch von Lumen Gentium*, 2. Edition (Frankfurt: Peter Lang, 2005); recently Heim has been awarded the Pope Benedict XVI prize for his work; Pablo B. Sarto, 'Joseph Ratzinger, pertito del Concilio Vaticano II (1962–1965)', in *Anuario de Historia de la Iglesia* 15 (2006) 43–66.

sired a fresh approach to the world. Now, the Council was a very large body, and while individuals certainly generated decisive impulses, the reason they could do so was that others desired the same thing. Perhaps others couldn't formulate it, but the willingness was there; people were on the lookout for something.[108]

Here we will focus only on his contribution to the draft of the constitution *"Dei verbum"* which was promulgated in November 18th 1965 with 2,344 *placet* and only 6 *non placet*. The historical and theological development of this document has been subjected to many scholarly scrutinies.[109] Ratzinger himself also commented on the theological achievements of this document in various locations.[110] According to many experts, the early debate about the schema *De fontibus revelationis* was one of the most decisive moments of Vatican II as the rejection of this proposed schema manifested and liberated a spirit of cooperation on various levels, among the Bishops, between the Pope and the Council fathers, between the Council fathers and *periti* and last but not least, among the *periti* themselves. While Pieter Smulders[111] was responsible for the composition of the final draft, he might also have been inspired by Ratzinger's theological position on the nature of revelation – a position which he had gained through his study of Bonaventure's concept of revelation. The

---

108 *SE*, 71.
109 Umberto Betti, *La trasmissione della divina rivelazione* (Roma: Pont. Athenaeum Antonianum, 1985); Riccardo Burigana, *La biblia nel concilio. La redazione della costituzione "Dei verbum" del Vaticano II* (Bologna: Il Mulino, 1998); Jared Wicks, 'Dei Verbum Developping: Vatican II's Revelation Doctrine 1963–1964', in *The Convergence of Theology. A Festschrift Honoring Gerald O'Collins*, edited by Daniel Kendall and Stephen T. Davis (New York: Paulist Press, 2001, 109–125; id., 'Vatican II on Revelation – From Behind The Scenes', in *Theological Studies* 71 (2010), 637–650; Karim Schelkens, *Catholic Theology on the Eve of Second Vatican Council (1958–1962). A Redaction History of the Schema de Fontibus Revelationis* (Leiden/Boston: Brill, 2010).
110 *CDV*, 155–272; *THV*, 40–48.
111 Jared Wicks, 'Pieter Smulders and Dei Verbum', in *Gregorianum* 82 (2001), 241–297. Wicks pointed out that Ratzinger had given a copy of his text to Smulders who then studied critically and used the critiques Ratzinger voiced against the schema *de fontibus revelationis*, in his theological service to the Indonesian Bishops.

analysis of the Ratzinger's talk to the German-speaking Bishops gathered at the German College S. Maria dell'Anima in Rome in October 1962 will confirm Bonaventure's influence. The text is published in *Gregorianum* by Jared Wicks.[112] According to Wicks,

> 'Prof. Ratzinger's incisive critique of the prepared draft anticipated many of the arguments made against its suitability as a conciliar text when the Council members took it up on November 12th, 1962, leading to the vote of November 20th in which 1,368 Fathers expressed their judgement that the text should go back to the doctrinal commission for extensive revision.'[113]

Thus Ratzinger's critique, voiced also via the authority of Cardinal Josef Frings of Cologne, who was at the same time a member of the preparatory commission and later also appointed member of the Mixed Commission for the revision of the text *de fontibus revelationis*,[114] opened ways for a more pastoral-historical account of revelation which subsequently determined also the pastoral and theological directions of other Council's constitutions and degrees, such as *Lumen Gentium, Gaudium et spes* or *Ad gentes*.[115]

---

112 Wicks, *Six texts*, 269–285 (English), 295–309 (German).
113 Ibid., 242.
114 'Kardinal Frings und das II. Vatikanische Konzil', in *Kardinal Frings: Leben und Werk*, edited by D. Froitzheim (Cologne: Bachem, 1980), 191–205; also Norbert Trippen, *Josef Kardinal Frings (1877–1978)* (Paderborn: Schöningh, 2005); *SE*, 72: 'The second thing ... was that, concretely, when the text on revelation was to be proposed for discussion, Cardinal Frings – and there, admittedly, I did play a part – explained that the text as it was then worded was not an adequate starting point.'
115 See the Pope's address to the Roman Curia in which he gave account on the reception of Vatican II, 'Ad Romanam Curiam ob omnia Natalia', in *Acta Apostolicae Sedis*, vol. XCVIII (Vatican: Libreria Editrice Vaticana, 2006), 45–52; also Wicks, *Vatican II on Revelation*, 643: 'thus, a letter penned by peritus Ratzinger and signed by Cardinal Frings was an early call for Vatican II to give to the Church and to the world an updated account of Catholic teaching on God's revelation.'

2.8 Ratzinger's Critical Assessment of "De fontibus revelationis"

Prior to the official opening of Vatican II on October 11th, 1962, the Central Preparatory Commission sent out seven draft schemas to the Council's participants. The correspondence also included a letter in which the Secretary of State invited the recipients to comment on the drafts. Having received the documents from Rome in August, Cardinal Frings forwarded them to Ratzinger with the request for a theological assessment of the schemas prior to September 15th. One of the seven documents dealt with the sources of revelation.[116] Since his *Habilitationsschrift* in 1955, Ratzinger was regarded as an expert on this topic, even though it was returned in the first instance by the theological faculty. In his account of the events surrounding the debates on the theological and pastoral suitability of the document on "the sources of revelation," Ratzinger recalled the spirit of the text which in his judgement was written rather in a scholastic and defensively condemning style than in a reconciling tone,

> The same cramped thinking, once so necessary as a line of defence, impregnated the text and informed with it a theology of negations and prohibitions; although in themselves they might well have been valid, they certainly could not produce that positive note which was now to be expected from the Council.[117]

Ratzinger's ecumenical sensitivity which he inherited from his principal supervisor Söhngen might be the reason behind his criticism of the narrowing perspective of the document. In similar tone Bishop De Smendt of Bruges, who was member of the Secretariat for the promotion of Christian Unity, regarded the text as a hindrance for ecumenical dialogue,

> The schema is a step backwards, a hindrance, it does damage. The publication of the theological schemata in the form of the drafts we had before us would destroy

---

116 For the historical process of the redaction of the document *de fontibus revelationis* see the detailed study of Karim Schelkens.
117 *THV*, 42.

all the hope that the Council could lead on the drawing together again the separated brethren.[118]

Ratzinger's intention was to modify the text in a positive way, such that it would open the Church to the world and to all Christians who are separated from Rome – a stand he has verbalized already in an earlier text which he composed – again at the request of Cardinal Frings – as a survey on the pre-Vatican situation of the world. The Cardinal used Ratzinger's verdict as his response to the Preparatory Commission,

> Councils always express God's word in ways influenced by contemporary circumstances which make it imperative to give Christian doctrine a new formulation ... But the past does not simply return, whatever may be the connections between the present and what was present in embryo in 1869–70. Our age is really different, and so we will try to characterize the basic currents of present-day culture and thought, which affect the task incumbent upon the teaching work of coming Council.[119]

As for the pastoral direction of the Council and the place of the Church in the world, Ratzinger stated further in the same text,

> The Council must serve this vitality of the Church, promoting the witness of Christian life more than issuing doctrines. This will show the world what is truly central, namely, that Christ is not merely "Christ yesterday", but is the one Christ "yesterday, today, and forever" (*Hebr* 13:8).[120]

In the document *De fontibus revelationis*, Ratzinger saw a direction which was counterproductive and which only repeated the anti-modernist stance particularly against some Catholic theologians. The document as it was in its original did not take history seriously – a point which Cardinal Frings also criticised when voting *non-placet* against certain articles of the schema.[121] Ratzinger, however, sub-

118 *DCV*, 160.
119 Wicks, *Six texts*, text 1, 254f.
120 Ibid., 261.
121 Schelkens, 244: 'Joseph Frings pointed out, upon voting *non placet*, that the articles twenty-one and twenty-two were too strict and that the schema maintained a concept of history that was ambiguous.'

jected the whole document to scrutiny by recurring in particular to the questions with which he had approached the theology of Bonaventure.[122] In accordance with the theological perspective that he had developed earlier in his doctoral and postdoctoral studies, he examined in the first place the correctness of the title of the document because 'the term used affects decisively the understanding of an object and in matters of faith the right use of terms is of major importance.'[123] According to him, the characterization of Scripture and tradition as sources of revelation carries in itself a danger deriving from an 'astounding narrowing the concept of revelation.'[124] In naming the Scripture and tradition as *fontes*, the document would identify revelation with its materiality causing a dangerous '"scripturalism", that is, holding *sola scriptura* [Scripture alone] and identifying Scripture and revelation.'[125] The identification of a reality with its material principles (Scripture and tradition) would mean that the divine revelation can be assessed and determined by a historical-critical exegesis of the Scripture and tradition. Ratzinger therefore recalled in his autobiography the danger which hid in this type of historical understanding of revelation,

> By its very nature, this method has no patience with any restrictions imposed by an authoritative *Magisterium*; it can recognize no authority but that of the historical argument. From its perspective, the concept of "tradition" had itself become questionable, since this method will not allow for an oral tradition running alongside scripture and reaching back to the apostles – and hence offering another source of historical knowledge besides the Bible.[126]

Ratzinger was not opposed to the application of historical-critical method – a point which he emphasizes in various publications.[127] As Christian faith is mediated historically through Scripture and tradi-

---

122 *DCV*, 159.
123 Wicks, *Six texts*, 271.
124 Ibid., 270.
125 Ibid., 271.
126 *Mi*, 124.
127 *JoN*, vol. 1, xv–xxiii.

tion, the historical-critical method is an important tool for a correct understanding of the Jesus' message. However, they cannot determine the contents of revelation whose only author is God. For that reason, Ratzinger also favoured an accurate understanding of the nature of the biblical exegesis which takes into consideration – as he said – the oral tradition. This oral tradition is called *"paradosis"* in the New Testament which is understood as the chain of a living preaching.[128] This *paradosis*, which is entrusted to the Church as *paratheke* under the double form of the living *kerygma* and its written expression in Scripture,[129] is the result of a reality which is named revelation as self-communication of God. Hence, divine revelation is an act of God who on the one hand unveils his inner being to human beings, and on the other hand illumines their minds at the same time. In Ratzinger's theology of revelation, the anthropological component is already included in the revelatory act of God. As such, revelation conveys to us not information, but the salvific will of God which is performative in human lives. For that reason, Ratzinger in his critique of the schema *De fontibus revelationis* argued that it is important not to conflate, but to differentiate between the order of reality and the order of knowledge, which is the result of reflection on the order of reality. Because of its significance for our context, I will repeat Ratzinger's argument in its full length,

> The reversal by which the composed and formulated expressions of revelation, Scripture and tradition, are made sources and revelation becomes something following them, probably became common in the early phase of historicism, when people everywhere were asking about sources and Christians came to call Scripture and tradition the sources in which they found revelation. This way of speak-

---

128 Josef R. Geiselmann, *The Meaning of Tradition* (*Questiones disputate* 15, London: Burns & Oates, 1966), 9: 'According to the New Testament, paradosis is the form in which the Gospel of Jesus comes to us (Jude 3). The second Letter of Peter (2:20) assumes that knowledge of our salvation in Jesus Christ is conveyed to us by paradosis.'; also Martin Hengel, *The Four Gospels and One Gospel of Jesus Christ. An Investigation of the Collection and Origin of the Canonical Gospels* (London: SCM Press, 2010).
129 Geiselmann, *Meaning of Tradition*, 23.

ing is flawed in failing to distinguish the order of reality from the order of our knowing. Scripture and tradition are for us sources from which we know revelation, but they are not *in themselves* sources, for revelation is itself the source of Scripture and tradition. Accordingly, it was traditional in the Middle Ages to call Scripture *fons scientiae* [the source of science], but never *fons revelationis* [the source of revelation]. While it is right that theological work have Scripture and tradition as its "sources", it is dangerous and one-sided to use here the title of a theological treatise on Scripture and tradition in a way wholly centred on the knowing subject, which does not depict the order of reality but instead only our approach to reality. For revelation is not something following upon Scripture and tradition, but is instead God's speaking and acting the one source that feeds Scripture and tradition.[130]

The designation of Scripture and tradition as sources cannot be referred back to the Council of Trent. In this context, Ratzinger referred to the study of Josef R. Geiselmann, Professor in Dogmatic theology at the University of Tübingen, who maintained that the Council of Trent in its final document had objected to the previous wording 'that the truths were contained '*partim* [partly] in written books, *partim* in unwritten traditions.'[131] In their objection to the *partim-partim* passage, the Fathers of the Council of Trent decided therefore not for one source against the other (Scripture vs. Tradition) and left open the question about the relationship between Scripture and tradition,

> Thus by not taking the position that Scripture and tradition each contain a proper part of the truth of revelation, Trent wanted to avoid censuring the position of others who held that all necessary content of faith is given in Scripture and so the relation has to be conceived more as a *totum* than a *partim-partim*.[132]

However, Ratzinger also admitted that at Vatican II he could not foresee the problem caused by many hasty and inappropriate interpretations of Geiselmann's position. Later on in his autobiography, Ratzinger

---

130 Wicks, *Six texts*, 270f.
131 Ibid., 271. Here Ratzinger cited Josef R. Geiselmann, 'Das Konzil von Trient über das Verhältnis der Heiligen Schriften und der nicht geschriebenen Traditionen', in *Die mündliche Überlieferung. Beiträge zum Begriff der Tradition*, edited by Michael Schmaus (Munich, 1957), 123–206.
132 Wicks, *Six texts*, 273.

was more critical against Geiselmann's position which considers Scripture as materially complete,

> The definitive text, however, avoided this "partially/partially", replacing it with an "and": in other words, Scripture and tradition *together* communicate revelation to us. From this, Geiselmann concluded that Trent wanted to teach that there can be no distribution of the contents of faith into Scripture, on the one hand, and tradition, on the other, but rather that both Scripture and tradition, each on its own, contain the whole revelation, hence that each is complete in itself. There was talk of the "material completeness" of the Bible in matters of faith.[133]

And Ratzinger now raised his critique against a wrong conclusion of Geiselmann's thesis,

> This *catch-word*, which was immediately on everybody's lips and was regarded as a great new realization, just as quickly became detached from its point of departure in the interpretation of the Tridentine degree. It was now asserted that the inevitable consequence of this realization was that the Church could not teach anything that was not expressly contained in Scripture, since Scripture was complete in matters of faith.[134]

Once again, the great achievement of Geiselmann was turned around into a prioritisation of the historical-critical exegesis which determined the contents of faith and therefore revelation itself. In order to avoid this one-sided conclusion, Ratzinger suggested that the schema ought to be modified in the sense which deals first with the divine revelation; otherwise as Ratzinger wrote in his theological assessment of the schema *De fontibus revelationis* revelation can become only historical truths.[135] He also opposed to an idea of tradition which is defined as the 'communication of unwritten affirmations.'[136] Here, Ratzinger referred to the example of the dogma of Mary's assumption which – as others argued – is proved only by tradition and not by Scripture.[137]

---

133 *Mi*, 125.
134 *Mi*, 125.
135 Wicks, *Six texts*, 271.
136 Ibid., 275.
137 Ibid., 274.

As it is with the limitation of historical-critical method so here it is with tradition seen as positive historicism: Tradition as positive historical proof of a dogma is in itself insufficient. For that reason, dogma is meaningful only if it is related to the one living organism of the Word of God, which is Christ who lives on in the Church. This Church is based upon three realities, namely Scripture, Tradition and the Church's *Magisterium* which together form the symphony from which the Church's dynamic teaching comes forth. From this understanding of revelation, the Bible can still develop in meaning as a 'process of spiritual appropriation and of elaboration of the mystery of Christ.'[138] Therefore, revelation is God's self-communication entrusted to the Church which is an assembly of pilgrims who are on the way to God with one heart and mind.

Accordingly, Ratzinger recommended a change of the document's title to *De revelatione* or *De verbo Dei*, because Revelation itself is the source of both Scripture and divine tradition. He proposed this to the German-speaking Bishops as they gathered on September 10th, 1962, in the German college S. Maria dell'Anima under the presidency of Cardinal Frings. The reason for this suggestion was that Scripture and tradition are not sources of revelation itself, but only sources of knowing.[139] This call for a modification of the structure and title of the schema was heard by members of the Mixed Commission, created by Pope John XXIII and to which Cardinal Frings was also appointed as member, 'In session between 25 November and 7 December 1962, general agreement was reached on the structure of the schema as well on the new title, *De divina revelatione*.'[140]

In its totality, the constitution reveals traces of many comprises. Nevertheless, it is a very significant document which sets the tone for further debates at Vatican II,

> The text, which was solemnly proclaimed by the Pope on this day, naturally reveals traces of its difficult history; it is the result of many compromises. But the

---

138 Ibid., 275.
139 Ibid., 272.
140 *DCV*, 161.

fundamental compromise which pervades it is more than a compromise; it is a synthesis of great importance. The text combines fidelity to Church tradition with an affirmation of critical scholarship, thus opening up anew the path that faith may follow into the world of today. It does not entirely abandon the position of Trent and Vatican I, but neither does it mummify what was held to be true at those Councils, because it realizes that fidelity in the sphere of the Spirit can be realized only through a constantly renewed appropriation.[141]

According to Ratzinger, Vatican II can therefore be interpreted as a combination of continuity in discontinuity. This point of view is reverberated in his Papal Christmas address to the Roman Curia delivered on December 22nd, 2005, thus forty years after the conclusion of Vatican by Pope Paul VI,

> It is precisely in this combination of continuity and discontinuity at different level that the very nature of true reform consists. In this process of innovation in continuity we must learn to understand more practically than before that the Church's decision on contingent matters – for example, certain practical forms of liberalism or in free interpretation of the Bible – should necessarily be contingent themselves, precisely because the refer to a specific reality that is changeable in itself. It was necessary to learn to recognize that in these decisions it is only the principles that express the permanent aspect, since they remain as an undercurrent, motivating decisions from within. On the other hand, not so permanent are the practical forms that depend on the historical situation and are therefore subject to change.[142]

2.9 Ratzinger's Comments on the Achievements of "Dei Verbum"

Among the aspects of discontinuity and modifications made at various stages during the discussion of the text,[143] which later became the Constitution *"Dei Verbum"*, Ratzinger singled out the most important one with regard to the understanding of interrelation between revelation and the Church,

141 Ibid., 164f.
142 'Ad Romanam Curiam ob omnia natalicia', in *Acta Apostolicae Sedis*, vol. XCVIII (Vatican: Libreria Editrice Vaticana, 2006), 50.
143 See Wicks, *Verbum Dei Developing: Vatican II's Revelation Doctrine 1963–1964*, 109–135.

> In retrospect one can see that this decision was absolutely right. The Council would otherwise have risked falling victim to a kind of ecclesio-monism in its texts, whereas the Constitution on Revelation now stressed the importance of listening, thus moving beyond everything that was said at the Council in order to take up an attitude of listening, an attitude in which the Church transcends itself, for it is not there for its own sake, but only to lead to him to whom all honour is due, God the Lord.[144]

It is quite evident that this close connection between the divine revelation and the nature of the Church represented a new perspective which had been neglected before. This view is re-echoed in Ratzinger's comment on the first article of the Constitution on Divine Revelation which opens with the phrase *'Dei verbum religiose audiens et fidenter proclamans'* [The word of God calls for reverent and confident proclamation].[145] Ratzinger praised this formulation as one of the happiest formulations in the text of the Constitution on Divine Revelation because it exactly avoids the sort of ecclesio-monism as it describes the Church 'in its double role of listening and proclaiming.'[146] This same phrase is reiterated in article ten where the text with regard to the interpretation of the Scripture states, *'pie audit, sancte custodit et fideliter exponit'* [as it devoutly listens, reverently preserves and faithfully transmits the word of God].[147] The Church does not proclaim herself nor does she have a program of her own, except that which she has received from the word of God. She is primarily defined by what she hears from God's word, and therefore, she only proclaims what is given to her in the word which comes from God. In this sense, the Church also does not come together by her own decision, but rather is gathered by a call through the word of God. Through this call human beings are invited to participate in the Trinitarian fellowship. In this sense, the Church's mission is consumed by the word of God. The Church therefore is related internally to

---

144 *DCV*, 162.
145 Translation taken from Norman P. Tanner (ed.), *Decrees of the Ecumenical Council*, vol. 2: Trent – Vatican II (London: Sheed & Ward, 1990), 971.
146 *DCV*, 167.
147 Tanner, 975.

God and externally to the world. She does not exist for her own sake, but proclaims the Crucified Christ to the world. The significance of this passage rests in the fact that therein theology and pastoral care are intertwined. This is plainly verbalized in the phrase taken from Augustine's *de catechizandis rudibus* 4, 8, '*ut salutis praeconio mundus universes audiendo credat, credendo speret, sperando amet.*' [that the whole world may hear the message of salvation, and thus grow from hearing to faith, from faith to hope, and from hope to love].[148] Here we can see with clarity that priority was given to revelation – a modification which Ratzinger had requested in his theological assessment of the schema *De fontibus revelationis*. Ratzinger noted in his commentary on the Constitution on Divine Revelation that this prioritization appears from Text E onwards as a special chapter headed as *De ipsa revelatione*.[149] However, Ratzinger also noted that the Vatican II text was not only a continuation of the councils of Trent and Vatican I, but it also decisively deepened the theology of earlier councils through the insertion of the word "Sacramentum" in the text of Vatican II. The comparison below will illustrate these changes:

Vatican I – *De revelatione*	Vatican II – *De revelatione*
Eadem sancta mater ecclesia tenet et docet, Deum, rerum omnium principium et finem, naturali humanae rationis lumine et rebus creates certo cognosci posse; invisibilia enim ipsius, a creatura mundi, per ea quae facta sunt, intellecta, conspiciuntur: attamen placuisse eius sapientiae et bonitati, alia, eaque supernaturali via, se ipsum ac aeterna voluntatis suae decreta human generi revelare…	Placuit Deo in sua bonitate et sapientia seipsum revelare et notum facere sacramentum voluntatis suae (cf. Eph 1, 9), quo homines per Christum, Verbum carnem factum, in Spiritu sancto accessum habent as Patrem et divinae naturae consortes efficiuntur (cf. Eph 2, 18; 2 Pt 1, 4). Hac intaque revelatione Deus invisibles (cf. Col 1, 15; 1 tm 1, 17) ex abundantia caritatis suae hominess tamquam amicos alloquitur (cf. Ex 33, 11: Io 15, 14–15) et cum eis conversatur (cf. Bar 3, 38), ut eos ad societatem Secum invitet in eamque suspiciat.

148 Tanner, 975.
149 *DCV*, 170.

[The same holy mother church holds and teaches that God, the source and end of all things, can be known with certainty from the consideration of created things, by the natural power of human reason: ever since the creation of the world, his invisible nature has been clearly perceived in the things that have been made. It was, however, pleasing to his wisdom and goodness to reveal himself and the eternal laws of his will to the human race by another, and that a supernatural, way][150]	[It has pleased God, in his goodness and wisdom, to reveal himself and to make known the secret purpose of his will (see Eph 1, 9). This brings it about that through Christ, god's Word made flesh, and in his holy Spirit, human beings can draw near to the Father and become sharers in the divine nature (see Eph 2, 18; 2 Pt 1, 4). By revealing himself God, who is invisible (see Col 1, 15; 1 Tm 1, 17), in his great love speaks to humankind as friends (see Ex 33; Jn 15, 14–15) and enters into their life (see Bar 3, 38), so as to invite and receive them into relationship with himself][151]

At its first glance both texts differ from each other in their theological structure. While Vatican I at the beginning of its text mentions the teaching role of the Church and therefore logically interprets revelation as the communication of divine laws, the text of Vatican II gives priority to God who communicates himself to human beings. The Constitution on Divine Revelation also reverses the statement of Vatican I which prioritizes *"sapientia"* over *"bonitas"*. In doing so, Vatican II gives

> a far greater emphasis to the personal and theocentric starting-point when compared with Vatican I: it is God himself, the person of God, from whom revelation proceeds and to whom it returns, and thus revelation necessarily reaches – also with the person who receives it – into the personal centre of man, it touches him in the depth of his being, not only on his individual faculties, in his will and understanding.[152]

This comment stands in line with what he has learnt from Bonaventure for whom God is diffusive because he is essentially good *(bonum diffusivum)*. Thus God in his goodness freely communicates himself

---

150 Tanner, 806.
151 Ibid., 972.
152 *DCV*, 171.

to human beings. The divine communication is not primarily expressed in eternal laws, but – as we can see in Vatican II – in the form of an invitation,

> From this there follows an understanding of revelation that is seen basically as dialogue, as indicated in the words *alloquitur* and *conversatur* ... This also indicates the element of actuality that is contained in dialogue: the dialogue of God is always carried on in the present; his address "no longer do I call you servants ... but ... friends" (Jn 15:15) is given here and now with the intention of forcing us to reply.[153]

Consequently, this concept of revelation which rests in the divine goodness includes already the anthropological dimension as a speech is directed to a hearer (friends) who in his freedom can answer to it. This dialogue which is described as mystery *("sacramentum")* cannot be objectified and reduced to doctrinal formulations,

> Instead of the legalistic view that sees revelation largely as the issuing of divine decrees, we have a sacramental view, which sees law and grace, word and deed, message and sign, the person and his utterance within the one comprehensive unity of mystery.[154]

This unity of mystery is not something which can only be fully realized in the future, but according to *Eph* 1:10 is already real in the person of Jesus Christ, 'For the mystery of God is ultimately nothing other than Christ himself – it is the person (Col 1:27).'[155] This Christocentric revelation stands in line with his *Habilitationsschrift* in which Ratzinger argued that Bonaventure had interpreted Christ as the centre of history, in contrast to Joachim de Fiore's view. Nevertheless, Ratzinger also warned its readers from a one-sided Christocentric view which is too focussed on its incarnational dimension by which one interprets revelation and salvation history over-optimistically, neglecting the fact of the cross through which the sinners are justi-

---

153 *DCV*, 171.
154 Ibid., 171.
155 Ibid., 171.

fied.[156] Hence a correct understanding of Christology must be supplemented by a pneumatological dimension which emerges naturally

> from a Christology of the resurrection as a correction to a one-sided Christology of the incarnation ... the theocentric position is given appropriate emphasis, towards which the Christocentric view, properly understood, is necessarily orientated.[157]

Ratzinger is opposed to a Christocentrism which neglects its Trinitarian dimension. An incarnational Christology would only cement the rigid concept of tradition which in return would counter the pastoral ecumenical intention of Vatican II. In fact, only within a theocentric frame of Christology, thus in its Trinitarian context, can history become salvation history. In citing Karl Rahner,[158] Ratzinger wrote,

> Christ no longer speaks merely of God, but he is himself the speech of God; this man himself and as an entity the Word of God that has made himself one of us. Thus the perfection of revelation in Christ is here removed from the domain of positivist thinking: God does not arbitrarily cease speaking at some point of history and at some point of his discourse ... but Christ is the end of God's speaking, because after him and beyond him there is nothing more to say, for in him God has, as it were, said himself.[159]

From this theological angle, Ratzinger also rightly criticised Vatican II for missing the opportunity to treat tradition in a critical fashion, 'Consequently, tradition must not be considered only affirmatively, but also critically.'[160] Hence one needs to take in consideration the 'possibility of a *deficere*, and in fact, this possibility is constantly being realized.'[161] For Vatican II and for Ratzinger as well, Scrip-

---

156 Ibid., 174.
157 Ibid., 172.
158 Karl Rahner, 'The Development of Dogma', in *Theological Investigations*, vol. 1 (New York: Herder and Herder, 1961), 49.
159 *DCV*, 175.
160 Ibid., 185.
161 Ibid., 185.

ture can be critical against theological distortions. Once again, one senses here the ecumenical sensitivity of Ratzinger, which went back at least as far as the time of his doctoral thesis. Through Bonaventure's theology of revelation, Ratzinger endeavoured to open the windows to the Lutheran Christians by introducing an inclusive concept of revelation which would permit a dynamic and authentic interpretation of Scripture and tradition. Thus, tradition and Scripture do not exclude each other, but tradition is concerned wholly with Scripture; at the same time Scripture is placed within the framework of tradition.[162] As Scripture and tradition originate in the one divine revelation, they therefore interpenetrate each other. While this interconnection between Scripture and tradition is recognized in contemporary biblical exegesis and theological investigation,[163] the debate on how the two sources of theology are related to each other is still continuing. This hermeneutical "openness" makes the implementation of the Council to some extent problematic. According to Pope Benedict XVI, the blockage of renewal which Vatican II desires for the Church and the world can only be lifted by the application of a right hermeneutic.[164]

---

162 Ibid., 190.
163 Alan Kirk – Thomas Thatcher (eds.), *Memory, Tradition, and Text. Uses of the Past in Early Christianity* (Atlanta: Society of Biblical Literature, 2005); James D. G. Dunn, *A New Perspective on Jesus. What the Quest for the Historical Jesus Missed* (Grand Rapids: Baker Academic, 2005); Martin Hengel, *The Four Gospels and the One Gospel of Jesus Christ. An Investigation of the Collection and Origin of the Canonical Gospels* (Harrisburg: Trinity Press, 2000).
164 'Ad Romanam Curiam ob omnia Natalia', in *Acta Sedis Apostolicae* (2006), 52: 'if we interpret and implement it guided by a right hermeneutic, it can be and become increasingly powerful for the ever necessary renewal of the Church.'

2.10 Ratzinger's Concept of Revelation and Contemporary Approaches to Theology

In his Christmas address to the members of the Roman Curia in 2005, Pope Benedict XVI indicated two contrary hermeneutics which 'came face-to-face and quarrelled with each other.'[165] The first type of hermeneutic is named as 'a hermeneutic of discontinuity and rupture'. In assuming a split between the pre-conciliar and post-conciliar Church, it endeavours to complete the very spirit of the Council. Within this point of view, the supporters of the hermeneutic of discontinuity interpret the conciliar texts as compromises which still uphold many superfluous rudiments of the past.[166] Therefore, the true spirit of the Council can be found not in the texts, 'but instead in the impulses toward the new that are contained in the texts.'[167] As a consequence, one should courageously move beyond the texts as well. In the end, it would come down to the local congregation or communities that become the interpreters of the true spirit of the Council,

> In a word: it would be necessary not to follow the texts of the Council but its spirit. In this way, obviously, a vast margin was left open for the question on how this spirit should be subsequently be defined and room was consequently made for every whim.[168]

---

165 Ibid., 42; similar position can be found also in *Salt of the Earth*, 75 f.; for further debate on this topic see also the valuable contribution of Neil Ormerod, 'Vatican II – Continuity or Discontinuity? Toward an Ontology of Meaning', in *Theological Studies* 71 (2010), 609–636. Ormerod states that the categories continuity and discontinuity appear not to be sufficient to describe the changes which occur in the post-conciliar period. In referring to Bernard Lonergan, Ormerod argues that 'A full response to the issue of change and Vatican II would therefore need to be expanded upon the categories of authenticity/unauthenticity and their relationship to change and development of meaning.' (613)

166 Ormerod, 609 f.: 'On one side is the Bologna approach to church history that, while not denying deep continuity, emphasizes the "rupture" of the council, the ways in which the council was discontinuous with what went before ... Its critics claim that it sets the "style" or "spirit" of the council over and against its official texts that are full of "compromises" to appease conservatives.'

167 *Ad Romanam Curiam*, 43.

168 Ibid., 43.

The second type of hermeneutic is what Pope Benedict XVI called the "hermeneutic of reform",

> of renewal in the continuity of the one subject-Church that the Lord has given us. She is a subject that increases in time and develops; yet always remaining the same, the one subject of the journeying People of God.[169]

From this question, it is evident that a true and authentic renewal can only bear fruits if one gives priority to the Lord who reveals himself by acting in and with the Church. As we have said earlier, revelation involves communication and action. Moreover, in revealing himself God also acts in a particular way by illuminating our hearts and minds so that we can have faith in Him. In repeating our earlier discussion, it is evident that priority is given to revelation from where renewal can come forth. As a consequence of a theocentric comprehensive view of revelation, history as a whole becomes then salvation history. Thus, tradition is not merely a deposit of the past memory, but it still continues to grow and to develop in the course of time. Even within the Sacred Scriptures one can observe a growth from the Old Testament to the Christocentric focus of the New Testament. Within this salvation history, the Church necessarily grows and develops because time, in contrast to Gnostic and platonic view, is not seen as a fall, but as a place in which God freely incarnates himself. The renewal in terms of a commitment to the world of today is also a clear 'commitment to expressing a specific truth in a new way', which 'demands new reflection on this truth and a new vital relationship with it.'[170] Pope Benedict XVI therefore sees in the combination of continuity and discontinuity at different levels the valid component of true reform. Within this hermeneutical frame, changes and modifications can occur in contingent matters, while the essential principles which derive as the consequences of the truth are permanent. As a matter of fact, the openness to the world should not be understood as disruption, but rather as both continuity and discontinuity. For this

---

169 Ibid., 43.
170 Ibid., 44.

reason, Scripture and tradition must complement each other when one interprets contemporary human experiences. Thus, theology as an attempt to understand and translate faith into contemporary context evolves in dialogue with Scripture and tradition. In this regard, Pope Benedict XVI concludes his speech,

> This dialogue must now be developed with great open-mindedness but also with that clear discernment that the world rightly expects of us in this very moment. Thus, today we can look with gratitude at the Second Vatican Council: if we interpret and implement it guided by a right hermeneutic, it can be and can become increasingly powerful for the ever necessary renewal of the Church.[171]

All renewal and reforms, however, must rest on a correct understanding of the concept of revelation, in particular if one undertakes the burden of interpreting Ratzinger's writings and theology that have gained momentum in recent years, since his election into the office of St. Peter in 2005. Among the many publications on Ratzinger's theology,[172] I would like to single out Tracey Rowland's work which was published in 2008 by Oxford University Press.[173] Since its publication, Rowland continues to divide the world of Ratzingerian scholarship. Her affiliation to John Milbank's circle of "Radical Orthodoxy" which often uses or abuses the thoughts of Augustine may add to the ongoing controversy. Rowland's association with the "Radical Orthodoxy" also determines her view on Ratzinger's hermeneutic of Vatican II. According to her, Ratzinger and the "Radical Orthodoxy" share 'a common core, and a very similar reading of cultures of modernity

---

171 *Ad Romnam Curiam*, 52.
172 See Joseph Lam C. Quy, *Theologische Verwandtschaft: Augustinus von Hippo und Joseph Ratzinger/Papst Benedikt XVI* (Würzburg: Echter, 2009); Hanjürgen Verweyen, *Joseph Ratzinger – Benedikt XVI. Die Entwicklung seines Denkens* (Darmstadt: Primus, 2007); Florian Trenner (ed.), *Joseph Ratzinger – Benedickt XVI* (Vatican: Libreria Editrice Vaticana, 2007); Alfred Läpple, *Benedikt XVI. Und seine Wurzeln. Was sein Leben und seinen Glauben prägte* (Augsburg: Pustet, 2006); Thomas Weiler, *Volk Gottes – Leib Christi. Die Ekklesiologie Joseph Ratzingers und ihr Einfluß auf das Zweite Vatikanische Konzil* (Mainz: Grünwald, 1997).
173 Tracey Rowland, *Ratzinger's Faith. The Theology of Pope Benedict XVI* (Oxford: Oxford University Press, 2008).

and post-modernity.'[174] This is evident in her interpretation of *Dei verbum* in chapter three of her book where she also quoted from a book edited by John Milbank.[175] With regard to revelation, Rowland maintains that 'Ratzinger underscored the principle that *actio* (action) is an antecedent to verbum (speech).'[176] Rowland's emphasis on action results in the static interpretation of tradition which serves her as an anchor against the liberal modern and post-modern cultures. In the course of this book, I will show that this assumption is insupportable because it would assume a temporal procedure in God and therefore would separate God's words and action. In line with patristic and medieval Fathers, Ratzinger perceives revelation as *actio* and *verbum*, without introducing a temporal difference in God. The simultaneity of action and speech secures the dynamic characteristic of Tradition and allows a positive dialogue with culture.

One of the criticisms directed against Rowland's approach to Ratzinger's theology is the fact that her interpretation of Vatican II rests upon an insufficient reading and knowledge of the documents. Joseph Komonchack has made this point very clear in this reaction against Rowland.[177] To this we may add that Rowland in her discussion of Ratzinger's concept of revelation did not refer to the latter's *Habilitationsschrift* at all, although she had mentioned its English version at the beginning of her book. To her credit we have to say that the English edition of the *Habilitation* published in 1971 contains only the second part of the original version submitted to the Munich Faculty of Theology in 1955. The original version of the *Habilitation* has been only recently published in German by Herder in 2009. With-

---

174 Ibid., 43.
175 She quoted the work of John Montag, 'Revelation: The False Legacy of Suárez', in J. Milbank, C. Pickstock and G. Ward (eds.), *Radical Orthodoxy* (London: Routledge, 1999), 58.
176 Rowland, 65.
177 Joseph Komonchack, 'A Postmodern Augustinian Thomism? in *Augustine and Postmodern Thought: A New Alliance against Modernity?*, edited by L. Boeve, M. Lamberigts, and M. Wisse (Bibliotheca Ephemeridum Theologicarum Lovaniensium, 219; Leuven: Peeters, 2009), 123–46.

out a more complete familiarity with the context, the interpretation of the role of tradition and Scripture risks being too narrow. Rowland's reading of Ratzinger in the Augustinian-Thomistic tradition ignored the fact that Bonaventure also departed from Augustine, in particular in the question of Trinitarian salvation economy. Rowland, however, maintained that Bonaventure was influenced by Augustine's work on the Trinity.[178] But her understanding of the "opus laboriosum" of Augustine is insufficient. In this regard she is very economical in giving references to back up her claims. Here we must instead argue that the *Seraphic doctor* differed from Augustine in the sense that he took over the idea of the Trinitarian communion *(perichoresis)* which derives from the Cappadocians, instead of aligning himself with Augustine's concept of the unity of the divine persons. In a similar way, Bonaventure not only accepted, but also refused many ideas found in the theology of the *Angelic doctor* Thomas Aquinas. According to Ratzinger, Thomas' concept of the *unitas* of the tradition of faith did not leave sufficient room for history. Furthermore, Rowland seems not to consult the texts and interventions which Ratzinger made prior to or during the debate on *Dei verbum*. Her only source in this regard was Ratzinger's commentary on the "Dogmatic Constitution of the Divine Revelation" edited in 1969 by Herbert Vorgrimler. This has led her to interpret Ratzinger in a narrow sense as if Ratzinger was in opposition to the secular world. In this context, Rowland focussed too much on the discussion of the role and function of tradition which is mostly opposing to secular culture. Despite her emphasis on the dialogical dimension of revelation (personal encounter), Rowland's work seems to play down the personal dimension of revelation – an element which Ratzinger in his *Habilitation* ascribed to the divine revelation itself.[179] In this sense, she contrasted Ratzinger's emphasis on tradition with that of Rahner. She described his theology in terms of an account of nature and grace which has 'a tendency to naturalize

---

178 Rowland, 60.
179 Rowland sees revelation merely in terms of an encounter and ignores that revelation for Bonaventure is also operating actively in each individual believer. Revelation is at the same time illumination of the mind which enables faith.

the supernatural ... a similar tendency to place little value on the medium of a Christian culture.'[180] Here we can reiterate Komonchak's critique of Rowland that a more attentive reading of the Vatican II documents and works of Rahner would reveal many similarities between Rowland's position and that of Rahner against whom she argued. In his biography Ratzinger attested that between Rahner and himself were both dissimilarities and similarities,

> In questions such as liturgical reform, the new place of exegesis in the Church and in theology, and in many other areas, he [Rahner] stood for the same things as I did, but for entirely different reasons.[181]

Of course Rahner was Heideggerian in his anthropology and his theology was more speculative, which in consequence gives little attention to what is historically real and unique. The disagreement between Ratzinger and Rahner rests on the fact that history did not play a significant role in Rahner's theology, although the subjective dimension forms an intrinsic part of Rahner's theology. And yet, this difference cannot be taken as absolute in terms of a black and white judgment. In Rowland's view, however, Ratzinger would rather agree with von Balthasar in this one point where Ratzinger maintains, 'that Revelation can only be mediated from a standpoint of "engraced" participation within the horizon of faith.'[182] This statement is rhetorically very rich, but is theologically confusing. For Ratzinger, faith and grace are at their deepest level two pairs of shoes. Faith, as Ratzinger wrote in his *Habilitation* in 1955, is the outcome of the apparition (historical event) and *illuminatio/revelatio* by God's word (meaning of the event).[183] Therefore, faith in its totality is the conclusive manifestation of the historical event and its meaning. Thus revelation in its strictest sense

180 Rowland, 61.
181 *Mi*, 128.
182 Rowland, 50.
183 *JRGS* 2, 106f.; for Augustine the *illuminatio* is primary *the visio intellectualis* through which one gains insights into the truth. This visio intellectualis is the source for knowledge; see Wolfgang Wieland, *Offenbarung bei Augustinus* (Mainz: Grünewald, 1978), 64–66.

is linked with the illumination (light) of the real meaning of the historical event. The manifestation as the outcome of revelation is an event of grace which enables faith.[184] For that reason, faith is primarily not a human virtue. Here, Bonaventure locates himself within the Augustinian tradition. For the Bishop of Hippo the *"initium fidei"* comes with the divine call *(vocatio)*. In order to understand this call, the human minds and heart must also be illuminated first. In contrast to the Aristotelian view, this illumination is not effected by intermediation, but is a direct divine intervention in the human mind. Both the *vocatio* and *illuminatio* go hand in hand and therefore underline the mystery *("sacramentum")* of the divine revelation.[185] Revelation means that, in a first step, God reveals himself, and, in a second step, he makes himself known by illuminating the human hearts and minds. It is now clear that revelation includes already an anthropological-historical dimension. Ratzinger's view on revelation, therefore, was the result of his reading of Bonaventure which was crucial for his interventions during the process of drafting the Constitution *Dei verbum*. Finally, there is the title of Rowland's book. The subtitle "The Theology of Pope Benedict XVI" suggests that Ratzinger had endeavoured to create a theology of his own. However, Ratzinger said from himself that he never had the intention to write a theology of his own,

> I have never tried to create a system of my own, and individual theology. What is specific, if you want to call it, is that I simply want to think in communion with the faith of the Church, and that means above all to think in communion with great thinkers of the faith. The aim is not an isolated theology that I draw out of myself but one that opens as widely as possible into the common intellectual pathway of the faith.[186]

Ratzinger's theological efforts are not defensive and merely apologetic, but oriented towards the world as they seek 'at the same time

---

184 Dulles, *Models of Revelation* (Dublin: Gill and MacMillan, 1983), 280, expresses similar view.
185 Gerhard Ring, 'Initium fidei', in *Augustinus-Lexikon*, edited by Cornelius Mayer, vol. 3, fasc. 3/4 (Basel: Schwabe, 2006), 205–210.
186 *SE*, 66.

to bring contemporary thought into the discussion.'[187] For him the service to the primacy of truth requires

> our humility and our obedience and can lead us to the common path ... the primacy of the truth ... can't be grasped in a purely abstract way but naturally demands integration into wisdom.[188]

This truth which comes with God's word is inexhaustible, although it is spoken in an historical context,

> The word revealed in history is definitive, but it is inexhaustible, and it unceasingly discloses new depths. In this sense, the Holy Spirit, as the interpreter of Christ, speaks with his word to every age and shows it that this word always has something new to say.[189]

In this sense, revelation is not concluded and cemented in Scripture and tradition: 'If Christian faith is tied to a revelation that was concluded long ago, isn't it condemned to look backward and to chain man to a past time?'[190] This phrase therefore should prevent us from a restrictive interpretation of tradition. A more balanced dynamic and yet critical reflection on the relationship between revelation tradition and Scripture is offered by Lieven Boeve who took up with Ratzinger as his theological sparring partner.[191] In agreement with Ratzinger and the "Dogmatic Constitution on Divine Revelation" Boeve called for a hermeneutic which includes

> the ability to cope with both continuity and discontinuity in order to safeguard the church's faithfulness to tradition. Mere continuity may run the risk of being a deadly self-enclosure without a future.[192]

---

187 Ibid.
188 Ibid., 67.
189 Ibid., 62.
190 Ibid.
191 Lieven Boeve, 'Revelation, Scripture and Tradition: Lessons from Vatican II Constitution *Dei verbum* for Contemporary Theology', in *International Journal of Systematic Theology* 13 (2011) 3, 416–433.
192 Boeve, *Revelation*, 420.

Crucial for this understanding is the perception that revelation is a salvific event realized in the incarnation of the *Logos* in the Person Jesus Christ, and experienced as the true life by the believer. In its very nature, revelation is dialogical. This soteriological nature of revelation therefore forms the very criterion for our understanding of Scripture and tradition. From this point of view, one should recognize the limitation which is inherent in Scripture and tradition, namely both are witnesses to the one divine revelation. Thus, prior to witness was the continual preaching of Jesus Christ as the Saviour and Redeemer,

> As a consequence, Scripture, so to speak, belongs to tradition – to the church's handing-on of the gospel. At the same time, tradition should be understood as proclamation, explanation and diffusion of the Word of God as it has been written down under the inspiration of the divine Spirit in Scripture, entrusted by Christ and the Holy Spirit to the apostles, and transmitted to their successors.[193]

As the preaching of the good news is an ecclesial event, the Church is therefore the first interpreter of the Scripture. This means that revelation surpasses Scripture in both directions,

> *from above* by the words and deeds of God fulfilled in the mystery of Christ, and *from below* by what revelation makes present in the occurrence of faith in the church beyond the borders of Scripture.[194]

From this point of view, Scripture and tradition are of dynamic nature because they are witnesses, and as such, they cannot be identified absolutely with revelation – a point which was not so clearly verbalized in Rowland's book. Her strong anti-liberal overtone has placed Ratzinger in a theological corner which seems to undermine his very intention, namely to conduct a dialogue between faith and culture. In citing Kurt Hübner,[195] Ratzinger concludes his response to Jürgen Habermas,

---

193 Ibid., 422.
194 Ibid.
195 *Das Christentum im Wettstreit der Religionen* (Tübingen, 2003), 148.

Kurt Hübner has recently formulated a similar demand. He writes that such a thesis [reason has its proper limitation] does not entail a "return to faith"; rather, it means "that we free ourselves from the blindness typical of our age, that is, the idea that faith has nothing more to say to contemporary man because it contradicts his humanistic idea of reason, Enlightenment, and freedom". Accordingly, I would speak of a necessary relatedness between culture and faith and between reason and religion, which are called to purify and help one another. They need each other, and they must acknowledge this mutual need.[196]

After this sideline commentary, let us now return to Boeve's dialogue with Ratzinger. In his theological reading of *Dei verbum* Boeve argues that Vatican II in its re-reading of earlier Councils calls for a greater recognition of the historical dynamic dimension inherent in the divine revelation. In his view, the incarnation of the *Logos* makes history a revelatory component of Christian faith. This historical dimension therefore allows tradition to be understood in a much broader sense than the earlier Councils would have permitted. This means that the transmission of tradition is now a task which involves both the whole Church, including the ecclesial hierarchy and the laity. This task demands a dynamic dialogue between the theological scholarship and the *magisterium* whose task is to listen to God's words and to learn from the world. In this context, Boeve then underlines the need for a greater freedom in exegetical and theological investigation – a freedom which goes beyond its ancillary function to the *magisterium*.[197] In this point Boeve believes that the "older" Ratzinger is too restrictive. It appears to him that Ratzinger in his fear of a too optimistic alignment of Vatican II to the world, has closed up prematurely the dialogue between the theologians and the *magisterium*. From this perspective, the historic dynamic nature of revelation as it has been understood by the Fathers of Vatican II is becoming more and more 'truncated'. In Boeve's view, this approach threatens the "spirit" of Vatican II whose aim was to open its windows to the world in a combined effort of *aggiornamento* and *resourcement*. Thus, Ratzinger's fear of relativism has reversed the "spirit" of Vatican II into a closure of the Church from the world.

196 *DoS*, 78.
197 Boeve, *Revelation*, 429.

Boeve's attitude differs from that of Rowland as he confidently emphasizes the important role which exegesis and theology can make to the ecclesial teaching. Boeve voices an important problem for theological research which exists already in the New Testament. This tension cannot be solved in an easy manner, particularly in a time of scientific progress. However, one should ask the question whether it is correct to claim that Ratzinger has changed his fundamental view with regard to Vatican II. To be sure Boeve's critique of Ratzinger's attitude towards exegesis and contemporary theological approaches is not new, as Maximilian H. Heim has already demonstrated in his book.[198] In this regard, Ratzinger will remain a focal point of an ongoing debate, which is often overshadowed by prejudices and suspicions. Nevertheless, one must always make an attempt to understand Ratzinger in his overall intention, regardless of one's personal attitude or preference. In this context, Ratzinger maintained on various occasions that the fundamentals in his life have remained unchanged, although he admitted that individual perspectives are not excluded from correction when the surrounding life coordinates undergo changes. In an interview Ratzinger answered to the common conjecture of two Ratzingers, namely the progressive young theologian and the conservative stern guardian of the faith, with the following statement,

> I think I have already made the essential point, that the basic decision of my life is continuous ... This decision unfolds in the process of life, and in that sense I think it's also good that it didn't freeze at some point or another ... I want to be true to what I have recognized as essential and also remain open to seeing what should change ... I don't deny that there has been development and change in my life, but I hold firmly that it is a development and change within a fundamental identity and that I, precisely in changing, have tried to remain faithful to what I have always had at heart.[199]

The continuous fundamentals of his life are united in the faith in God, in Christ as it is lived in the Church. Of course faith, as we have seen earlier, is enabled through the light which comes from the di-

---

198 Heim, 184–197.
199 *SE*, 116.

vine revelation. This faith is certain as it rests upon the divine promise of salvation which gives hope. For this reason, Ratzinger did not attempt to create a theology of his own, but to stay faithfully in the tradition of the Church. According to him, the construction of an individual theology will remain always an "individual knowledge".[200] For Ratzinger, this confidence in individual expertise can lead to a sectarian arrogance, 'as if we were the new, the true Church, an alternative magisterium with a monopoly on the truth of Christianity.'[201] What Ratzinger has expressed in this quotation summarizes also his experience at Vatican II where the voices of theologians became more important than the voices of the Bishops,

> The role that theologians had assumed themselves to be the truly knowledgeable experts in the faith and therefore no longer subordinate to the shepherds. For, how could the Bishops in the exercise of their teaching office preside over theologians when they, the Bishops, received their insights only from specialists and thus were dependent on the guidance of scholars?[202]

The dependence on historical theological expertise brings with it a risk that makes faith reliant on human decision and knowledge. In this case faith is no longer certain as it is now open to historical scrutiny, revision and change. Accordingly, faith becomes then detached from divine revelation. The magisterial intervention of Ratzinger which appears to some theologians too restrictive and *"instruktionstheoretisch"* (theoretically instructive) must also be judged from this point of view. His intention is not to disregard the importance of theology or historical-critical method or academic freedom,[203] but

200 *LW*, 197: 'Nur solange man von den Einzelerkenntnissen berauscht ist, sagt man: Mehr geht nicht; wir wissen damit alles.'
201 *RREP*, 18f.
202 *Mi*, 133.
203 *LW*, 200: 'Die Anwendung der historischen Methode auf die Bibel als einen historischen Text war ein Weg, der gegangen werden musste. Wenn wir glauben, dass Christus wirkliche Geschichte und nicht Mythos ist, muss das Zeugnis von Ihm auch geschichtlich zugänglich sein. Insofern hat die historische Methode uns auch vieles geschenkt. Wir sind wieder näher am Text und seiner Ursprünglichkeit, sehen genauer, wie er gewachsen ist und vieles mehr;' see also *NTM*, 31–41.

rather to re-introduce a balance which safeguards the gracious-existential nature of faith by linking it back to the living God,

> Revelation has its instruments; but it is not separable from the living God, and it always requires a living person to whom it is communicated. Its goal is always gather and unite men, and this is why the Church is a necessary aspect of revelation. If, however, revelation is more than Scripture, if it transcends Scripture, then the "rock analysis" – which is to say, the historical-critical – cannot be the last word concerning revelation; rather, the living organism of the faith of all ages is then an intrinsic part of revelation. And what we call "tradition" is precisely that part of revelation that goes above and beyond Scripture and cannot be comprehended within a code of formulas.[204]

If Scripture is not absolutely identical with revelation, then historical-critical exegesis or theology can only be seen as possibilities of understanding.[205] And yet tradition should not be understood in a static manner, but entirely in the dynamic sense of the *Dogmatic Constitution on Divine Revelation*,

> Tradition properly understood is, in effect, the transcendence of today in both directions. The past can be discovered as something to be preserved only if the future is regarded as a duty; discovery of the future and discovery of the past are inseparably connected, and it is this discovery of the indivisibility of time that actually makes tradition.[206]

Tradition therefore is dynamic as it looks towards the future which transcends the past. At the same, it is historically embedded in the witnesses of the past which likewise transcends a pure look at the future. This concept of tradition on the one hand considers the dialogue with the world a necessity; on the other hand it is also critical towards the world. Therefore, a tradition which is an intrinsic part of revelation is both dialogue and critique. It is evident that Ratzinger did not have it in mind a break up with the world; even some of his

---

204   *Mi*, 133.
205   *LW*, 201: 'Die historisch-kritische Methode wird immer eine Dimension der Auslegung bleiben.'
206   *PCT*, 87, see also Heim, 184–186.

later comments may have led us in this direction. What he aims at is the liberation of faith from the dominance of scientific method which in the end leaves little room for faith.[207] The truth which is revealed in faith can never be fully materialized,

> It leaves simply space for the freedom of the human decision-making and consent ... God's being is an encounter, which reaches to the depths of human beings, but which can never be fully grasped by an merely explication of material sources. From this perspective it is clear, that faith is a gift of freedom. This gift of freedom, nevertheless, comprises the certainty, that it carries in itself the truth of reality.[208]

Thus, it is not scriptural exegesis or theological investigation; it is not a theory or *gnosis*, but faith which gives certainty. In today's atmosphere the certainty of faith seems to be debatable. Faith is often judged from its psychological or historical perspective. This view is repeated recently by the Australian psychologist and social researcher Hugh Mackay who wrote in his recent comment on the relationship between faith and doubt,

> Faith is also about trust ... But faith can never be rooted in certainty. It evaporates under the pressure of rigid dogma. It is no basis for being judgemental, because it is about seeking, not knowing. Certainty denies the very essence of faith.[209]

For Mackay the claim of certainty is a sign of fundamentalism. From his psychological-historical interpretation faith can only be uncer-

---

[207] *IC*, 182 f.: 'Sometimes one can get the impression from contemporary theology that it is so pleased with its progress – certainly very welcome – ..., and so glad that it is succeeding in moving old boundary stones ..., they quite often simultaneously slip into watering down Christianity into sweet sounding generalities, which certainly flatter the ears of their contemporaries but deny them the strong meat of faith to which they [the believers] are entitled.'

[208] *LW*, 204: 'Es ist einfach der Freiheit des menschlichen Entscheidens and Ja-Sagens Raum gelassen ... Sein Dasein ist eine Begegnung, die bis ins Innerste und Tiefste des Menschen hineinreicht, die aber nie auf die Greifbarkeit einer bloß materiellen Sache reduziert werden kann. Deshalb ist von der Größe des Geschehens her klar, dass Glaube ein Geschenk der Freiheit ist.'

[209] Hugh Mackay, 'Where there's faith, so too doubt', in *The Sydney Morning Herald – News Review*, Christmas Weekend Edition December 23rd, 2011, 14.

tain because of human limitations. Mackay points to human doubt which is part of the human psyche. As a consequence, human being is never sure of the absolute truth. As a seeking being, human person is always a semi-sceptic. Ratzinger would oppose to this view. From the theological perspective, he argued that faith is certain because of the promise given by God who is the Lord of history. For Ratzinger, theology must therefore begin with the certainty of faith; otherwise theology can only rely on suppositions and hypotheses which in the end would contradict the very foundation of theology itself,

> Many people probably think that this meaning of "believing" is also applicable in the realm of religion, so that the contents of the Christian faith are imperfect, preliminary stage of knowledge. When we say, "I believe in God", this, they think, is just an expression of our not knowing anything definite about the matter. If this were so, theology would be a rather strange discipline – indeed, the concept of an academic discipline dealing with faith would actually be a contradiction in itself. For how could one construct a real academic discipline upon suppositions?[210]

With regard to the biblical interpretation, Ratzinger suggests a faith hermeneutic which can be combined with a historical hermeneutic, 'aware of its limits, so as to form a methodological whole.'[211] According to the Pope, this combination would put into practice the methodological principles outlined in *Dei verbum* 12,

> Now since in the Bible God has spoken through human agents to humans, if the interpreter of Holy Scripture is to understand what God has wished to communicate to us, he must carefully investigate what meaning the biblical writers actually had in mind; that will also be what God chose to manifest through their words ... Consequently, a right understanding of the sacred texts demands attention. No less than that mentioned above, to the content and coherence of scripture

---

210 'Address on the Occasion of the Conferring of an Honorary Doctorate in Theology by the Theological Faculty of Wroclaw/Breslau', in *PFF*, 18.
211 *JoN*, vol. 2, xv; also in *LW*, 198: '... eine Exegese vorzulegen, eine Auslegung der Schrift, die nicht einem positivistischen Historismus folgt, sondern den Glauben als Element der Auslegung mit einbezieht. Das ist natürlich in der gegenwärtigen exegetischen Landschaft ein ungeheures Risiko. Aber wenn Schriftauslegung wirklich Theologie sein will, dann muss es das geben.'

as a whole, taking into account the whole church's living tradition and the sense of perspective given by faith.[212]

For that reason, Ratzinger prefers the "canonical" exegesis to the quest for the "historical Jesus" which 'is focussed too much on the past for it to make possible a personal relationship with Jesus.'[213] Once again, Ratzinger is not opposed to the historical-critical method, if it is aware of its limitation. The Pope, however, underscores the need for a faith hermeneutic which includes the historical-critical exegesis,

> We must be clear that about the fact that historical research can at most establish high probability but never final and absolute certainty over every detail. If the certainty of faith were dependent upon scientific-historical verification alone, it would always remain open to revision.[214]

3. Summary

When Ratzinger commenced in 1953 his *Habilitation* project, the theological concept of revelation was determined by denominational colours. While the Lutheran-Protestant side encountered in the revelation a God who acts in human history, the Catholics interpreted it as communication of divine truths. Lutherans would therefore refuse the neo-scholastic concept *"analogia entis"* which in their view would amount to a sort of *"theologia speculativa"*, whereas the Catholics would regard the *"analogia fidei"* as insufficient. It was Söhngen who entered into this debate, in particular with Emil Brunner, against whom he argued that the penetration of revelation necessitates a twofold light, which includes *ratio* and *fides*. Against this backdrop

---

212 Tanner, 976.
213 *JoN*, xvi.; for the usefulness of canonical exegesis see also James D.G. Dunn, *A New Perspective on Jesus. What the Quest for the Historical Jesus Missed* (Grand Rapids: Baker Academic, 2005).
214 *JoN*, vol. 2, 104.

Söhngen maintained that *"analogia fidei"*, in so far it is *"analogia"*, is also *"anlogia entis"*. Faith and metaphysics are complementary because faith always relies on the certainty of truth. Thus, Söhngen made efforts to reconcile both directions. In this ecumenical endeavour, he asked his "favourite" student to investigate the Bonaventurian concept of revelation. Ratzinger's study on Bonaventure confirmed the expectations of his teacher, not only because he and his teacher shared the same philosophical background. At the same time, Ratzinger also went beyond his teacher's hope. With Bonaventure he intended to answer the following fundamental questions: Firstly, what is the nature of revelation? Is it action or dogma? Secondly, how is revelation connected to history? Thirdly, what is the relationship between revelation and "natural theology"? Fourthly, how can we experience the divine revelation? According to the *Seraphic Doctor*, revelation includes both word and action. God's deeds can only be understood with the assistance of divine enlightenment. Therefore, revelation is primarily a theological concept. Revelation is evidently the manner through which God communicates Himself, He who is word and act together. For this reason, revelation in so far it is a theological quality, is always more than its witnesses. It can be absolutely indentified neither with Scripture alone nor with tradition. These are orders of knowledge, while revelation is the reality of this knowledge. Hence, faith, which is an outcome of a personal encounter with this divine reality, precedes its witnesses. As a consequence, historical theology, including the biblical exegesis, cannot fully penetrate the real meaning of revelation. It can clarify the context of the witnesses, but not the divine reality itself. This divine reality reveals itself in the incarnate *Logos*, in whom the truth, already promised in Old Testament, is now fulfilled in a definitive manner. History is now Christ-centred because the divine Word took place in history. History is not fall, but is seen as saving time because it emerges from God's word and will return through the Word which became flesh. Thus, the meaning of revelation is not to dissolve time, as the Gnostics taught, but rather to bring history to its proper integrity. Within the presence of the *Logos*, history can develop and progress towards its fulfilment. Tradition is an element of this continual development. Thus, tradition becomes the dynamic force of the Church that makes the words of God present. Through it, the Church delves deeper into the profound mystery which is God. The Church is the *locus* where we come to experience the continuous self-communication of God. In short, it is through the Church that the Scriptures, which give witness to the divine revelation, are brought back to the life of the people.

His study of Bonaventure provides Ratzinger with the theological insights that made him one of the main contributors at Vatican II. If it is correct, that the constitution *Dei verbum* was one of the theological cornerstones of the Council, then Ratzinger was perhaps one of the important builders who helped to ensure that this edifice has also a pastoral and ecumenical structure. If revelation is dialogical, then ecumenism is a responsibility. If revelation is dialogical because it is fulfilled through the *Logos*, then the dialogue must be based on truth without which a conversation would end up in banalities. For this reason ecumenical dialogue is more than the debate about the various differences which separate Christians from one another. Thus, dialogue is a process of spiritual appropriation and elaboration of the mystery of Christ. In this sense, a dialogue requires open-mindedness and discernment.

Chapter Two: *Christology*

1. Introduction

The theological methods have changed drastically since the Second World War. Christology is one of the theological disciplines which is exposed to changes. In a context which is dominated by the historical-linguistic turn in humanities, revelation not only comes under suspicion, but the traditional path of Christological reflection is also challenged by the preponderance of historical method. It appears that this historico-literal criticism has gained much prominence in the biblical scholarship. As a consequence, Christology, which has become more and more social-political anthropology, is now separated from revelation in the sense that it does not consider Jesus Christ as the definitive revealer of the divine truth. Thus, the divinity of Jesus Christ is reduced in favour of the human Jesus. It is against this historical reduction that Ratzinger proposed an alternative approach to Christology which is more inclusive than the exclusive reliance of historical-critical method. According to him, only a spiritual Christology can lead to the true knowledge of the real Jesus. Ratzinger came to it only in 1981, although his earlier theological publications contain traces of this new approach. The spiritual Christology culminates in the Pope's recent three volumes on *Jesus of Nazareth* in which he offered his personal spiritual reflection of the faith in Jesus Christ. There is no doubt that Ratzinger's spiritual Christology is a theological-practical consequence of his earlier study of the Bonaventurian concept of revelation.

In his *Habilitation* thesis on Bonaventure's concept of revelation, Ratzinger touches the central problem of theology which has been divisive since the Council of Trent (1545–1563). Is revelation an act by which God either discloses eternal truth to humankind (in an informative manner), or intervenes directly in the world and humans (in a more performative acitivity)? The answer to such a question depends on denominational perspective. For the Franciscan theologian revelation, is not merely a statement about God, but describes the divine action in relation to the human subject. As we have seen in the first chapter of this book, this divine action is Christo-centric – for at least two reasons. Firstly, Ratzinger's Christology is situated within the divine dialogue, for God is never without his *Logos*. Christology and revelation are intrinsically connected. Secondly, this *Logos* becomes *sarx* (flesh). History turns therefore into salvation history centred on Jesus Christ. Time is now saving time. As a consequence of this Christological mediation, history and faith must be seen as complementary factors. Only in connection with faith can history on the one hand transcend the confinement of its past and influence the present; and, on the other hand, faith through its embodiment in history gains concreteness.

Ratzinger's Christo-centrism[1] is in sharp contrast to Rahner's transcendental method.[2] It is not, therefore, a system, either from "below" or from "above".[3] In this context, Ratzinger draws attention to two theological difficulties which arise from the historical-literal approach to the Scriptures. A Christology from "below" can run into the Nestorian trap,

> in which, when one reflects on the humanity of Christ, his divinity largely disappears, the unity of his person is dissolved, and reconstructions of merely the human Jesus dominate, which reflect more the idea of our times than the true figure (Gestalt) of our Lord.[4]

1 See Emery De Gáal, *The Theology of Pope Benedict XVI. The Christocentric Shift* (New York: Palgrave Macmillan, 2010).
2 Roman A. Siebenrock, 'Christology', in *The Cambridge Companion To Karl Rahner*, edited by Declan Marmion – Mary E. Hines (Cambridge: Cambridge University, 2005), 120: 'In his final stage there is a shift in Rahner from a Christology from above to a Christology from below.'
3 Ratzinger notes in the second volume of his work *JoN*, vol. 2, xvi, that his Christology has been labelled as 'an example of Christology from above.'
4 *NSL*, 10.

And a Christology from "above" can end up in a kind of Monophysite Christology which minimises the human in Christ.[5] According to Ratzinger, a solid Christology must embrace both the condescending and ascending natures of Jesus Christ. Such a Christological method has exegetical consequences. For Ratzinger, Christology is a theological spiritual reflection of the meaning of Jesus Christ. Historical exegesis alone is quite insufficient for the understanding of the real Jesus Christ:

> If scholarly exegesis is not to exhaust itself in constantly new hypotheses, becoming theologically irrelevant, it must take a methodological step forward and see itself once again as a theological discipline, without abandoning its historical character.[6]

Only as theologically interpreted can the cross and resurrection of Jesus become meaningful events of God's revelation. Within this theological framework, as Ratzinger repeatedly emphasizes, theology evolves from a constant dialogue with the faith of Church. Christology then cannot rest only on historical premises or analyses, but must also be done with a shared spiritual insight. Referring to the historical-biblical exegesis, the Prefect of CDF was convinced that only a spiritual Christology can offer a full knowledge of the real Jesus Christ.[7] As far as the Cardinal saw it, this spiritual Christology also fulfils the ecumenical and pastoral intention of Vatican II[8] because the foundation of renewal and hope lies in the salvific revelation in the Word-Son: 'As I read the texts it become clear, much to my astonishment, that the achievement of a spiritual Christology had also been the Council's ultimate goal.'[9] Clearly, this spiritual Christology is the concrete practical application of his study of the Bonaventurian concept of revelation.

---

5   *NSL*, 7.
6   *JoN*, vol. 2, xiv.
7   *PO* (San Francisco: Ignatius, 1986).
8   Perhaps *GS* no. 22 best expresses the link between spirituality and Christology.
9   *PO*, 9.

A few theologians branded Ratzinger's Christology as an approach from above, which, in their view, is nothing else than a systematic Christological anthropology. Robert Krieg observed in Ratzinger's *Introduction to Christianity* an idealism à la Max Scheler which risks conflating Christology with anthropology; thereby the historical is submitted to systematic universalism.[10] As a consequence, he believed that Ratzinger's Christology marginalises the historical individuality of Jesus. To this criticism one must reply that the recent publication of the two volumes on Jesus of Nazareth has shown the Pope's concern for the historical,[11] in sharp contrast to Rahner who paid only little attention to the biblical historical context. This transcendental method therefore can only end up in an anonymous Christianity.[12] And yet the Pope is also convinced that historical facts can only gain meaning if they are incorporated into a global perspective, which can come only from faith.[13] However, Krieg's criticism reflects once again the tension between faith and history that has been introduced into theology since the nineteenth century. Other theologians endeavoured to solve this problem by ascribing to history a judicial role in the relation to faith. They argued that in many cases historical facts not only contradict the faith's claim, but historical research also reveals that the beginning of faith's tradition was not uniform, but rather multi-layered.[14] Thus,

10 Robert Krieg, 'Cardinal Ratzinger, Max Scheler and Christology', in *Irish Theological Quarterly* 47.3 (1980), 205–219. Ratzinger's theological methodology unfolded in *Introduction to Christianity* is critically examined by Hans Albert, 'Joseph Ratzingers Apologie des Christentums: Bibeldeutung auf der Basis einer spiritualistischen Metaphysik', in *ZfRG* 59.1 (2007), 14–35.
11 *JoN*, vol. 1, xv: 'If we push this history aside, Christian faith as such disappears and is recast as some other religion. So if history, if facticity in this sense, is an essential dimension of Christian faith, then faith must expose itself to historical method – indeed, faith itself demands this.'
12 Here Ratzinger disagrees with Rahner's thesis of anonymous Christianity whose foundation Ratzinger saw in the latter's unbiblical theology, see *PCT* (San Francisco: Ignatius, 1987), 162–171.
13 *LW* (Freiburg: Herder, 2010), 198.
14 Terrence W. Tilley, *History, Theology and Faith: Dissolving the Modern Problematic* (New York: Orbis, 2004).

the only solution is by pass the problem by acknowledging the variety of constitutive factors in Christian faith. In their view, ecclesial dogmatism has tended to eliminate the colourful origins of faith. But according to Ratzinger, this type of historical theology is doomed to fail because it neglects the most important feature of human existence, namely the presence of a collective memory.[15] It is not the pure knowledge of facts, but rather the collective memory which gives meaning to historical events, and therefore establishes the identity of a group. However, memory does not exist in a vacuum. According to Maurice Halbwachs and Jan Assmann, human memory does not only retain historical facts, but these facts are embedded and reconstructed within sociological and cultural frameworks.[16] By applying the notion of social-cultural memory to Christian history, it becomes obvious that the core encounter with Christ is experienced and relived through the liturgical worship and faith practices which Christians call tradition. In the liturgical commemoration, where the faith in Jesus Christ is professed, the historical events of Jesus Christ are re-experienced. It is through the faith-memory that the past transcends its boundaries, and, connected to the present. The present, however, already participates in the future. In this way, the memory of the early Christianity retained on the one hand the historical traces of its founder; and on the other hand it continually reconnects the tradition of the past to the present time. This dynamism arises from the eschatological dimension of biblical faith:

---

15 Recent cultural and biblical scholarships considered the memory as indispensable element of the formation of faith and tradition about Jesus; see Dale C. Allison, *Constructing Jesus: Memory, Imagination and History* (Grand Rapids: Baker Academic, 2010); Mark Smith, *The Memoirs of God: History, Memory and the Experience of the Divine in Ancient Israel* (Minneapolis: Fortress, 2004); James D.G. Dunn, *A New Perspective on Jesus: What the Quest for Historical Jesus Missed* (Grand Rapids: Baker Academic, 2005).
16 See Maurice Halbwachs, *On Collective Memory*, edited, translated and with an Introduction by Lewis A. Coser (Chicago: Chicago University, 1992); Jan Assmann, *Religion and Cultural Memory* (Stanford: Stanford University, 2000).

> But the tradition of Israel also oriented Christian thought toward the future... Christianity moreover juxtaposes, in reality superimposes the Eucharist and the spiritual exercises... onto the Jewish cult which has been unburdened in this manner.[17]

For Ratzinger, memory is the indivisible centre of communication in which faith and historical knowledge are mutually mediated and interwoven. Only in this way can there be a meaningful reliving of Jesus' history. Referring to the Christological context of *Heb* 13:8: 'Jesus Christ is the same yesterday and today and forever,' Ratzinger comments:

> This was the profession of those who had known Jesus on earth and had seen the Risen One. This means that we can see Jesus Christ correctly today only if we understand him in union with the Christ of "yesterday" and see in the Christ of yesterday and today the eternal Christ. The three dimensions of time as well as going beyond time into that which is simultaneously its origin and future are always a part if the encounter with Christ.[18]

Faith-memory therefore reveals the many dimension of the real Jesus, which a narrow scope of historical-critical exegesis cannot achieve. Alan Kirk pleads for a return to the importance of memory. He notes the failure of the nineteenth-century quests for the historical Jesus and limitations of a notion of tradition that marginalises faith-memory:

> A glance at a key text for Christian memory, the *anamnesis* passage in 1 *Cor* 11:23–26, shows memorializing practices of early Christian communities implicated in ritual and ethics, in issues of oral tradition and transmission, and accordingly in historical Jesus questions as well.[19]

---

17 Halbwachs, 96.
18 *NSL*, 11; see also *PCT*, 22–25, in particular 23: 'God is memory per se, that is, all-embracing being, in whom, however, being is embraced as time. Christian faith, by its very nature, includes the act of remembering; in this way, it brings about the unity of history and the unity of man before God, or rather: it can bring about the unity of history because God has given it memory. The seat of all faith is, then, the *memoria Ecclesiae*, ... It exists through all ages, waxing and waning but never ceasing to be the common sites of faith.'
19 Alan Kirk – Tom Thatcher (eds.), *Memory, Tradition and Text. Uses of the Past in Early Christianity* (Atlanta: Society of Biblical Literature, 2005), 1.

Only through constant communication of the past with the eschatological memory of community (worship, practices and teaching) can the real Jesus become accessible to the believers, who are distant from the original context. Thus, in memory, the *Kerygma* in the form of a confession is fused directly with the unique story of Jesus.[20] In this sense, the confessional memory is expressed in the narrative traditions apparent in the gospels. On the other hand, the gospel narratives can be understood only on the basis of the collective memory. Ratzinger prioritizes the "canonical exegesis" which aims to read 'individual texts within the totality of the one Scripture, which then sheds new lights on all the individual texts'.[21] In this, he is consistent with his understanding of revelation and Church, which he learned respectively from Augustine[22] and Bonaventure.

2. The Church's Remembrance as the Realm of Understanding

On various occasions, Ratzinger maintains, that since the conclusion of Vatican II, the theological panorama has fundamentally changed. While certain frameworks remained unchallenged in theological controversies prior to Vatican II, these fundamentals themselves are now 'widely matters of dispute.'[23] For example, Ratzinger singles out the

---

20 Martin Hengel, *The Four Gospels and the One Gospel of Jesus. An Investigation of the Collection and Origin of the Cannonical Gospels* (Harrisburg: Trinity International, 2000), 92 f.
21 *JoN*, vol. 1, xviii.
22 See Joseph Lam Cong Quy, *Theologische Verwandtschaft. Augustinus von Hippo und Joseph Ratzinger/Papst Benedikt XVI.* (Würzburg: Echter, 2009).
23 'Seven Theses on Christology and the Hermeneutic of Faith', in *The Hermeneutic of Continuity: Christ, Kingdom and Creation*, edited by Scott Hahn (Steubenville/Ohio: St. Paul Center for Biblical Theology, 2007), 189. The same seven theses can be found in Ratzinger's book *PO*, 13–46.

Christological debate which he sees as being reduced to a historical analysis. Indeed, the historical approach to biblical sources has produced many images of Jesus which cause confusion among Christians. Like the people in the time of Jesus, Christians and non-Christians today raise the same fundamental question with which Jesus once has challenged his disciples: 'Who do the people say that I am?'[24] And the disciples reported to Jesus what the people said about him: 'John the Baptist, and others say Elijah; but others, that one of the prophets of old has risen again.'[25] Commenting on the answers by the Apostles, Ratzinger argues that the people depicted Jesus according to their historical knowledge or categories which were available to them.[26] He writes,

> The answers of the people in the time of Jesus, as reported in the gospels, reflect the attempt to find, in the arsenal of the known and nameable, categories in which to describe the figure of Jesus.[27]

The answers of the people of Jesus' time are comparable to the attempts of the historical-critical method attempts to reconstruct the historical nucleus ("historischen Kern") of Jesus' identity. Instead of moving towards the eschatological future of the Reign of God, faith in Jesus Christ becomes, in effect, regressive.[28] When history is interpreted backwards, the mysteries of faith are confined to the past, 'in such a way that it is made incapable of speaking to us in the present.'[29]

24 *Mk* 8:27 || *Mt* 16:13 || *Lk* 9:18.
25 *Lk* 9:18.
26 *PCT*, 23: 'catalogue of things to be believed.'
27 Hahn, 190.
28 This point represents Ratzinger's main criticism against the theology of liberation: 'The essential mistake in best known attempts at a liberation theology was reading this history backwards. This means that instead of progressing on the path of the history of liberation as the Bible describes it, from Moses to Christ and with Christ toward the kingdom of God, liberation theology went in the opposite direction;' see *NS L*, 5 f.
29 Jesús Martínez Gordo, 'The Christology of J. Ratzinger – Benedict XVI in the Light of His Biography', in *Edition Cristianisme y Justicía*, 1–31, here 5; see <www.fespinal.com> (accessed on 14 April 2012).

Fixation only on the past would suggest that the New Testament did not intend to promote a living and world transforming faith. Jesus is reduced to a merely Jewish man, intent only on renewing his own Jewish religion. Ratzinger maintains, then, that historical retrospection is precisely the cause for the many contradictory portraits of Jesus. Without an interpretative frame, historical sources can be construed differently, depending on individual ideologies. Even those titles which were given to Jesus by the people, such as prophet, priest, Paraclete, Lord, Son of God or Messiah, can carry different meanings. Reflecting on Peter's confession of Jesus as the Messiah, Ratzinger argues:

> Although Peter's confession provided a fundamental orientation, regarded by believers as pointing in the right direction, the single formula, "Jesus is the Christ, the Messiah" was not sufficient by itself. In the first place, the title "Messiah" had many different meanings ... Peter's confession ... clearly shows the need for explanation and clarification.[30]

It is obvious that this reconstruction, which is based upon historical hypotheses, cannot lead the readers into the knowledge of the real Jesus. Historical-critical exegesis cannot move beyond or transcend the past. As a consequence, it can see in Jesus only a human being in whom God operates. From this reduced historical perspective it seems impossible that a man, who lived in a particular context and place, could act as God, let one be God among us.[31] At most, Jesus would appear as a moral-religious person who lived his life in complete confidence of his God. He was the man who taught the way to liberation, but was not the one who brought salvation, even though he superseded the prophets. Jesus, the human being, may appeal more to modern people traumatized and depressed by their own weaknesses. Because Jesus is understood as human, he can be imitated by his

---

30   Hahn, 190.
31   *UChr*, 61: 'Dieser Voraussetzung gemäß ist es nicht möglich, daß ein Mensch wirklich Gott ist und Taten vollbringt, die göttliche Macht erfordern und den allgemeinen Ursachenzusammenhang sprengen würden."

fellow human beings. For this reason, Christology is now becoming separated from soteriology which is ascribed solely to God. This separation has an enormous practical impact on Christian life:

> Discipleship of Jesus, however, concentrates on the man Jesus who opposes all forms of authority; one of its features is a basically critical attitude to the Church, seen as a sign of its faithfulness to Jesus. This in turn goes beyond Christology and affects soteriology, which must necessarily undergo a similar transformation. Instead of salvation we find liberation taking pride of place, and the question, 'How is the liberating act of Jesus to be mediated?' automatically adopts a critical stance over against the classical doctrine of how man becomes a partaker of God.[32]

According to Ratzinger, it is only within the framework of the ecclesial faith tradition that one can gain access to the real history of Jesus:

> We could put it like this: the Church's tradition is the transcendental subject in whose memory the past is present. As a result of this, as time moves on and in the light of the Holy Spirit who leads men to the truth, what is already present in the memory is seen more clearly and better understood.[33]

Of course, one can question the accuracy of memory. Is memory not already a second revision of past events? Though Ratzinger would not deny this, he would not accept the liberal hypothesis that ecclesial faith is necessarily a 'falsification of the original phenomenon simply because the historical distance is too great.'[34] In his view, faith is not a falsification, but rather a process of simplification and concentration of the many historical experiences deriving from a personal encounter with Jesus Christ and kept in the memory of the first generation of Christians. Indeed, ecclesial faith is the participation in the vision of Jesus' own vision:

> Of its essence Christian faith is sharing in the vision of Jesus, mediated by his word, which is the authentic expression of his vision. Jesus' vision is the point of reference of our faith, the point where it is anchored in reality.[35]

32 *PO*, 14.
33 *PO*, 31.
34 Hahn, 191.
35 *LoChr*, 32.

As we have seen, the earliest believers made great efforts to capture Jesus' reality by exploiting a repertoire of familiar categories and titles. On this point, Ratzinger argues, that among the many titles ascribed to Jesus, the early Church considered "sonship" as the most comprehensive category to express the basic historical experience of eyewitnesses. In fact, "sonship" is the concentration of all other titles. Ratzinger clarifies this point:

> Since the title *Christ* (Messiah) became more and more associated with the name Jesus and had little clear meaning outside a Jewish milieu; and since *Lord*, too, was not as clear as *Son*, a further concentration took place. The title *Son* comes in the end to be the only comprehensive designation for Jesus. It both comprises and interprets everything else ... In bringing the many strands of tradition together in this one word and thus imparting an ultimate simplicity to the fundamental Christian option, the Church was not oversimplifying and reducing: in the word Son she had found that simplicity with is both profound and all-embracing.[36]

Ratzinger agrees with van der Leeuw,[37] the great expert on the phenomenology of religion: the profundity and all-embracing nature of the Christian faith originates in the fact 'that in the history of religion God the Son was there before God the Father.' Transferring this thesis into Christianity, Ratzinger adds, 'It would be more accurate to say that God the Saviour, God the Redeemer appears earlier than God the Creator.'[38] This primordial experience of redemption, which appears in the Son, was the all-embracing category for interpreting all titles given to Jesus:

> Calling Jesus the Son, is far from overlaying him with the mythical gold of dogma ... To the contrary, it corresponds most strictly to the center of the historical figure of Jesus. For the entire gospel testimony is unanimous that Jesus' words and deeds flowed from his most intimate communion with the Father ... Luke, of all the evangelists, lays stress on this feature. He shows that the essential events

---

36 Hahn, 191.
37 Here he cites Gerardus van der Leeuw, *Phänomenologie der Religion*, 2nd edition (Tübingen: 1956), 103.
38 *IC*, 68.

of Jesus' activity proceeded from the core of his personality and this core was his dialogue with the Father.[39]

Thus, all Christological titles and formulations are only meaningful if they are interpreted from the perspective of salvation through Jesus Christ – and this forms that remembrance on the part of the Church that Jesus commanded:

> This being so, fellowship with Jesus and the resultant knowledge of Jesus presupposes that we are in communication with the living subject of tradition to which all this is linked – in communication with the Church. The message of Jesus has never been able to live and mediate life except in this communion ... It grew in and from the Church; its unity comes solely from the Church's faith, which brings together diverse elements into a unity ... This remembrance on the part of the Church lives by being enriched and deepened by the experience of love which worships.[40]

From this perspective, faith is a dynamic factor. It leads history into the future where history will be fulfilled and God's love will be all in all.

3. The Faith in Jesus Christ

Ontologically speaking, God's dialogical nature is grounded in his being as love. But this love is not merely a feeling or emotion which can dissipate. Since God is love because he is good, the divine communication is neither a psychological nor a mental act by which God actualizes himself. Rather, the basis of God's communicative nature lies in his self-giving character *(bonum diffusivum sui)*. Gerald O'Collins identified in this self-giving quality of divine love a redemptive aspect:

---

39   Hahn, 191.
40   *PO*, 30f.

> Self-giving also marked this redemptive initiative of God. Sometimes it is said that 'when we love, we give the best of ourselves'. Certainly the three divine persons gave the best of themselves through the sign and presence of the Son of God among us ... The free self-giving entailed a new presence that effected a communion of life and love.[41]

As divine gift of salvation, Jesus Christ is the centre of salvation history. O'Collins continues in this direction: 'Visibly sharing his presence, Christ brought about results that were and remain life-giving and life-enhancing – in a word, salvific.'[42] In Jesus Christ, salvation is achieved for all: 'There can be no bypassing Christ when we come to the goal of salvation and revelation. He will be there for everyone as Saviour and Revealer.'[43]

But is this claim really so evident? Can Christians make this assertion with a tranquil conscience vis-à-vis the hard reality which surrounds them? With this problem in mind, Ratzinger observes that,

> Modern negativity is located not in any transcendent realm but in the hard reality before us: ... the First and Second World Wars, from the killing fields at Verdun to the Nazi furnaces and swift annihilation of thousands in Hiroshima and Nagasaki, the carpet bombing of Vietnam and Cambodia, the massacres from Setif and Soweto to Sabra and Shatila, and list goes on and on. There is no Job who can sustain such suffering.[44]

If people live only by facts, and if facts represent the totality of what human can know and experience, the only reaction is dread. Mere facts can paralyse human beings. There can be no Job to withstand such meaningless and overwhelming suffering. There is no denying the importance of the *factum* (or factual situation), especially when the incarnation is precisely the sign of divine concern for the

---

41 O'Collins, *Jesus*, 183 f.
42 Ibid., 184.
43 Ibid., 225.
44 Antonio Negri – Michael Hardt, *Empire*, (Boston/MA: Harvard University, 2000), 46; cited according to Karen Armstrong, *The Case For God* (New York: Anchor, 2010), 278.

factum.[45] Nonetheless, Ratzinger maintains that Christianity is also decisively shaped by a faith reality. As Pope, he designates it as substance or *hypostasis*,[46] through which one stands firm on a specific ground, despite the hard and terrifying facts. He distinguishes a theory of "know-make"[47] from the Christian concept of "stand-understand".[48] The knowing-making relationship is an outcome of human action through which human agents knowingly construct their world. In contrast, standing-understanding relationship points to given order created by a personal God to whom we turn in faith: Faith, then,

> is a way of taking a stand in the totality of reality, a way that cannot be reduced to knowledge and is incommensurable by knowledge; it is the bestowal of meaning without which the totality of man would remain homeless on which man's calculations and actions are based.[49]

The whole reality is love which 'embraces the whole of existence in each of its dimensions, including the dimension of time.'[50] Thus one stands firm in this love. In its deepest dimension love is a gift which opens up to human being 'the space of meaningful existence,'[51] despite the hard reality of sufferings and despair. This space of meaningful existence is Jesus Christ, who with his cross answers to Job's cry. Ratzinger concludes:

---

45   *IC*, 38: "Christian belief really is concerned with the *factum*; it lives in a specific way on the plane of history and it is no accident that history and the historical approach grew up precisely in the atmosphere of Christian belief. And indubitably belief also has something to do with changing the world, with shaping the world, with the protest against the lethargy of human institutions and of those who profit from them."
46   See *SpS* no. 7.
47   Ibid., 39: "the act of believing does not belong to the relationship 'know-make,' which is typical of the intellectual context of 'makability' thinking."
48   Ibid., 39.
49   Ibid., 42.
50   *DC*, no. 6.
51   *LoChr*, 84.

> The cross of Christ means that he precedes us and that he accompanies us on the painful way of our healing and salvation ... a form of accompanying people on the difficult but beautiful way to new life that is also the way to true and lasting joy.[52]

Since Christ's cross reveals God's unconditional love, it 'discloses the fullness of all being in its breadth and depth.'[53] If we return to Job and his experience of the overpowering sufferings, then it becomes clear that only God's love can be the answer. Such love not only takes seriously the burden which derives from the experience of evil, but it also gives hope and real comfort to humans in a desperate situation. Ratzinger continues:

> What is the meaning of the cross of the Lord? It is a form of the love that has totally taken hold of humanity and as a result has also descended into the sin and death of humanity. This love has become a 'sacrifice': a love without limits that has taken up humanity – a lost sheep – onto his shoulders and brought it back to the Father through the night of sin. Ever since then there has been a new way of suffering that is not a curse but a love that transforms the world.[54]

This transforming love manifests at the same time Job's 'smallness and ... the poorness of the perspective from which he looked at the world. He learned how to quiet down, how to be silent, and to have hope.'[55] Thus, God's love is an action, or better, an act of compassion which 'was not like a simple act of feeling, but it was a reality. The compassion of God took on flesh ... God entered into our suffering.'[56] This compassion of God is therefore the foundation of faith on which Job can stand firm: despair is conquered by God's indestructible love:

> The worst anxiety of all, as we have already said, is the fear of not being loved, the loss of love: despair is thus the conviction that one has forfeited all love

---

52 Ibid., 89f.
53 Ibid., 66.
54 *GChr*, 47–48.
55 Ibid., 44.
56 Ibid., 45.

forever, the horror of complete isolation. Hope in the proper sense of the word is thus the reverse: the certainty that I shall receive that great love that is indestructible and that I am already loved with this love here and now.[57]

Accordingly, the certainty of faith goes beyond the facts of visible reality because it is based upon a truth which is not somehow out there, but rather this truth appears as a person who bears us up and the world. For this reason, faith is more real than objective facts because it involves the act of entrusting oneself to a person who does not remain apathetic vis-à-vis our hard reality, and that this person knows us and loves us; and that in his empathy with those who suffer and are tormented by despair, he would do his best, even beyond what humanly is unimaginable:

> Christ descended into "Hell" and is therefore close to those cast into it, transforming their darkness into light. Suffering and torment is still terrible and unbearable. Yet the star of hope has risen – the anchor of the heart reaches the very throne of God. Instead of evil being unleashed within man, the light shines victorious: suffering – without ceasing to be suffering – becomes, despite everything, a hymn of praise.[58]

In Jesus Christ, God does not only make comprehensible to Job that He loves him, but also manifests the fact that He *is* really love.[59] It is so because Jesus Christ is not simply a witness 'whose evidence we trust,' but rather he is the 'presence of the eternal itself' in this world.[60] This worldly presence of the eternal therefore is not a product of human making; rather it is God as person who comes to meet us:

---

57 *LoChr*, 67.
58 *SpS*, no. 37.
59 *PCT*, footnote 172: 'In view of the fundamental meaning of this "is", I would stress…the irreplaceability and pre-eminence of the ontological aspect and, therefore, of metaphysics as the basis of any history. Precisely as a confession of Jesus Christ, Christian faith…is faith in a living God. The fact that the first article of faith forms the basis of all Christian belief includes, theologically the basic character of the ontological statements and the indispensability of the metaphysical, that is, of the Creator God who is before all becoming.'
60 *IC*, 48.

> The essence of faith, however, is that I do not meet with something that has been thought up, but that here something meets me that is greater than anything we can think of for ourselves.[61]

In Ratzinger's theological reasoning, faith is certitude resulting from divine revelation in Jesus Christ who gave his life for those he loves. Faith is therefore a higher level of understanding.

4. The God of Jesus Christ

Ratzinger's concept of faith rests clearly on a communicative model. This matches with his philosophical preference of *personalism* with which Ferdinand Ebner and Martin Buber reacted against the depersonalizing rationalism of the Enlightenment and the Hegel's system. According to the online *Stanford Encyclopedia of Philosophy*,

> Personalism posits ultimate reality and value in personhood – human as well as (at least for most personalists) divine. It emphasizes the significance, uniqueness and inviolability of the person, as well as the person's essentially relational or communitarian dimension.[62]

Accordingly, Ratzinger observes:

> The act of faith is a profound personal act … But precisely because it is so completely personal it is also an act of communication. In its profoundest nature the "I" always refers to the "thou" and vice versa: real relationship that becomes "communion" can only be born in the depths of the personality.[63]

61 *GW*, 29.
62 Thomas D. Williams and Jan O. Bengtsson, 'Personalism', *The Stanford Encyclopedia of Philosophy* (Summer 2011 Edition) by Edward N. Zalta; <http://plato.stanford.edu/archives/sum2011/entries/personalism/>; Joseph Ratzinger in his biography admitted that he discovered the personalist philosophy through the writings of Martin Buber; see also Markus Rutsche, *Die Relationalität Gottes bei Martin Buber und Joseph Ratzinger* (München: Grin, 2007).
63 *LoChr*, 37.

Hansjürgen Verweyen has convincingly showed that this communicative model, which Ratzinger first encountered in the *Confessions* of Augustine, is deepened through his studies of Bonaventure's concept of revelation.[64] In asserting that God's being is necessarily personal, Ratzinger is affirming the inseparability of truth and faith. Faith without truth would be a blind surrender to irrationality. And yet, truth without faith would remain a hypothesis whose value for human life still needs to be proven *a posteriori*. Faith adds to truth an existential level of certainty which can take the form of a personal conviction. Consequently, knowing truth is consecutive of Christian existence. It is so strongly connected to human nature that one would give one's own life for the sake of this truth. Through faith the truth is removed from the purely objective realm. Ratzinger therefore distinguishes the philosopher's God from the God of the Bible:

> ... the God of the philosophers ... who had previously existed as something neutral, as the highest, culminating concept ... who had been understood as pure being or pure thought, circling round for ever closed in upon itself without reaching over to man and his little world; this God of the philosophers, whose pure eternity and unchangeability had excluded any relation with the changeable and transitory, now appeared to the eye of faith as the God of men, who is not only thought of all thoughts, the eternal mathematics of the universe, but also *agape*, the power of creative love.[65]

It is not a surprise that Ratzinger considers 1 *John* 4:8: 'Whoever does not love does not know God, because God is love' as the best summary of God's nature. In the communicative theology, love is seen as a process of reciprocal giving which aims at the creation of communion between the giver and the recipients of this gift.[66] Hence the mystery of love includes 'the element of the personal, of proximity, of invocability, of self-bestowal, an element which is heralded in

---

64 Hansjürgen Verweyen, *Ein unbekannter Ratzinger. Die Habilitationsschrift von 1955 as Schlüssel zu seiner Theologie* (Regensburg: Friedrich Pustet, 2010).
65 *IC*, 99.
66 See Gisbert Greshake, "Der Ursprung der Kommunikationsidee", in *Communicatio Socialis* 35 (2002), 8: "bonum est communicativum et diffusivum"

the idea the God of our fathers, of Abraham, Isaac and Jacob.'[67] Since God is love, He is therefore not a platonic isolated being or a mere idea of pure thought. Rather the Christian God is 'basically defined by the category of relationship.'[68] Thus God is not the unmoved or the first principle of being, but is a person, whom we call Father. Trust therefore presupposes knowledge. And yet, in revealing his name, is not reduced completely to the human world, for divine love always maintains its freedom: 'On the other side is the fact that this proximity, this accessibility, is the free gift of what stands above space and time, bound to nothing and binding everything to itself.'[69] According to Ratzinger, God's love seems to be paradoxical. On closer inspection, the paradox is not so apparent. Since God is not confined to time and space, He is close to all. Ratzinger considers that the story of the burning bush in *Exodus* 3 best explains God's personal being. To Moses, who asked for God's name, the reply is simply: 'I am who I am.' (*Ex* 3:14) What seems to be a riddle for Moses expresses God's sovereign nature. But paradoxically this sovereignty manifests God's true and ever-present proximity. God's 'I am' means at the same time, 'I am there for you'. Ratzinger explains: 'His Being is expounded not as Being in itself, but as a Being-for.'[70] This pro-existence originates in the inner Trinitarian love of the divine persons who recognize and embrace each other as persons:

> The Father and the Son do not become one by dissolving into one another. They stay face to face, for love is established as a face-to-face meeting, which is not suppressed. If then each of the Persons stays in himself, and if they do not mutually eliminate each other, the unity cannot consist of each Person by himself but in the fruitfulness in which each of them offers himself and is himself. They are one inasmuch as their love is fruitful and goes beyond them. In the Third Person the Father and the Son give themselves to each other, and in this gift they bring it about that each of them is himself and that they are also one.[71]

67 *IC*, 92.
68 Ibid., 102.
69 Ibid., 93.
70 Ibid., 87.
71 *GChr*, 28.

What we experience in God is nothing else than the unity *in* plurality. In opposition to the Platonic view which considered plurality as a fall and sin, Christianity welcomes plurality because it is already inclusive in God's being. Once again, love unites, but, at the same time preserves freedom. Because God is triune, the conversation is a true exchange between the persons, for the Trinitarian nature excludes a monologue to which even a human dialogue can be reduced. Thus, plurality is not secondary to unity; rather 'plurality has its inner ground in God.'[72] For this reason, God is communicability and relatedness, unity *in* plurality Ratzinger explains: 'It is the nature of the Trinitarian personality to be pure relation and so the most absolute unity.'[73] When in God unity and plurality are complementary, the consequence is that God's relation to Jesus derives completely from the love of the Father, who gives to the Son all what love can entail: 'Once again ... being is interpreted as being "from" and as being "for".'[74] Consequently, the inner Trinitarian processions are the preconditions for the external missions of the second and third divine persons. Christ is sent for he is the Word of the Father:

> He who is here is Word; he is consequently "spoken" and hence the pure relation between the speaker and the spoken to. Thus *"Logos"*-Christology, as *"word"*-theology, is once again the opening up of being to the idea of relationship.[75]

Christology is closely related to theology of revelation in the sense that one can speak from God correctly only from the Christological perspective. In Jesus Christ 'God is no longer the Wholly Other, the incomprehensible One, but he is now also the One who is near us, who has become identified with us, who touches us and is touched by us.'[76] This being the case, Jesus Christ is then the revealer of God for he is the saviour.

72 *IC*, 128.
73 Ibid., 135.
74 Ibid., 136.
75 Ibid., 136.
76 *GW*, 221 f.

5. The Spiritual Christology of Joseph Ratzinger

Having clarified the theological-spiritual preconditions of Ratzinger's Christology, we can now attempt to describe Ratzinger's fundamental Christological positions. In the *Introduction to Christianity* he discusses Christology in a more systematic manner. He is concerned about the uncritical acceptance of the historical theology of 1960s, which 'gradually watered down the demands of faith.'[77] He writes,

> to help understand faith afresh as something which makes possible true humanity in the world of today, to expound faith without changing it into small coin of empty talk painfully labouring to hide a complete spiritual vacuum.[78]

Ratzinger's *Introduction,* though foreshadowing a development of a spiritual Christology, provoked also many critiques. The criticism of a "latent idealism" made earlier by Kasper against Ratzinger is taken further by Robert Krieg. He argued that Ratzinger's reliance on Max Scheler's idealism contributed to the conflation of Christology and anthropology. It fails to distinguish the historical Jesus from the Christian faith: 'Ratzinger's explicitly Christological discussions, his reflections on baptism, and his meditations on the life of Jesus of Nazareth fail to distinguish Jesus from those who call themselves Christian.'[79] As proof of Ratzinger's dependence on Scheler, Krieg refers only to Ratzinger's *Glaube, Geschichte und Philosophy*, page 543, where Scheler is listed together with other influential thinkers, such as Augustine of Hippo. Ratzinger himself mentioned Scheler only three times in his earlier works.[80] In all three occasions, Ratzinger rejects both Scheler's separation of metaphysical from religious cognition,

---

77   *IC*, 11.
78   Ibid., 12.
79   Robert Krieg, 205.
80   Scheler is mentioned twice in his doctoral dissertation *VHG* on page 511 and 523 f. However, in his *Habilitation* thesis Scheler is named only one time on page 553 f.

and Scheler's interpretation of the Augustinian epistemology. Scheler believed that Augustine's epistemology is fundamentally based on the primacy of love. According to Ratzinger, however, this view is alien to Augustine.[81] Relying solely on love would reduce a being to will. For the Bishop of Hippo, however, will without truth is reduced to emotion and feelings. Will without truth is blind, just as will is complemented by reason, and in faith will and reason come together. Though Krieg's criticism lacks a solid basis, Hans Albert sees in Ratzinger's theological method a spiritualized metaphysics which is more apologetic than historical-critical. He writes,

> He [Ratzinger] is more interested in the incorporation of the Christian faith in his spiritualistic metaphysics, that he would accept the results of historical research only if they match for this theological purpose. One can therefore speak here properly of a non-critical but apologetic use of history.[82]

Ratzinger himself recognized that not all exegetes would agree with every detail of his book on *Jesus of Nazareth*. However, many biblical scholars – and Ratzinger named the distinguished German exegetes Peter Stuhlmacher, Franz Musser and Martin Hengel (†) – endorsed in general the content and theological method of his book.[83] For the Pope, the Holy Scripture is not merely a historical book, but is also a book which describes the salvation revealed and actualized in the person of Jesus Christ. As Martin Hengel said earlier, in the memory of the early Christians the *kerygma* in the form of a confession is fused directly with the unique story of Jesus. From this perspective

81 *OGB*, 553 f.: 'Seit Max Scheler hat man sich vielfach angewöhnt, von einem Primat der Liebe im Denken Augustins zu sprechen, so wie man vorher schon von einem Primat des Willens geredet hat, ja selbst die Lehre, dass die Liebe dem Erkennen vorausgeht, wurde auf Augustin zurückgeführt. Wer Augustin selbst kennt, weiß indessen, dass solche Gedanken in seinem Werk keinen Platz haben.'
82 Hans Albert, 29: 'Es geht ihm so sehr um den Einbau des christlichen Glaubens in seine spiritualistische Metaphysik, daß er Resultate der historischen Forschung nur dann gelten läßt, wenn sie sich für diesen Zweck verwerten lassen. Man darf daher hier mit Recht von einer nicht kritischen, sondern apologetischen Verwertung der Geschichte sprechen.'
83 *JoN*, vol. 2, xiii.

Hans Albert's question, e.g. whether Ratzinger's sacrificial reading of the cross would do justice to the real mind of Jesus, must be affirmed positively because the early Church preached this saving message right from the very beginning. Furthermore, who can really know what the mind of Jesus is really about, except Jesus himself? Albert's question therefore can never be answered satisfactorily except in the knowledge of faith. Hence, Ratzinger suggests that the results of historical research, which offers only a partial access to the real Jesus, should also be read in the spirit in which the Bible was written. This spirit is the collective faith memory without which history remains merely a category of the past. It is this spirit of faith that sees the development of history not as regression ("Abfall"),[84] but as sign of hope because faith carries history towards its fulfilment.[85] Thus, Ratzinger's theological program was to combine exegesis with the dimension of faith which is the spiritual foundation of theology.

For Ratzinger, who like Augustine and Bonaventure before is both theologian and shepherd, exegesis is not an end in itself, but serves faith which is a pre-given existential in the life of a Christian. It is through faith that one enters into the intimate friendship with Christ. It is through faith that one immerses into the Christ-reality and becomes Christ-like. Of course it is self-evident that one cannot follow Christ blindly without any knowledge of him. One can enter into a personal relationship only if one knows the person whom one is supposed to follow. Nevertheless, the knowledge, which is required, is an existential knowledge which cannot be ascertained solely by academic exegesis. In Ratzinger's view the question of "who Jesus

---

84 Marianne Schlosser – Franz-Xaver Heibl (eds.), *Gegenwart der Offenbarung. Zu den Bonaventura-Forschungen Joseph Ratzingers* (Regensburg: Friedrich Pustet, 2011), 15.
85 *LW*, 201: 'Das Vatikanum II hat dies deutlich gemacht, indem es einerseits die wesentlichen Elemente der historischen Methode als notwendigen Teil des Zugangs zur Bibel darstellt, aber gleichzetig hinzufügt, die Bibel muss in dem Geist gelesen werden, in dem sie geschrieben wurde. Sie muss in ihrer Ganzheit, in ihrer Einheit gelesen werden. Und das ist nur möglich man wan sie als ein Buch des Volkes Gottes betrachtet, das voranschreitend auf Christus zugeht.'

is" can be answered appropriately only through a Christological *"vademecum"* which includes faith, worship and martyrdom. In this context, Ratzinger suggests that only a spiritual Christology can lead into the "indivisible inner unity" of Jesus and Christ.[86] Since Christian existence is communal and therefore necessarily evolves in the Church,[87] the main task of a spiritual Christology is to understand and to interpret the common faith of the Church, 'not as reconstructing a vanished Jesus, as long last piercing together his real history.'[88] This is precisely the point which Ratzinger wanted to make in his two volumes on *Jesus of Nazareth* published respectively in 2007 and 2011, as he writes,

> I have attempted to develop a way of observing and listening to the Jesus of the Gospels that can indeed lead to personal encounter and that, through collective listening with Jesus' disciples across the ages, can indeed attain sure knowledge of the real historical figure of Jesus.[89]

Without the hermeneutic of faith assisted by the Creed of the Church, the historical-critical method would not be capable of transposing history into the Christian life.[90] Indeed, it is faith which establishes the inner unity within the books of the New Testament and that of the two Testaments:

> Since the inner unity of the books of the New Testament, and that of the two Testaments, can only be seen in the light of faith's interpretation, where this is lacking, people are forever separating out new components and discovering contradictions in the sources.[91]

86　*PO*, 9: 'to consider Christology more from the aspect of its spiritual appropriation that I had previously done.'
87　See Heim, 148: "Accordingly, the individual does not believe out of his own resources but, rather as Ratzinger stresses, always believes along with the whole Church ... the profession of the triune God in the ecclesial *communio* constitutes the faith of the Church."
88　*PO*, 14.
89　*JoN*, vol. 2, xvii.
90　*LW*, 198.
91　*PO*, 44.

In Ratzinger's opinion only faith holds together the entire canonical texts:

> It is the only hermeneutics which is in a position hold fast the entire testimony of the sources; it is also the only one which is able to comprehend the sources' different nuances and their pluriformity, because it alone has a vision of unity which is wide enough to accommodate the apparent contradictions.[92]

Thus Ratzinger's overall goal was to unite faith and reason for faith commitment always demands an intellectual assent.[93] In line with the philosophy of personalism, Ratzinger develops a spiritual Christology which sees in Jesus Christ, the Church and history as an indivisible inner unity.[94] This unity is the theological constant in Ratzinger's theology which covers his entire academic and pastoral ministry, from his doctorate on Augustine's ecclesiology to his recent publications on Jesus Christ.[95]

6. Christology and Prayer

Ratzinger's spiritual Christology is the outcome of a development which owes much to Augustine and Bonaventure. Both men were academics and pastors. Like the Bishop of Hippo who was called away from his academic desk to priestly ministry in 391, so Bonaventure, who held the Franciscan chair of theology in Paris, was

---

92 Ibid., 45.
93 *UChr*, 66: 'Denken und Existenz sind in den letzten Fragen für den Menschen nicht mehr zu trennen. Die Entscheidung für Gott ist eine Entscheidung des Denkens und des Lebens zugleich – beides bedingt sich gegenseitig;' see also Lam, 103–105.
94 *PO*, 15: 'My intention is more modest, namely to put forward in a few theses certain fundamental characteristics of the indivisible inner unity of Jesus Christ, Church and history.'
95 See Lam, 106: 'Diese Einheit von Lehre und Leben geht bereits auf die Arbeiten der sechziger Jahre des vergangenen Jahrhunderts zurück.'

called into the office of Minister General of his order in 1257. This event – as Ratzinger observed – has also brought with it a significant shift from academic to the spiritual awareness of theology. The office of shepherd requires a new theological form and language.[96] Theology now is embedded in proclamation for both activities are centred on the divine Word which is not merely informative, but also performative as it signals and demands a conversion of people's thoughts and actions. Moreover, theology is now complemented by prayer.[97] It is in this context that Ratzinger declared explicitly in 1981 that only a spiritual Christology can capture the whole significance of Jesus Christ. It was only in connection with the Eucharistic Congress held 1981 at the Marian Shrine in Lourdes that Ratzinger took up the opportunity to 'consider Christology more from the aspect of its spiritual appropriation than [he] had previously done.'[98] This spiritual appropriation involves 'a certain degree of empathy, by which we enter, so to speak, into the person or intellectually concerned, become one with him or it, and thus become able to understand.'[99] According to Ratzinger, the fundamental act of religious empathy is prayer through which one deepens the fellowship with God.[100] It is through prayer that one partakes in the

---

96   *OGB*, 78.
97   See also the Pope's catechesis on Bonaventure which he delivered during the audience general in March 10th 2010: 'Thus we see that for St Bonaventure governing was not merely action but above all was thinking and praying. At the root of his government we always find prayer and thought; all his decisions are the result of reflection, of thought illumined by prayer. His intimate contact with Christ always accompanied his work as Minister General and therefore he composed a series of theological and mystical writings that express the soul of his government.' – <http://www.vatican.va/holy_father/benedict_xvi/audiences/2010/documents/hf_ben-xvi_aud_20100310_en.html> (accessed on April 30th 2012).
98   *PO*, 9.
99   Ibid., 25.
100 *JoN*, vol. 1, 130: 'Praying actualizes and deepens our communion with God'; also *UChr*, 67: 'in Lebensgemeinschaft mit ihm standen.'

inner realities of Christ[101] whom the gospels often portray as a man who through prayer was in constant dialogue with his Father. Walter Brueggemann, the great scholar of the Old Testament, argued that prayer is a form of dialogue which seeks "common interest" between God and man and which ultimately leads to a real communion between God and the petitioner. Referring to Moshe Greenberg's study on prayer,[102] Brueggeman concludes that prayer is not a psychological exercise, but rather it is a 'genuine dialogical real transaction' between the engaged partners.[103] This genuine real transaction, which is based upon a common interest between partners, is concretely shown in the garden scene of Gethsemane, where Jesus rises above himself into the will of his Father:

> And he came out and proceeded as was His custom to the Mount of Olives; and the disciples also followed him. When he arrived at the place, he said to them, 'Pray that you may not enter into temptation.' And he withdrew from them about a stone's throw, and he knelt down and began to pray, saying, 'Father, if you are willing, remove this cup from me; yet not my will, but yours be done'.[104]

In Ratzinger's view, it was Luke in particular who considered prayer as the channel which gives access to the inner reality of Jesus:

> According to Luke, we see who Jesus is if we see him at prayer. The Christian confession of faith comes from participating in the prayer of Jesus, from being drawn into his prayer and being privileged to behold it … only by entering into Jesus' solitude, only by participating in what is most personal to him, his communication with the Father, can one see what this most personal reality is; only thus can one penetrate to his identity.[105]

---

101 *JoN*, vol. 1, 130: 'It aims to form our being, to train us in the inner attitude of Jesus.'
102 Moshe Greenberg, *Biblical Prose as Prayer as a Window to the Popular Religion of Ancient Israel* (Berkeley: University of California, 1983).
103 Walter Brueggemann, *Great Prayers of the Old Testament* (Louisville: Westminster John Knox, 2008), xxi.
104 *Lk* 22:39–42.
105 *PO*, 19.

Brett Doyle is correct in attesting to the Pope's teaching on prayer a Christological dynamism.[106] Prayer is an event of the *Logos* who as the Word not only precedes human words, but is at the same time also a person who through the sending of the Holy Spirit prays in and with the faithful.[107] Being Word and Son, he draws all into his prayer. It becomes clear that Jesus' prayer reveals also his inner reality as the Word of the Father. Thus, in his prayer Jesus manifests himself truly as Son who is the Word through which the Father communicates himself irreversibly to the world. It is only through the prayer that the identity of Jesus is fully revealed to the mind of the believer. Through prayer, one enters into that 'intimacy which Jesus reserved for those who were his friends.'[108] It is through this intimacy that Jesus' inner realities are revealed: 'Jesus thereby involves us in his own prayer; he leads us into the interior dialogue of triune love.'[109] Prayer is for Pope Benedict XVI the activity which actualizes and deepens the human communion of being with the God who is in us and above us: 'It is an encounter with the Son and the Holy Spirit and thus a becoming-one with the living God who is always both in and above us.'[110] It is through this communion of being that the true nature of Jesus Christ is revealed. For that reason, Ratzinger maintains that Christology is nothing else than the interpretation of Jesus' prayers.[111]

---

106 Brett Doyle, 'Ratzinger on Prayer', in *Australian Catholic Record* 86.3 (2009), 328–346.
107 *JoN*, vol. 1, 131.
108 *PO*, 22.
109 *JoN*, vol. 1, 132.
110 Ibid.,
111 *PO*, 19: 'it interprets the experience of Jesus' prayer, and its interpretation is correct because it springs from a sharing in what is most personal and intimate to him.'

7. The Lord's Prayer and Gethsemane as Distinguished Manifestation of Jesus Christ's Inner Reality

Jesus Christ's inner reality is best disclosed in the so-called Lord's Prayer[112] and in the prayer uttered by Jesus in the garden of Gethsemane on the eve of his trial.[113] These prayers, according to Ratzinger, are a special type of conversation which comes forth from the most intimate exchange between Jesus and his Father. In both prayers Jesus called God his "Abba" (Father) which conveys to the readers the unique relationship between Son and his Father:

> Whereas there is not a single instance of God being addressed as *Abba* in the literature of Jewish prayer, Jesus always addressed him in this way ... that is the way a child address his father within the family ... Jesus's use of *Abba* in addressing God reveals the heart of his relationship with God.[114]

The qualification of God as Father has two implications. Firstly, it is a statement about the existence of God as person. Secondly, it expresses the special relationship of Christ to his Father. As a person, God is the creator because He is Father. However, God's creation differs from the ancient mythology. In contrast to ancient *mythos* which portrays God as a being who creates simultaneously the cosmos, the Bible depicts God as a person who created each individual human being:

> Every human being is unique, and willed as such by God. Every individual is known to him. In this sense, by virtue of creation itself man is the "child" of God in a special way, and God is his true Father.[115]

It is through this particular relationship that human beings turn towards God. This conversion to God is only possible because of the

---

112 *Lk* 11:1–4 ǁ *Mt* 6:9–13.
113 *Lk* 22:39–46 ǁ *Mt* 26:36–46 ǁ *Mk* 14:32–42.
114 *JoN*, vol. 2, 161–162. Here Ratzinger quoted Joachim Jeremias, *Abba: The Prayers of Jesus* (London: SCM, 1967), in particular pages 57 and 62.
115 *JoN*, vol. 1, 138.

divine love which makes God turn even against his own justice. It is only in this turn that mercy is imaginable for us. The essence of God as Father is therefore nothing else than love. For this reason, God cannot but create "good things".[116] Moreover, the Father's love for his children endures "to the end", otherwise God's love would not be perfect. This enduring love includes the cross of the Son who 'had loved those who were his in the world, but now he showed how perfect his love was.'[117] For Ratzinger, creation and cross are inseparable constituents of Christology. While the first reveals Christ's divine nature as the Word, the second affirms his true human nature. The Word, through which the human beings were created, is the same Word which the Father in the fullness of time,

> 'speaks intimately, as one man to another' by descending into the depth of human sufferings. As Word of God, who 'sees with total clarity the whole foul flood of evil ... all the wiles and cruelty of evil', Christ hence is the only one who can endure and drink the "chalice" [118] prepared for him: 'All this he must take into himself, so that it can be disarmed and defeated in him.'[119]

In the prayer of Gethsemane, which leads to the acceptance of the will of his Father, Christ shows himself as the faithful Son who exists totally in and for the love of his Father. In this context, the Pope meditated:

> Thus the prayer "not my will, but yours"[120] is truly the Son's prayer to the Father, through which the natural human will is completely submitted into the "I" of the Son. Indeed, the Son's whole being is expressed in the "not I, but you" – in the total self-abandonment of the "I" to the "you" of God the Father.[121]

116 Here Ratzinger cites *Mt* 7:9–11: 'Would any of you give a stone to your son when he asks for bread? Or give him a snake, when he asks for a fish? As bad as you are, you know how to give good things to your children. How much more, then, will your Father in Heaven give good things to those who ask him.'
117 *John* 13:1.
118 *Lk* 14:36: 'Abba, Father, all things are possible to you; remove this chalice from; yet not what I will, but what you will.'
119 *JoN*, vol. 2, 155.
120 *Lk* 22:42.
121 *JoN*, vol. 2, 161.

In this context, Ratzinger noted in Jesus Christ a synergy of the divine and human wills, which at the same time reinstates human greatness:

> The drama of the Mount of Olives lies in the fact that Jesus draws man's natural will away from opposition and back toward synergy, and in doing so he restores man's true greatness.[122]

It is through this synergy of wills, which derives from the intimate dialogue between Jesus and his Father, that salvation is made possible. Consequently, the recognition of Christ's redemptive identity cannot be achieved other than from within prayer through which one is configured into the image of the Son who is the true image of his Father. By praying with Jesus, one participates in the intimacy of dialogue between the Son and the Father. Only through this intimacy can one gain insights into Jesus Christ' identity:

> Only by entering into Jesus' solitude, only by participating in what is most personal to him, his communication with the Father, can one see what this most personal reality is; only thus can one penetrate to his identity. This is the only way to understand him and to grasp what "following Jesus" means ... it is prayer, only yielding its meaning within prayer. The person who has beheld Jesus' intimacy with his Father and has come to understand him from within is called to be a "rock" of the Church.[123]

Participating in Jesus' prayer is for Ratzinger more than a mere spiritual exercise. It is rather a soteriological event; prayer is, in the words of Walter Bruggemann, a 'genuine dialogical real transaction.'[124] Prayer is the manifestation of Jesus's obedience to the will of his Father, whereby redemption becomes a reality. The more the disciple is united with Jesus Christ in prayer, the more the cross and resurrection is truly transposed into the life of the disciple. Quoting "It is no longer I who live, but Christ who lives in me" (Gal 2:20), Ratzinger observes that 'the disciple is bound to the mystery of Christ. His life

---

122 Ibid., 161.
123 *PO*, 19.
124 Brueggemann, xxi.

is immersed in communion with Christ.'[125] The cross is henceforth a sign of the transformative love, as Paul confidently proclaimed to the Ephesians:

> But God loved us with so much love that he was generous with his mercy: when we were dead through our sins, he brought us to life with Christ – it is through grace that you have been saved – and raised us up with him and gave us a place with him in heaven, in Christ Jesus.[126]

8. Christology and Soteriology

For Ratzinger, prayer is 'the clue linking together Christology and soteriology, the person of Jesus and his deeds and sufferings.'[127] And yet he recognizes how difficult it is for the modern mind to reconcile history with redemption in Jesus Christ:

> Can we cling at all to the straw of one single historical event? Can we dare to base our whole existence, indeed the whole history, on the straw of one happening in the great sea of history?[128]

Obviously, this modern hesitation is based upon an understanding of history only as a monotonous progression. It fails to reckon with events whose meanings point to a reality which is beyond historical verification. To the modern mind, therefore, the resurrection of a dead person must be dismissed as "unhistorical".[129] The meaning of salvation history cannot be grasped. Ratzinger therefore suggests that exegetical-historical research ought to be done also from the perspective of faith 'which is not a reconstruction or a theory but a

---

125 *JoN*, vol. 1, 74.
126 *Eph* 2:4–6.
127 *PO*, 22.
128 *IC*, 142.
129 *UChr*, 61.

present, living reality.'[130] This Christian reality is lived and made visible in the liturgy through which the believers enter into living communion ("Lebensgemeinschaft") with Jesus Christ,[131] whose death represents the true sacrifice restoring the communication between God and humanity:

> 'Death, which by its very nature, is the end, the destruction of every communication, is changed by him into an act of self-communication, and this is man's redemption, for it signifies the triumph of love over death.'[132]

Ratzinger clearly saw a close connection between Christology and soteriology, with worship being the visible bridge between them. In this respect, particularly highlights the significance of Christ's priestly prayer in John 17. The structure of this prayer resembles the Jewish rituals of the Day of the Atonement.[133] Jesus recites it within the context of his farewell discourse, after having celebrated the Last Supper with his disciples. It ought to be taken as a form of Christ's consecration – and surrender – to his Father as his death approaches.[134] Noting the sacrificial undertones of this prayer, Pope Benedict sees it the consummation of the ritual of the Atonement because Christ's sacrifice was the definitive realization of Israel's hope:

> The ritual of the feast [of Atonement], with its rich theological content, is realized in Jesus' prayer – "realized" in the literal sense: the rite is translated into the reality that it signifies. What had been represented in ritual acts now takes place in reality, and it takes place definitively ... Jesus' high-priestly prayer is the consummation of the Day of Atonement, the eternally accessible feast, as it were, of God's reconciliation with men.[135]

Through Christ's priestly prayer, the ritual of the atonement's sacrifices was spiritually transposed into the Eucharist ("thysia logike")

130 *IC*, 148.
131 *UChr*, 67: 'weil sie in Lebensgemeinschaft mit ihm standen.'
132 *PO*, 25.
133 See *Lev* 16.
134 *PO*, 24.
135 *JoN*, vol. 2, 77.79.

through which all people are recognized as disciples of Christ: 'Eternal life is gained through recognition, presupposing here the Old Testament concept of recognition: recognizing creates communion; it is union of being with the recognized.'[136] Christ's priestly prayer unveils his identity to the readers. He is the saviour as he is both priest and victim who bore the guilt of all sinners by giving up his life as a sin-offering, thus reconciling humanity with God. In this regard, Jesus Christ is the true worship of God. Quoting *Jn* 17:17–19,[137] Ratzinger emphasizes the relational dimension of the sacrifice:

> Here, Jesus designates himself as the one sanctified and sent into the world by the Father. Hence we are dealing with a triple "sanctification": the Father has sanctified the Son and sent him into the world; the Son sanctifies himself; and he asks, on the basis of his own sanctification, that the disciples be sanctified in the truth.[138]

First of all, Christ sanctifies himself in virtue of being the Son – which is 'something quite distinct from the concept of son of God.'[139] This sonship indicates a new form of intimacy with God. Christ as Son, who calls his Father "Abba", which is a more colloquial form and includes an intimate familiarity,[140] belongs completely to the sphere of his Father. As Son, Christ lives completely for his Father; his existence is "pro-existence" in relation to the Father. This ontological relationship between Father and Son is transformed into a Christology of service:

> The "servant" aspect is no longer explained as a deed, behind which abides the person of Jesus; it is made to embrace the whole existence of Jesus, so that his *being* itself is service … because this being, as a totality, is nothing but service, it is sonship.[141]

---

136 Ibid., 83.
137 'Sanctify them in truth; your word is truth… For their sake I consecrated myself, that they also may be consecrated in truth.'
138 *JoN*, vol. 2, 85–86.
139 *IC*, 165.
140 Ibid., 166.
141 Ibid., 168.

Through his service, Christ is sanctified by his Father. But sanctification in this context means being consecrated as sacrifice. Christ's sacrifice is considered as a process through which all people can be drawn to his sanctification. The sanctification resulting from Christ-centred worship involves the act of submission of oneself to God. Such a personal consecration to God is the true meaning of sacrifice in regard to God and others.[142] Christ's sacrifice therefore constitutes a new form of existence. Being configured to the image of Christ means pleasing and praising God: 'It is no longer I who live, but Christ who lives in me.'[143] Spiritual communion with Christ secures human freedom as the indispensable condition of genuine service.

9. *Excursus:* Christian Worship vs. Roman Cult: Charity as Form of Christ's Sacrifice

Ratzinger's location of Christ' sacrifice in the realm of relationship between God and mankind shows parallels to Augustine's concept of worship. This may be the logical consequence of his doctoral thesis in 1951 on Augustine's ecclesiology. Already in this early work, Ratzinger observed in Augustine's writings[144] an existential dimension of the Christian worship in contrast to the "mechanical" rituals of the Roman religion. Roman cult was less interested in establishing a communion between God and humanity. Rather, it sought to secure divine protection and ongoing prosperity for its people through the accurate performance of rituals. Thus, the personal belief or relationship with the gods was not essential for the well-being of the State. As long as the rituals were upheld meticulously, the protection and continuation of the State were assured by the gods, even though

---

142 Ibid., 86.
143 *Gal* 2:20.
144 In particular in Augustine's opus magnum *De civitate Dei*.

123

the faith of the worshippers differed from each other. It was therefore the responsibility of the State to encourage its citizens to carry out the sacrificial rituals for the prosperity of the State. For this reason, Christians were accused of profanity when they rejected the sacrificial rituals of the Gods. The Christian attitude therefore would endanger the well-being and survival of the State. It was in 410 that the accusation of disloyalty against the Christians reached its peak. In that year Rome was invaded and sacked by the Vandals. The Roman aristocrats blamed the Christians for this humiliating defeat because the Christian renounced the cult of the Gods. Hence, the Roman aristocrats demanded the resumption of the cult for the sake of the *beatitudo* of the State. Augustine agreed that prosperity and happiness of the State and its people can come only from the true God. However, he also argued that the well-being of the State and humanity cannot be achieved through the mere observance of rituals, but only through the loving union with the one and true God.[145] In contrast to the Roman concept of salvation, which is ensured through the mechanical performance of rituals, Augustine emphasized the personal, dialogical dimension of Christian worship. Salvation is granted by God through an act of personal adherence to God's will ("adhaerere Deo").[146] Accordingly, sacrifice is an act of conformity to God's will, and an act of self-abandonment to God.[147] The essence of true sacrifice, therefore, is not the performance of rituals, but a life pleasing to God. Salvation is the fruit of union with God. However, Augustine was also aware of the gap between God and humans cut off from God through sin and its lethal social consequences – death of body and spirit. In Augustine's theology, sin is the outcome of the obsession with the self ("Ich-heit"), so that sinners cannot reach beyond themselves into the divine sphere. Consequently, their sacrifice is fruitless and void, and even intensifies their self-enclosure.

---

145 *JRGS* 1, 265: 'Liebesvereinigung mit dem einen Gott.'
146 Here Ratzinger quoted Augustine's *exp in ps* 72, 28: 'Mihi autem adhaerere Deo bonum est.'
147 *JRGS* 1, 266.

For Augustine, sin not only has negative consequences for the individual, but also has damaging impact on the entire cosmic order in that humans are part of creation in which everything is ordered to the will of God.[148] Through sin, humans descend into an inferior position within the cosmic order, and the balance of the cosmic order is disturbed. Spirit and body lose their integrity. The cosmos is thereby brought into an imbalance. The more sin invades a human person, the further will he/she be separated from God. Having lost the "forma dei" through sin, humans cannot be regarded as worthy of God: 'A human being has sinned. He has lost contact with God.'[149] Consequently, they cannot offer themselves as a worthy sacrifice to God. The main question for Augustine is this: How can sinful humans enter into communion with the all-holy God? The answer is evident: It is only through the mediator Jesus Christ that the communion with God can be restored. The task of the mediator is twofold. Firstly, he needs to re-establish human integrity. Secondly, the establishment of human integrity also must restore the balance and order of creation. Because the cosmos is not a mere physical reality, but includes an ethical-moral order, this restoration cannot come from ritualism, for a saving sacrifice must be offered by a holy and innocent person – namely, Jesus Christ.[150] Hence, a sacrifice is worthy only if it is united to the sacrifice of Jesus Christ: 'For what is the spirit of Christ other than the grace of Christ, as *caritas*, which is poured into our hearts by the Spirit given to us?'[151] Love is therefore the essential criterion for the worthiness of sacrifice by humans. Only through love can human beings become *homines spirituales*, acceptable to God. Because of the indwelling of Christ's spirit in human hearts ("in corde")[152],

---

148 Ibid., 268: 'Durch die Sünde ist zwischen Gott und Mensch eine Kluft entstanden – wobei immer der ethische und kosmische Gedanke parallel zu nehmen sind.'
149 Ibid., 269.
150 Here Ratzinger cited from Augustine's *tract in Io* 84, 2: 'Unus est solus, qui et carnem hominis habere et peccatum potuit non habere;' see also *JRGS* 1, 283.
151 *Rom* 5:5; see *JRGS 1*, 287.
152 Heart is the symbol which stands for the entire human existence. It includes both dimensions of human existence, namely soul and body.

the faithful become temples of God. Insofar as they have become the temple of God, they are sanctified in the sight of God, and consecrated to his service. Faith, then, is an act of love and self-surrender to God.[153] Sacrifice in the form of faith and charity establishes real ontological relationship between God and humanity and union with Christ.[154].

Augustine, like Ratzinger later, developed his understanding of sacrifice from the notion of relationship with Christ because sacrifice is an act of pro-existence. This existence for others entails an existential basis deriving from an inner encounter with Christ whose transformative *caritas* dwells in the human hearts. For Augustine and Ratzinger, there is an intrinsic link between the inner attitude and outer action of human existence. Worship is the inner foundation of an ethical life.[155] For St Paul, this intrinsic connection is the essence of Christianity:

> I appeal to you therefore, by the mercies of God, to present your bodies as a living sacrifice, holy and acceptable to God, which is your spiritual worship. Do not be conformed to this world, but be transformed by the renewal of your mind, that by testing you may discern what is the will of God, what is good and acceptable and perfect.[156]

And both worship and ethics originate from an existential certainty founded in the covenantal relationship between God and humanity. Understandably, Ratzinger is opposed the relativistic views which consider any claim of religious truth as mere presumption.[157] Rela-

---

153 *JRGS 1*, 286: '… die im Glauben sich vollziehende Akteinheit.'
154 Ibid., 286: 'Aber die Einheit zwischen Christus und den Christen verläuft eben für Augustinus in einer Dimension des Seins, in der das Sein frei und bewusst ist, in einer Seinsschicht also, in der es keine Seinseinheit geben kann, die nicht bewusst und bejaht ist.'
155 See Anselm J. Gribbin, *Pope Benedict XVI and the Liturgy. Understanding recent liturgical developments* (Herefordshire: Gracewing, 2011), 6: "Worship – the right way to relate to God – is essential to right kid of existence in the world."
156 *Rom* 12:1–2.
157 *UChr*, 68.

tivism would make the human search meaningless because it could never achieve its goal.[158] As Prefect of the Congregation of Faith, Ratzinger felt the need to reaffirm with vigour the Church's faith in Jesus Christ. In an interview published in the *Frankfurter Allgemeine* on September 22nd 2000 he underlined the necessity of the Church's profession in the Lordship of Christ as expressed in the declaration *Dominus Iesus*:

> The document begins with the words *Dominus Iesus*; this is the brief formula of faith contained in the First Letter to the Corinthians (12:3), in which Paul has summarized the essence of Christianity: Jesus is Lord.

10. Christology in *Dominus Iesus*

After the publication of the declaration *Dominus Iesus* on August 6th, 2000, many critiques were raised against its ecclesiology. The Prefect of the CDF was annoyed that such criticisms had missed the Christological essence of the document. He understood the declaration to be an 'invitation to all Christians to open themselves anew to the recognition of Jesus Christ as Lord, and thus to give a profound meaning to the Holy Year.'[159] Such recognition is the logical consequence of the inner communion of the Church with Jesus Christ. Only union with Christ guarantees the Church's existence despite her failures and mistakes. No triumphant judgment on other religions is implied, but a wholehearted commitment to the truth revealed fully in Jesus Christ, the hope of the pilgrim Church, is expressed. Thus the declaration is primarily christological, and only secondarily ecclesiological. In the previously mentioned interview in the *Frank-*

---

158 Ibid., 69: 'Aber – so muss man dagegen fragen – was ist das für eine Suche, die niemals ankommen darf?'
159 See *Frankfurter Allgemeine* no. September 22nd 2000.

furter Allgemeine, the Cardinal underlined this Christological nature of the declaration:

> The ecclesiological and ecumenical issues of which everyone is now speaking occupy only a small part of the document, which it seemed to us necessary to write in order to emphasize Christ's living and concrete presence in history.

Thus the declaration's theological position on the nature of the Church must be judged from the Church's faith in Jesus Christ.

According to the Cardinal, there are two forms of the Christological faith which complement each other, despite their contextual differences. While the first Petrine formula took the shape of prayer, the second Pauline formula was a Spirit-filled credo which the ecclesial community professes in the liturgy, and expresses her identity and mission to the world.[160] In the form of prayer, the Petrine credo emphasizes the inner communion with Christ. This is the foundation for the Pauline formula because through the prayers of the faithful, the Church participates in the Spirit of Christ. Thus, the Petrine formula derives from an inner familiarity with Christ whom Peter confessed to be the Christ as the definitive redeemer of Israel. Relying on the faith of Peter, Paul professes in explicit terms the Lordship of Jesus, at the same time the Son of God. For Paul and the emerging Church, Jesus is the Christ, not just a human being graced by God, but God from God.[161] Prayer and the creed therefore are the two sides of the one coin. In Jesus Christ, truth is made visible and made known to the people of God. And yet the truth concerned is first and foremost divine revelation. Not the possession of the Church or the product of individual genius, but graciously given to all the faithful and preserved authentically in the Church. Only truth communicates truth. And this truth is most real because Christ is the in-

---

160 *UChr*, 56: 'Die petrinische Form ist Anrede an Jesus, ist "Gebet"; die paulinische Formel ist ein geistgegebenes Credo, das die Gemeinde im Gottesdienst vor Gott spricht, aber doch auch vor die Welt hinstellt als Ausdruck ihrer Identität und als Kern dessen, was sie der Menschheit zu sagen hat.'
161 Ibid., 57.

carnate wisdom of God. Revelation and incarnation are the theological foundations of the Church's responsibility and mission. If truth is not the product of the Church, but is given to her in love as a divine commandment, then it is the Church's responsibility and obligation to serve others in humility.[162] Faith in Jesus Christ always involves social responsibility. The Church is the prolongation of Christ's pro-existence. Of course, Ratzinger recognised the difficulty of modern human beings with regard to faith. To relativism, any truth claim, especially if it is of a religious nature, is mere presumption because no one can penetrate God's mind. The negation and indifferentism in regard to questions relating to religious truth lead to the denial of the universal redemptive role of Jesus Christ:

> On the basis of such presuppositions, which may evince different nuances, certain theological proposals are developed – at times presented as assertions, and at times as hypotheses – in which Christian revelation and the mystery of Jesus Christ and the Church lose their character of absolute truth and salvific universality, or at least shadows of doubt and uncertainty are cast upon them.[163]

From relativistic presuppositions, it is not evident that truth and salvation should depend on one single human being who lived 2000 years ago in Palestine and who was known as the son of the carpenter named Joseph.[164] As a human being, Jesus might be an inspired prophet who had enjoyed a special experience of enlightenment similar to Buddha or other prominent "enlightened" ones. But Jesus is not God since "God" is not, for enlightenment reason, an objective verifiable category. Even Jesus' personal experience of enlightenment is only fragmentary, for no human being can ever experience the entire truth. Relativism, therefore, questions the essence of Christian faith and its

---

162 Ibid., 69–70: 'Wenn es mir gegeben ist, so ist es Verantwortung, die mich auch für den anderen in Dienst nimmt... daß wir solche Erkenntnis nicht als unsere Leistung ansehen, sondern der Wahrheit treu bleiben, daß die Begegnung mit dem Wort auch für uns nur Geschenk ist, das uns gegeben wurde, damit wir es weitergeben, umsonst, wie wir es empfangen haben.'
163 *Dominus Iesus*, no. 4.
164 See *Mt* 13:55.

missionary nature. In a reaction against relativism, the Cardinal stated that relativistic theories degrade human beings and cause despair; relativism ultimately offers to hearts and minds no hope for the discovery of truth and salvation. Ratzinger is clear that no one can ever see God except by divine initiative: 'Only God knows himself completely. Only God sees God. Therefore only he, who is God, can lead us to the true knowledge of God.'[165] This knowledge of God is revealed fully in the life and deeds of Jesus Christ:

> As a remedy for this relativistic mentality, which is becoming ever more common, it is necessary above all to reassert the definitive and complete character of the revelation of Jesus Christ. In fact, it must be *firmly believed* that, in the mystery of Jesus Christ, the Incarnate Son of God, who is 'the way, the truth, and the life' (*Jn* 14:6), the full revelation of divine truth is given: 'No one knows the Son except the Father, and no one knows the Father except the Son and anyone to whom the Son wishes to reveal him' (*Mt* 11:27); 'No one has ever seen God; God the only Son, who is in the bosom of the Father, has revealed him' (*Jn* 1:18); 'For in Christ the whole fullness of divinity dwells in bodily form' (*Col* 2:9–10).[166]

The humanity of Jesus Christ is not a mere human existence; but rather in him God and humanity, the Infinite and finite, the Creator and creature come together. Only Jesus Christ can close the infinite gap between God and humanity. For this reason the Cardinal regarded faith in Jesus Christ as the only accessible way to God. Through faith one stands in the living communion with Christ who reveals his Father to those he loves. Faith in Jesus Christ is a firm foundation of the hope which enables Christians to take responsibility for others. The link between the certainty of hope and social responsibility is clearly restated in the second encyclical that Pope Benedict XVI issued as *Spe salvi* in 2007:

> According to the Christian faith, "redemption" – salvation – is not simply a given. Redemption is offered to us in the sense that we have been given hope, trustwor-

---

165 *UChr*, 67–68: 'Nur Gott kennt sich selbst ganz. Nur Gott sieht Gott. Und daher konnte nur der, der Gott ist, wirklich Kunde bringen von ihm.'
166 *Dominus Iesus*, no. 5.

thy hope, by virtue of which we can face our present: the present, even if it is arduous, can be lived and accepted if it leads towards a goal, if we can be sure of this goal, and if this goal is great enough to justify the effort of the journey.[167]

Thus, Jesus Christ's universality is the basis for the universal commitment to service.

Is this Christological universal claim not a hindrance for interreligious dialogue which is often based on the presupposition that all religions are equal? Is it presumptuous to uphold that Christianity is the unique form of salvation? Is it not rather that each religion represents a specific way to salvation? And is Christianity therefore not only one of the many forms? In his reply, Ratzinger distinguishes religion and philosophy. From a religious perspective, the Cardinal admitted the possibility of salvation for other faiths if their followers seek to please God with a good and moral life. And yet, this recognition should not lead automatically to the conclusion that all religions are *per se* equal. The history of religion has clearly shown that within certain religions there were also religious practices which ignited irrational fear; and therefore must be deemed destructive: 'There are various levels [of religion], and there are religions that are obviously sick, religions which can also be destructive for man.'[168] Ratzinger points to the ancient ritual sacrifices which aroused fear rather than peace in the human mind and heart. Such religious ritualism is cruel. Yet, the Pope also acknowledged that Christian sacrifice as form of atonement can also be viewed in this way: 'Again and again people say: It must be a cruel God who demands infinite atonement.'[169] For Ratzinger, religion is only true if it is purified from all destructive forces which oppress and alienate human beings. His argument for Christianity as true religion should be seen against this background. But Christianity is only true because in Jesus Christ the Word of God appeared as normative measure and purifying force against ideologies and systems which cause oppression and alienation:

167 *SpS*, no. 1.
168 *SE*, 23.
169 *JoN*, vol. 2, 232.

> I would say that if Christianity, appealing to the figure of Christ, has claimed to be the true religion among the religions of history, this means ... that in the figure of Christ the truly purifying has appeared out of the Word of God ... it furnishes the criterion and the orientation for the purifications that are indispensable for keeping religion form becoming a system of oppression and alienation, so that it may become really a way for man to God and to himself.[170]

Hence, Jesus Christ is the truth and the way which liberates human beings. This truth leads to the fulfilment in God who is love. For this reason, Christianity is from its very beginning critical of religions ("religionskritisch"). As an example of its critical stance against conventional ritualism of sacrifice, Ratzinger points to Jesus whose death has put an end to all forms of animal or human sacrifices:

> God himself becomes the locus of reconciliation, and in the person of his Son takes the suffering upon himself ... God himself "drinks the cup" of every horror to the dregs and thereby restores justice through the greatness of his love, which, through suffering, transforms the darkness.[171]

Thus Jesus' death establishes a new form of worship of God which involves human life and conduct in its entirety. Citing *Heb* 10:5–7 the Cardinal interpreted the worship of God as obedience to and as doing the will of the Father:

> Living within and on the basis of God's word has been recognized as the right way to worship God ... So here the idea of spiritual sacrifice, or "sacrifice in the manner of the word, was formulated: prayer, the self-opening of the human spirit to God, is true worship.[172]

This liturgical notion is, for Verweyen, the constant of Ratzinger's theology.[173] The orientation towards the *Logos* purifies religions. Christianity finds in philosophical reasoning *(Logos)* a dialogical partner that directs human intelligence towards the truth. As a conse-

---

170 *SE*, 24.
171 *JoN*, vol. 2, 232.
172 Ibid., 233;
173 Verweyen, *Entwicklung*, 135.

quence, Christianity is not primarily grounded in external ritualism, but in the redemptive truth revealed in the deeds and words of Jesus. For Ratzinger, truth and redemption overlap directly with one other. Thus the faith in Jesus Christ, through which one is placed on the level of the salutary truth, demands from a Christian a true conversion. This contrasts with the idea of "absolute self-determination, which acts according to the principle of 'everyone according to his own truth.'[174] Christians cannot accept the pluralistic idea, that all religions were somehow true and that they were therefore salutary, because – as Ratzinger argued – Christ as the *Logos* is the absolute revelation of God: 'The revelation is not an accumulation of clauses, but is Christ himself. He is the Logos, the all-encompassing Word, in which God expresses himself, and which we call the Son of God.' Ratzinger tirelessly reminds Christians of this truth: 'Christians should not be content with Christianity of habits, or of naked ritualism and customary routines. They, too, must break with the habits, in order to see the truth, which appeared in human flesh.'[175] Ratzinger's understanding of the uniqueness of Jesus Christ clearly accords with the Christological nature of the Dogmatic Constitution *Dei Verbum* (DV), in particularly with the article four.[176] In his commentary on *DV* and in agreement with Karl Rahner,[177] Ratzinger saw in Jesus Christ the

---

174 Lieven Boeve, "'La vraie reception de Vatican II n'a pas encore commence". Joseph Ratzinger, Révelation et autorité de Vatican II', in *EphTL* 85.4 (2009), 305–339, here 317.
175 *UChr*, 76.
176 This Christocentric nature of revelation probably went back to the pen of Daniélou who composed on behalf of the French Archbishop Garrone a text of seven paragraphs entitled with "On Revelation and the Word of God". According to professor Jared Wicks, this text found its way into *Dei Verbum*'s teaching; see Jared Wicks, 'Vatican II on Revelation – From Behind the Scenes', in *Theological Studies* 71.3 (2010), 637–650, here 647–649; with regard to the dogmatic evolution of chapter four of *DV* see also Brendan Cahill, *The Renewal of Revelation Theology (1960–1962). The Development and Responses to the Fourth Chapter of the Preparatory Schema De deposito Fidei* (Roma: Gregorian University, 1999).
177 Ratzinger cited here Karl Rahner, 'The Development of Dogma', in *Theological Investigations*, vol. 1 (1961), here in particular page 49.

perfection of God's revelation: 'Christ is the end of God's speaking, because after him and beyond him, there is nothing more to say, for in him God has, as it were, said himself. In him, the dialogue of God has attained its goal.'[178] Because Christ is the Word incarnate, revelation in Jesus Christ cannot be supplanted by 'any new development in the history of religion or of mankind.'[179] And yet, God's dialogue with humanity has not ceased. The Spirit of Christ opens the human "I" so that the self can be constantly addressed by God. This pneumatological dimension of Christology is influenced by the Eastern Orthodox Churches represented at Vatican II,[180] thus countering a one-sided extrinsic Christocentricism focussing solely on the positivist finality of the divine revelation. Commenting on article no. 2 of *DV*, Ratzinger therefore points to the Trinitarian concept of revelation:

> Another important thing in our text is the markedly Trinitarian conception: the movement of revelation proceeds from God (the Father), comes to us through Christ, and admits us to the fellowship of God in the Holy Spirit. Thus although our text has been composed in definitively Christological terms – Christ is described finally as the mediator of revelation and the fullness of revelation itself – it does not present a one-sided Christocentric view ... Thus, on the one hand, the pneumatological dimension is not overlooked here, this emerging naturally from a Christology of the resurrection as a correction to a one-sided Christology of incarnation, and at the same time the theocentric position is given appropriate emphasis, towards which the Christocentric view, properly understood, is necessarily oriented.[181]

The incarnational and pneumatological nature of Christology therefore respects both the historical-incarnational character of the revelation, and safeguards its eschatological perfection towards which human history necessarily moves:

178 *CDV*, 175.
179 Ibid., 176.
180 In his lecture published as 'Kirche als Tempel des Heiligen Geistes', in *Vom Wiederauffinden der Mitte – Grundorientierungen: Texte aus vier Jahrzehnten*, edited by Stephan O. Horn, Vinzenz Pfnür and others (Freiburg: Herder, 1997) 148–157, Ratzinger suggested this possibility.
181 *CDV*, 172.

The Christological foundation for Christian claim to finality has become clearer and the eschatological relation brought in, which now shows from within faith the provisional character of Christianity and hence its relatedness to the future, which exists together with the connection with the Christ event that has taken place once and for all, so that it is impossible to state the one without the other.[182]

Hence, promise and hope are brought together in Jesus Christ. It is precisely the latter that transforms the "gentiles" into co-heirs of the promise given first to the children of Israel. The participation in this hope, however, comes from faith which entails trust 'with which it sets out on a path the end of which cannot yet be seen.'[183] Faith confesses Christ as saviour and revealer:

> Faith proclaims Christ as the one who has come and as the one who is to come and thus bears within itself both the infinite openness of man and the finality of the divine answer that does not put an end to man's development, but makes him conscious of his true, infinite nature.[184]

11. *Jesus of Nazareth* – A Spiritual-Theological Exploration into the Real Jesus

The Spiritual Christology that Ratzinger had just discovered for himself in the year 1981 is fully elaborated in the last three volumes he published on *Jesus of Nazareth* between the years 2007–2012. According to the Pope, the Christological events reported in the New Testament are not only historical, but they are also "mysteries" which cannot be explained completely by historical-critical exegesis, although it is indispensable. Ratzinger argued therefore for a methodological whole which combines the historical hermeneutic with the hermeneutic of faith. In joining the two hermeneutical methodologies

---

182 Ibid., 177.
183 Ibid., 176.
184 *CDV*, 177.

together, he adds to the objective history an existential personal adherence:

> In the combination of the two hermeneutics of which I spoke earlier, I have attempted to develop a way of observing and listening to the Jesus of the Gospels that can indeed lead to personal encounter and that, through collective listening with Jesus' disciples across the ages, can indeed attain sure knowledge of the real historical figure of Jesus.[185]

The Pope advocates for an Christological approach, which respects the historical context and the sacramental character of the biblical texts. Ratzinger's courage to pursue his spiritual Christology is endorsed by Marius Reiser's book on biblical criticism and interpretation of the Scriptures in which the author promotes a spiritual-theological exegesis.[186] Accordingly, Reiser maintains that biblical exegesis is also theological exegesis because its referential object is Christ. Thus, Christ is the key to the riddles and secrets contained in the biblical texts.[187] In agreement with Reiser, Ratzinger calls on the biblical exegesis 'to take a methodological step forward and see it as a theological discipline, without abandoning its historical character.'[188] This means that biblical exegesis should take into account the revelatory character of the biblical texts. Biblical exegesis ought to be conducted as a dialogue which arises from the living faith in Jesus Christ. It is therefore legitimate to incorporate the entire living tradition of faith into the reading of biblical texts. It means concretely that one should read the scriptural texts synchronically, but without neglecting their historical context. Ratzinger suggests further that, where the historical contexts of the scriptural passages or where the

---

185 *JoN*, vol. 2, xvi–xvii; see also Hans Boersma, 'History and Faith in Pope's Benedict XVI *Jesus of Nazareth*', in *NV* 10.4 (2012), 985–991.
186 Marius Reiser, *Bibelkritik und Auslegung der Heiligen Schrift: Beiträge zur Geschichte der biblischen Exegese und Hermeneutik* (Tübingen: Mohr Siebeck, 2007).
187 Id., 'Hat die spirituelle Exegese eine eigene Methode?', in *Studies in Spirituality* 10 (2004), 431.
188 *JoN*, vol. 2, xiv.

biblical texts seem to contradict each other, one should also refer to the richness of the deposit of faith, such as the teaching of the Fathers of the Church etc. Explaining his own method, Ratzinger writes:

> In this sense, I have taken pains to enter into dialogue with the texts. In doing so I have been conscious that this conversation, drawing in the past, the present and the future, can never come to end, and that every exegesis must fall short of the magnitude of the biblical text.[189]

That the historical context of many scriptural texts cannot be completely reproduced by historical-critical exegesis becomes clearly evident in the many texts which the biblical authors employed to express the theological significance of Jesus. As an example Ratzinger points to Matthew's and Luke's infancy narratives which defy to certain degrees the literary historical criticism. This applies especially to the genealogy of Jesus. Having explained the agreements and differences between Matthew and Luke, Ratzinger continues to affirm the impossibility to determine with absolute certainty the sources behind the traditions of the genealogy:

> Apart from elements drawn from the Old Testament, both authors have based themselves on traditions whose sources we cannot reconstruct. It seems to me utterly futile to formulate hypotheses on this matter.[190]

While acknowledging the historical traditions of the genealogy, Ratzinger moves towards a theological-spiritual interpretation of the genealogy of Jesus. For the Pope, the evangelists were not obsessed with the details, but more concerned with the symbolic-theological structure of the given traditions. In the various accounts of Jesus' genealogy he sees

> the intricacy with which he [Jesus] is woven into the historical strands of the promise, as well as the *new beginning* which paradoxically characterizes his origin side by side with the *continuity* of God's action in history.[191]

---

189 *JoN*, vol. 3, xi–xii.
190 *JoN*, vol. 3, 8.
191 Ibid., 8–9.

In the genealogy prominent figures, such as Abraham and David, serve as bridges for a theological interpretation of Jesus's significance. According to Ratzinger, Matthew saw in Abraham,

> a wayfarer, not only from the land of his birth into the promised land, but also on the journey from the present to the future. His whole life points forward, it is a dynamic of walking along the path of what is to come.[192]

The promise that Abraham would be the Father of all nations (*Gen* 12:2–3) is the condition which leads to the universal openness achieved in Jesus Christ who after his resurrection commanded his disciples to 'make disciples of all nations.'[193] This universality is, however, realized already in Jesus' birth. The inclusion of the four non Jewish women, Tamar, Rahab, Ruth and the wife of Uriah, in the genealogy clearly indicates this universality of Jesus' birth. In a spiritual reading of the infancy narrative, Ratzinger sees this universality not only as a continuation of Israel's history but also as a new beginning dawned at the virgin birth of Jesus. The biologically fatherless conception of Jesus makes Mary also a signpost of a new creation, conceived by the Holy Spirit: 'It is in the end Mary, the lowly virgin from Nazareth, in whom a new beginning takes place, in whom human existence starts afresh.'[194] Neither Abraham nor Joseph, but God is truly the father of all peoples. According to Ratzinger, this Matthean account of Jesus' genealogy proves the dual characters of Jesus' provenance. As son of Mary, he is also the Son of God whom he calls "Abba" (*Mk* 14:6). Jesus' dual origin is also the key to the understanding of the relationship between David and Jesus. In 2 *Samuel* 7:16, David received the blessing of Yahweh via the lips of the prophet Nathan: 'Your house and your sovereignty will always stand and secure before me and your throne be established forever.' Thus, David's kingdom shall endure forever. In the Matthean account of Jesus' genealogy the eternal kingdom, which God has

---

192   Ibid., 5.
193   *Mt* 28:19.
194   *JoN*, vol. 3, 8.

promised to David, was closely associated with the birth of Jesus. By stating that Jesus through Joseph was a descendant of the Davidic line, Matthew intended to show theologically the legal heritage of Jesus[195]: Christ is the true heir of King David. In Christ the eternal Kingdom is fully realized. The Old Testament therefore figuratively points towards the New Testament. Indeed Jesus Christ is the key to the understanding of the Old Testamentary prophesy. This becomes clearer in the Lucan version of Jesus' provenance which the evangelist presented at the beginning of Jesus' public ministry (Lk 3:23–38). A look at both genealogies reveals that Matthew and Luke agree on only a few names of Jesus' ancestry. Perhaps both evangelists were not interested in historical details, but in their symbolic theological significance. In presenting the genealogy at the beginning of Jesus' ministry, Luke signalled to us his theological-spiritual plan: Jesus' willingness to take 'upon himself the whole of humanity, the whole history of man, and he gives it decisive re-orientation toward a new manner of humanity.'[196] Thus, the presentation of Jesus' genealogy already includes the soteriological task designated for Jesus. In his spiritual-theological transposition of the biblical texts, Ratzinger interweaves the life of the faithful with the life of Jesus, 'who gives us a new origin, who brings us to birth "from God".'[197] Jesus's birth therefore, not only is the continuation of Israel's hope, but also contains a newness which goes beyond Israel's expectation.

Ratzinger, as we would have expected, expounds the soteriological implication of Jesus' ministry in the second volume of *Jesus of Nazareth* where he discusses the spiritual-theological significance of the Christological events from the entrance into Jerusalem to the resurrection. Due to the limitation of space, we cannot repeat here the controversies which arose since its publication in 2009. However, it is important to keep in mind the fact that Pope Benedict did not intend to offer only a historical approach to the life of Jesus, but rather

---

195 *Mt* 1:16.
196 *JoN*, vol. 3, 11.
197 Ibid., 13.

was interested in relating Jesus to the life of the faithful whose historical and spiritual context differs much from the time of Jesus. He is always interested in investigating both the person and message of Jesus: 'Exaggerating a little bit, one could say that I set out to discover the real Jesus, on the basis of whom something like a "Christology from below" would then become possible.'[198] Jesus' message therefore explains who Jesus really his. But the message can only be reappropriated within the scope of Revelation. The penetration of Jesus' message should be done also within the frame of the collective faith which arises out of the encounter with Jesus. We can still hear the message of Jesus because God did not cease to reveal himself, but continues to enlighten us. This is the reason why Jesus' message is constitutive for our life.

In the second volume of his book on Jesus of Nazareth, the Pope pays much attention to the events of the crucifixion and death of Jesus. The main problem can be abbreviated in this way: How can the faithful participate in the death of Jesus, which was an historical event of past? This question touches the heart of Christian faith because it is through Jesus' death that we are redeemed. Ratzinger solves this problem by proposing a reading of the historical events alongside the theology of the Word *(logos)*. Thus, he proposes, they must be read together in the light of God's revelation. From the background of Revelation, the death of Jesus is not seen as an isolated historical event[199], but is a part of the whole. Ratzinger sees Jesus' redemptive death already prefigured in the baptism administered by John. He reads the epiphany of Jesus reported in the synoptic Gospels, such *Mt* 3:17 3:22: 'This is my beloved Son, with whom I am well pleased' together with *Isaiah* 53:7 (Suffering servant) and 1 *Cor* 5:7 (Pascal Lamb). For Ratzinger, the baptism of Jesus anticipates already on the one side his willingness to undergo death for the forgiveness of sins; and on the other side it points also towards his resurrection.[200]

198 *JoN*, vol. 2, xvi.
199 It is not an event of coincidence.
200 *JoN*, vol. 1, 17–22.

Here the historical event is supplemented by a sacramental spiritual reading. The death of Jesus is then seen 'in the context of God's ongoing relationship with his people, from which it receives its inner logic and its meaning.'[201] The revelatory character of the *Logos* therefore unchains the historicism of an event and transposes it into the present. Through baptism the believer is now bound to Christ and is identified as Christian.[202] The Church becomes the indispensable *locus* where the encounter with Christ is made possible. For this reason Jesus' death differs from the death of a sinner, for he himself is the *Logos*:

> Insofar as Jesus' death can be located within this context of God's word and God's love, it is differentiated from the kind of death resulting from man's original sin, as a consequence of his presumption in seeking to be like God, a presumption that could only lead to man's plunge into wretchedness, into the destiny of death.[203]

Within God's revelation, Jesus' death already points towards his resurrection. Because God's revelation is understood as an ongoing relationship between God and humanity, Jesus' death and resurrection also affect us today:

> If we attend to the witnesses with listening hearts and open ourselves to the signs by which the Lord again and again authenticates both them and himself, then we know that he is truly risen. He is alive.[204]

The obscure meaning of the death and crucifixion can be enlightened by the fact that the *Logos* is alive. As such, he still communicates with us. From the perspective of the *Logos*, Jesus' death is beneficial for us. Jesus in his death died truly for *our* sins: 'Because his

---

201 Ibid., 252.
202 *JoN*, vol. 1, 18: 'to accept the invitation to be baptized now means to go to the place of Jesus' Baptism. It is to go where he identifies himself with us and to receive there our identification with him. The point where he anticipates death has now become the point where we anticipate rising again with him.'
203 *JoN*, vol. 2, 252–253.
204 Ibid., 277.

death has to do with the word of God, it has to do with *us*, it is a dying for *us*.'²⁰⁵ Thus his death is not only an act which completes or which ends a negative circle, but it also creates something new. Jesus is seen as the new Adam who through his dying, creates a new creation which he gathers in his Church. In a spiritual adaption of the early Fathers' theology, Ratzinger writes about the intrinsic relationship between Jesus's death and the foundation of the Church:

> In this double outpouring of blood and water, the Fathers saw an image of the two fundamental sacraments – Eucharist and Baptism – which spring forth from the Lord's pierced side, from his heart. This is the new outpouring that creates the Church and renews mankind. Moreover, the opened side of the Lord asleep on the Cross prompted the Fathers to point to the creation of Eve from the side of the sleeping Adam, and so in this outpouring of the sacraments they also recognized the birth of the Church: the creation of the new woman from the side of the new Adam.²⁰⁶

Ratzinger therefore sees the birth of the Church not as an outcome of the resurrection. He locates the origin of the Church already in the redemptive death of Jesus. Thus, the Church is truly intended by Jesus. This bond legitimates the missionary dimension of the Church. According to Ratzinger, it is John who saw a close connection between the Cross and the Church's mission:

> This brings us tho the great theme of Jesus' universal mission. Israel does not exist for itself; its election is rather the path by which God intends to come to all men. This idea of universality will turn up again and again as the real core of Jesus' mission. By referring to the Lamb of God that takes away the sins of the world, the Fourth Gospel places this idea right at the beginning of Jesus' journey … For this very reason, though, there is an arc joining this beginning of Jesus' journey and the words with which he sends his disciples into the world after his Resurrection: 'Go therefore and make disciples of all nations, baptizing them in the name of the Father and of the Son and of the Holy Spirit (*Mt* 28:19).²⁰⁷

---

205 Ibid., 252. *Italic* mine.
206 Ibid., 226.
207 *JoN*, vol. 1, 22–23.

In this sense, the Church is instituted from above, from the redemptive will of God. This is the reason why the liturgy is not made primarily for anthropological purpose, but primary for the worship of God. But it is a new worship which comes to the fore:

> The Cross and Resurrection give him authority as the one who ushers in true worship. Jesus justifies himself through his Passion – the sign of Jonah that he gives to Israel and to the world. ... The era of the Temple is over. A new worship is being introduced, in a Temple not built by human hands. This Temple is his body, the Risen One, who gathers the peoples and unites them in the sacrament of his body and blood. He himself is the new Temple of humanity. The crucifixion of Jesus is at the same time the destruction of the old Temple. With his Resurrection, a new way of worshipping God begins, no longer on this or that mountain, but "in spirit and truth" (Jn 4:23).[208]

The above quotation makes plain that the historical events reported in the Scriptures gain their full meanings only through the faith of the Church because Christ's spirit lives in her. The fullness of the inner relationship between Christ and his Church is manifested in the Eucharistic celebration. It is in the Eucharist that we participate in Jesus Christ's death and resurrection. The Church's martyrdom is therefore a visible manifestation of this inner bond with Christ.

12. Summary

Our reflections have shown that Ratzinger's spiritual Christology is inseparable from his insights into the Bonaventurian concept of revelation. Revelation involves a twofold action: the revelation in words and deeds with which God continuously illumines the human mind and moves the will. It is always more than Scriptures and tradition. Both are the wellsprings of the knowledge of the one revelation. For

---

[208] *JoN*, vol. 2, 22–23; see also Geoffrey Wainwright, 'The "New Worship" in Joseph Ratzinger's *Jesus of Nazareth*', in *NV* 10.4 (2012), 993–1013.

this reason, neither Scriptures alone nor tradition is *per se* sufficient. Because revelation is divine action, it can never be fully mastered by humans. Against this theological background, Ratzinger maintains that historical-critical exegesis alone cannot offer full access to the real Jesus. True knowledge to the identity of Jesus is possible only through an existential-spiritual friendship with Jesus Christ. Personal friendship with Jesus Christ is enhanced through faith and prayers. According to Bruggemann, prayer is a 'genuine dialogical real transaction.' Continual prayer effects a real ontological unity between those who pray, and the one to whom the prayers are addressed. It is through prayers that faith becomes an existential certitude which originates in the knowledge that God will keep his promise. Prayers therefore reveal, from within, the identity of the real Jesus Christ. In the New Testament, Jesus discloses his identity in his prayers. It is in these moments that the intimate relationship between Jesus and his God, whom he called his Father, is revealed. The prayers of Jesus manifest his identiy as the Son of his Father, just as his dying on the cross manifests his filial love. Obedient to his Father, Jesus becomes the redeemer and saviour of mankind. Jesus' prayers, then, must be seen as salvific events. Furthermore, in his prayers, Jesus truly converses with his Father because he is the Word of his Father. As *Logos* Jesus draws us into his inner dialogue with the Father in the sense that he, as Son, died for us and incorporates us into himself. Like Augustine, Ratzinger therefore states that we were also present at Jesus' prayers, for the Word prays in, and for, us. This Christological dimension gives a new meaning to the concept of sacrifice and consecration. The Eucharistic liturgy is not ritual or cult, but worship in terms of "thysia logike". It is a liturgy according to the *Logos*, the Word. In this context, sacrifice is consecration because it involves a right conduct and right love of a person towards God and the neighbours.[209] According to John, it is through love that one comes to know God:

---

[209] See *Dt* 6:5; *Mt* 22:37 ‖ *Lk* 10:27 ‖ *Mk* 12:30: 'And you shall love the Lord your God with all your heart and with all your soul and with all your mind and with all your strength.'

'Beloved, let us love one another, for love is from God, and whoever loves has been born of God and knows God.' (1 *John* 4:7) And this love is the foundation of the Church's mission which aims not to destroy, but to renew in truth the people's life. It is this love for truth that is critical of all what is inhuman.

Ratzinger's spiritual Christology is therefore inclusive. It takes into consideration various elements of Christian existence, namely faith, worship, Scriptures, tradition and human knowledge. Because of the mystery character of the divine revelation, the true and real identity of Jesus is revealed only through a spiritual relationship.

Chapter Three: *Ecclesiology*

1. Introduction

After more than three centuries of not having councils, Pope Pius IX opened the First Vatican Council on December 8th 1869. His intention was to strengthen the faith and the authority of the ecclesiastical *magisterium*, given the rise of secular ideologies and political liberalism. The outbreak of the Franco-Prussian and the invasion of the Vatican by Garibaldi's army of liberation left this council unfinished. And so, when Pope John XXIII convoked the Second Vatican Council, he wanted to complete the work of the previous Council. According to Cardinal Ratzinger, there was unanimity amongst the bishops that the Church should be the main theme of the Second Vatican Council. He recalled in his *Memoirs*:

> There was an implicit agreement that the Church herself should be the main theme of the gathering, which would take up again and conclude the work of First Vatican Council, which had been prematurely interrupted in 1870 by the Franco-Prussian War.[1]

Ratzinger's view accords with the Belgian *peritus* Gérard Philips who was influential in the deliberation of *Lumen Gentium*: 'When the Council made this theme its primary interest, it backs explicitly to the programme of the Council of 1870 and determined to take it further.'[2] However, Philips in his assessment of *Lumen Gentium* did not refer to the *Dogmatic Constitution on Revelation*, despite the fact

---

1   *Mi*, 122.
2   Gérard Philips, 'Dogmatic Constitution on the Church. History of the Constitution', in *Commentary on the Documents of Vatican II*, vol. 1, edited by Herbert Vorgrimler (London: Burns & Oates, 1967), 105; see also Ratzinger's assessment of the role of Philips during the process of the drafting of the text *PCT*, 44–45.

147

that he had mentioned the Christocentric focus of *Lumen Gentium*. For Ratzinger, the Church is deeply rooted in revelation because she is the collective subject[3] addressed by God in an intimate manner. For this reason, the Church is considered as *"sacramentum"* – a term which Philips, not without reservation, only introduced later in the new draft as *"veluti* sacramentum".[4] The Church as sacrament points clearly to its intimate relationship with God. Consequently, it is always through the faith of the Church that the spiritual meaning of the Scripture is fully captured.[5] The Church, in the words of Bonaventure, is intrinsically related to God who reveals himself completely through his only Word whose Spirit fills and inspires the Church.[6] Thus, the Church is radically located within the Trinitarian communion. To underline the intimate bond between God and the Church, Ratzinger reported a minor incident related to a communication between Cardinal Frings and himself during the preparatory phase of the Council. When the German Episcopal Conference met to discuss the main topics of the Council, the bishops had agreed that the Church should be the main theme. During the debate, the venerable Archbishop Buchberger of Regensburg, who was the co-editor of the well-known *Catholic Encyclopedia (Lexikon für Theologie und Kirche)*, intervened and proposed, to the consternation of the participating bishops, that the main focus of the Council should be God. This proposal left Cardinal Frings dissatisfied, so that he 'asked again and again how such a suggestion could possibly be carried out.'[7] His reaction was that of

---

3   Vorderholzer, 61: 'ekklesialer Subjektivismus.'
4   *PCT*, 45: 'The Belgian text is more cautious in its approach. It begins by defining *sacramentum* "as a sign and instrument" but even then introduces the word itself with circumspection and a qualifying *veluti* ('as it were'), thus characterizing the usage as figurative by comparison with the usual use of the term and explaining it at the outset;' also *JRGS* 8. 1, 244–247.
5   *JRGS* 2, 519: '"Offenbarung" gerade als Erfassen geistigen Sinnes.'
6   Ibid., 178: 'dass der Heilige, der die Kirche als Zeit des Heiligen Geistes betrachtet, ein offenbarendes Tun des Geistes kennt, das Christi Werk erst vollendet.'
7   *JRGS* 8.1, 574: 'Aber eine innere Unruhe ist da mindestens bei Kardinal Frings geblieben, der sich immer neu fragte, wie wir diesem Imperativ genügen könnten.'

an experienced pastor who looked at the Church from the perspective of her wholeness.[8] A biblical scholar himself, Frings intervened at Vatican II, emphasising that the Church

> must live from the whole, draw again and again directly from the Bible, drink again and again from the great, pure sources of all times. Only then does faith remain great and wide; only then does it reach into those depths and grow to height through which it binds heaven and earth.[9]

For Frings the renewal process, attempted by Vatican II, requires basically a 'trust in God who reveals himself … The good God obviously does not harm us; one needs to show him nothing more than some kind of primitive trust.'[10] This primitive trust must be grounded in the goodness of God, who communicates himself fully in his Son, and whose death and resurrection transform the people into members of his body. As Christ is ever present in his body, the Church is therefore present in Christ. This rediscovery of the Christological thrust of the Church's existence was one of the most important elements of renewal in Vatican II. Ratzinger writes:

> The Church means the presence of Christ, our contemporaneity with him, his contemporaneity with us. It lives from Christ's dwelling in our hearts; from there he forms the Church for himself. For that reason, the Church's first word is Christ and not itself; it is sound in the measure that all attention is directed towards him.[11]

According to Ratzinger, this contemporaneity is most visible in the Eucharistic celebration through which Christ establishes a new unity between God and humanity. In the Eucharist, two essential moments

---

8   'Cardinal's Frings's Speeches During the Second Vatican Council: Some Reflections Apropos of Muggeridge's The Desolate City', in *Pope Benedict XVI – Joseph Ratzinger in Communio*, vol. 1: The Unity of the Church, Introduction by David L. Schindler, translated by Peter Verhalen (Grand Rapids, Michigan: Eerdmans, 2010), 87.
9   Ibid., 90.
10 Ibid., 103–104.
11 *EV*, 64.

of the salvation history, namely God's word and action, fuse together.[12] In this sense, creation and revelation form an inseparable unity in the Eucharistic celebration. From there the Church is constantly renewed in conformity with Christ whose Spirit dwells in the heart of the Church. Thus, the renewal of the Church is a consistent feature in the pastoral concern of Vatican II. Of course, the adjective "pastoral" can be interpreted in various ways. According to Ratzinger, however, it should mean,

> speaking in the language of scripture, of the early Church Fathers, and of contemporary man. Technical theological language has its purpose and is indeed necessary, but it does not belong in the kerygma and in our confession of faith.[13]

Among the Fathers of the Church, Augustine, the African bishop of Hippo, was singled out. In a televised interview on December 28, 1998, conducted by the journalist, Lohmann, Ratzinger expressed his abiding admiration for Augustine with these words:

> My great personal encounter was Augustine, who, in my eyes, was not a man of the past. But his life and thought are so alive in our minds that I consider him as a contemporary fellow of my life.[14]

This attachment to Augustine was a constant in Ratzinger's theology and ministry.[15] In the school of Augustine, Ratzinger developed his ecclesiology.

---

12 *LW*, 157: 'This important point is that the Lord's Word and his real presence in the signs are inseparable in the Eucharist. It is important that we also receive instruction in the Word. That we answer through our prayer and that God's guidance, our following, and our allowing ourselves be changed thus form an interlocking whole – so that men themselves can be changed, which is the most important precondition for any really positive change in the world.'
13 *THV*, 45.
14 This interview can be seen online; see <www.br.-online.de/alpha/forum>.
15 In his catechesis on Augustine Pope Benedict XVI regarded Augustine as 'a friend, a contemporary who speaks to me, who speaks to us with his fresh and timely faith;' see *FoC*, 144.

2. Ratzinger in the School of Augustine

In his secondary school years, Ratzinger had already discovered his love for Augustine. As a lover of Latinity,[16] the teenage Ratzinger had probably read Augustine's *Confessions* or perhaps even the *City of God*. According to a testimony of an early roommate at the military base, Ratzinger used to read about Augustine in his spare time.[17] The Bishop of Hippo continued to influence Ratzinger as a priest, theologian and leader of the Church. Ratzinger might have seen in the life of Augustine a parallel to his own life. Like Augustine who was called from his academic chair to become a pastor, so was Ratzinger appointed Archbishop of Munich in 1977 at the peak of an academic career. Like Augustine, Ratzinger accepted pastoral office in the Church only reluctantly.[18] In his catechesis on Augustine, Pope Benedict XVI described Augustine's reluctance in accepting a pastoral office in the diocese of Hippo:

> In his city on the African coast he was ordained a priest in 391, despite his reluctance, and with a few companions began the monastic life which had long been in his mind, dividing his time between prayer, study and preaching. All he wanted was to be at the service of the truth. He did not feel he had a vocation to pastoral life but realized later that God was calling him to be a pastor among others and thus to offer people the gift of truth.[19]

This tension between pastoral responsibility and academic theology accompanies Ratzinger throughout his life. It is widely known that the then Cardinal Ratzinger wrote in 1997 a formal letter to Pope John Paul II, in which, due to the canonical age, he not only offered his resignation as Head of the CDF, but also expressed his desire to serve the Church as a retiree in the role of the Librarian of the Holy See, hoping to devote himself to study and theological research. Instead,

---

16 *Mi*, 29: 'The Greek and Latin classics filled me with enthusiasm.'
17 Lam, 18.
18 *Mi*, 152: 'I went back to the nuncio and again explained my reservations; but in the end, with him as my witness, I hesitantly wrote my acceptance…'
19 *FoC*, 139–140.

he was elected to be the universal Pastor of the Roman Catholic Church on April 16th, 2005. In referring to his election, he later used the image of a guillotine to describe his personal feeling. He compared his elevation to the highest office of the Catholic Church with the fall of the guillotine upon him, putting an end to his personal plans for retirement.[20] However, in his uncertainty, and now Pope Benedict, he felt the companionship of Christ and the example of Augustine encouraging him to accept the inevitable. In the Bishop of Hippo, Pope Benedict XVI observed the harmony between truth, faith and the service in the Church, and pointed to the importance of Augustine for him, for the Church and indeed for the entire Western world:

> I would like to speak of the greatest Father of the Latin Church, St. Augustine. This man of passion and faith, of the highest intelligence and tireless in his pastoral care, a great saint and doctor of the Church is often known, at least by hearsay, even by those who ignore Christianity or who are not familiar with it, because he left a very deep mark on the cultural life of the West and on the whole world.[21]

Ratzinger's Episcopal motto, *"co-operatores veritatis"*, evokes Augustine's search for truth in the service of the Church.

Reflecting on the influence of Augustine upon his theological thoughts, in particular for his ecclesiology, Cardinal Ratzinger reminisced during a book presentation in 2005:

> When I embarked on my dialogue with St. Augustine 50 years ago, I almost immediately found in him a contemporary, a man who does not speak from afar and from a totally different context from our own but who, having lived in a context very similar to ours, responds – in his own way, of course – to problems which are our same problems.[22]

---

20 *LW*, 3: 'Yes, the thought of the guillotine occurred to me: Now it falls down and it hits you. I had been so sure that this office was not my calling, but that God would now grant me some peace and quiet after strenuous years.'
21 Ibid., 136.
22 '*The Power and The Grace*. The presentation of the book by *30Days* on the actuality of Saint Augustine, with Cardinal Joseph Ratzinger, in the "Sala del Cenacolo" of the Chamber of Deputies, in *30Days* (2005) 5; see <http://www.30giorni.it/articoli_id_8926_l3.htm>; see also my book Joseph Lam Cong Quy (Würzburg: Echter, 2009), 14–23.

This quotation not only reveals Augustine's influence on Ratzinger, but also Ratzinger's dialogical reading of Augustine's writings. Both speaking and listening are necessarily involved:

> Dialogue first comes into being where there is not only speech but also listening. Moreover, such listening must be the medium of an encounter; this encounter is the condition of an inner contact which leads to mutual comprehension. Reciprocal understanding, finally, deepens and transforms the being of the interlocutors.[23]

This dialogical character of Ratzinger's listening to Augustine excludes treating the writings of Augustine in a detached academic fashion – indeed, it would be quite against Augustine's own intentions. In his *Confessions*, Augustine invites his readers not only to read about his past life,[24] but also to listen to the truth revealed beyond his *Confessions*. In paying attention to the truth, readers are called on to change their own lives.[25] In dialogue, the inmost being of the other is revealed: the listener's being is enriched and deepened 'because it is united with the being of the other and, through it, with the being of the world.'[26]

For Ratzinger, the deepest level of dialogue is achieved in conversation among friends. Augustine is seen here as an example:

> This is an element upon which the early Augustine set particular value. In fact, we can easily trace the story of Augustine's conversion in the records of his dialogues with his friends ... Analyzing these colloquies in retrospect, Augustine concludes that community of friends was capable of mutual listening and understanding because all of them together heeded the interior mater, the truth ... Dialogue without this interior obedient listening to the truth would be nothing more than a discussion among the deaf.[27]

But no one possesses the truth for himself alone. That is precisely why dialogue with the past is possible because the present and the past are seen together as a joint effort in the search for truth. The

23 *NTM*, 32–33.
24 This would be a kind of historical curiosity; see *Conf.* 10, 3: 'A race interested in finding out about the other man's life, slothful in amending their own.'
25 *Conf.* 10, 1–4.
26 Ibid., 33.
27 Ibid., 34.

connection between the past and the present is established through faith, a gift of the Holy Spirit which always looks for the whole truth.[28] It is only through the trans-historical spirit of faith that the past is opened up and the dialogue between the past and the present is made possible. The one Spirit joins historical particularity to the whole truth 'which in turn endows the particular, which hitherto had not been understood, with its genuine meaning.'[29]

With this, we touch on the theological method of Ratzinger. For him, history is dynamic because it is permeated by truth which is trans-historical. Hence the historical- critical approach is insufficient because the Spirit of truth is never static. This means that history in itself does not produce meaning. Historical analysis should therefore be complemented by theology.

When Ratzinger looked back to Augustine for guidance, he did not mean that, with Augustine, everything had been said; but rather that the dialogue with the Bishop of Hippo could contribute much to the contemporary understanding of the Church. It can broaden the contemporary narrowness. Here, theological tradition functions as a corrective to contemporary views. And perhaps a contemporary dialogue with Augustine may bring a systematic coherence to Augustine's theology unrealizable in his own time. Thus, Ratzinger's dialogue with Augustine has a double aspect of openness towards the past and the present.

Methodologies, of course, do not fall from heaven. Ratzinger has probably inherited his dialogical method from his teacher. In his autobiography, Ratzinger reports that the topic of his dissertation was assigned to him by his theological master.[30] In the "unwritten" German academic tradition, it is expected of the student that he takes over the methodology of his mentor. There is no doubt that Söhngen exercised a great influence on Ratzinger's theological method. This is

---

28 *NTM*, 56: 'truth becomes accessible only in the act of faith and that faith is the gift of a new beginning for thought.'
29 *NTM*, 55.
30 *Mi*, 97.

clearly voiced in Ratzinger's eulogy at the funeral of his teacher: 'Now he is gone from us. The direction he signposted remains.'[31] In the foreword to his dissertation, Ratzinger also spoke of a new systematic approach which he has inherited from his theological teacher.[32]

2.1 Excursus: The Open System in the Theological Methodology of Gottlieb Söhngen

Söhngen's theological methodology is perhaps best explained in his analysis of Augustine's *Confessiones* X, 6–27. Augustine became bishop of Hippo, the second most important city of North Africa, in the year 396. In book ten of his *Confessions*, composed between the years 397–400, he looked back on his life before his episcopal elevation.[33] Hence, Augustine dealt in the tenth book with the capacity of human memory. Söhngen compared Augustine's idea of memory with Thomas Aquinas' conception of reminiscence, to conclude that Augustinian notion is a more "open" system compared to Aquinas.[34] This Augustinian open system is the outcome of a spiritual wrestling typical of Augustinian memory. It displays a capability of self-questioning through which the past is transported back to the present. Moreover, Augustine's present is co-determined by both the past, and the present, so that the present itself is always oriented towards the future. The present is treated in a futuristic perspective.[35] As a result, memory encompasses the past, present and the future.

---

31 Excerpts from the sermon by Joseph Ratzinger at the funeral of his professor Gottlieb Söhngen, Cologne, parish of Saint Agnes, 19 November 1971; see <http://www.30giorni.it/articoli_id_10131_l3.htm>.
32 Ibid., 44.
33 Gottlied Söhngen, 'Der Aufbau der augustinischen Gedächtnislehre *Confessiones* X c. 6–27', in Id., *Die Einheit in der Theologie* (Munich: Zink, 1952), 63–100.
34 Ibid., 64.74–75. While Thomas Aquinas described the process of intellectual self-recognition as a deductive movement from outside to inside, Augustine recognized in the self-cognition the operation of the mind which is self-reflexive, meaning that it is in itself and by itself.
35 Ibid., 99.

Augustinian memory is an essential human capacity by which the human person is intimately exposed to divine truth. In contrast to Aquinas' more intellectual notion of reminiscence, Augustinian memory is less concerned with causal association, but intent on interior participation in the divine truth. Accordingly, the Augustinian reflexive self-knowledge involves an openness transcending all categories. For this reason, Söhngen claimed that the *Confessions* of Augustine is not without objectivity. But this objectivity of memory is located in a different dimension – in a deeper stratum that eludes the grasp of a strictly historical control and method. All earthly knowledge therefore is complete only through the truth which comes from above: 'Ultimately, the truth is the immutable truth which is the pure spiritual light that enlightens every human spirit.'[36] Clearly, history achieves its full meaning only through a transcendental interpretation which is assisted by faith.

His analysis of the Augustinian nature of memory provides Söhngen with a foundation on which he can now build up his own methodology. A characteristic of Söhngen's theological style was the capacity to radically combine philosophical questioning with a firm faith commitment. Ratzinger comments,

> Söhngen was one who questioned in profound and critical fashion. Even today one cannot question in a more profound way than he did. But at the same time he was a profound believer. What in him fascinated us students in an ever new way was precisely the unity of those two elements: the courage with which he posed each question, and the clarity with which he knew that, by so doing, faith has nothing to fear from a vast search for knowledge.[37]

As Ratzinger saw it, Söhngen's entire academic efforts aimed at reconciling and at anchoring the unity between philosophy and theology. Söhngen's early doctorates in philosophy and theology and his

---

36   Ibid., 97. This idea returns later in his studies of Bonaventure's conception of revelation.
37   Excerpts from the sermon by Joseph Ratzinger at the funeral of his professor Gottlieb Söhngen, Cologne, parish of Saint Agnes, 19 November 1971; see <http://www.30giorni.it/articoli_id_10131_l3.htm>.

subsequent *Habilitation* were concrete examples of this endeavour.[38] For him the *via media* is the appropriate method of Christian theology. Thus Ratzinger inherited from his master the radical and critical way of questioning which is an intrinsic part of the maturity of faith, because 'only those, who live by faith, can truly ask radical and critical questions.'[39] As we have seen already, this radicality, however, leads neither Ratzinger nor Söhngen to the theological arrogance of proposing a new system of theology of their own:

> Thus for him it was also clear that the theologian doesn't speak in his own name, albeit he must give himself, but that instead he affirms the faith of the Church, that he does not invent, but receives. The courage of his questioning sprang from the inward recognition that, as regards truth, we could not have questioned unless truth has not asked of us first, if beforehand we had not already been found by her.[40]

Accordingly, it is the faith of the Church which precedes and enables human questioning. For Söhngen, one can ask radical questions only from the 'pre-existing systematic knowledge'.[41] This antecedent systematic knowledge is the faith of the Church. And yet, faith also involves an intellectual assent. For this reason contemporary philosophical questions, which arises from the "systematic experience", are vital to the dynamic of faith, if faith is to remain a living reality in the life of the Church; otherwise faith can become merely a matter of

---

38   While his doctorate in philosophy in 1914 dealt with a pure Kantian topic *"Über analytische und synthetische Urteile. Eine historisch-kritische Untersuchung zur Logik des Urteils"*, the subsequent doctorate on a philosophical aspect of scholastic theology *"Sein und Gegenstand. Das scholastische Axiom ens et verum convertuntur als Fundament metaphysischer und theologischer Spekulation"* (1930) and the *Habilitation* in the discipline of Fundamental Theology on the subject *"Teilhabe am göttlichen Wissen"* (1931) were attempts to bring theology and philosophy together.
39   Lam, 27–28.
40   See the sermon by Joseph Ratzinger at the funeral of Gottlieb Söhngen. This sermon is re-edited in the monthly magazine *30Days*; see <http://www.30giorni.it/articoli_id_10131_13.htm>.
41   *JRGS* 1, 43: 'Fragen aber kann er nur aus seiner eigenen vorbestehenden systematischen Erkenntnis heraus.'

continuing restoration in the sense that it is cemented by the past.[42] Thus, questioning opens up the past for the present, which in turn can lead to fresh answers, and new questions. Thus, faith and philosophy can enter into a genuine dialogue with mutual benefits.[43] Faith can serve both as question and answer, even open to new questions. Clearly, truth is for Ratzinger not static, but dynamic, bringing new aspects of truth to light.

This tension between openness and certainty of truth in Augustine's *Confessions* fascinated Söhngen. Augustine did not conceive faith and philosophy as antinomies, but rather as complementary sides of the same coin.

In this context, Söhngen criticised the theological method of his time which sought to rely only on Neo-scholasticism: 'To build our theological research purely on Neo-scholastic concept would mean this: the dead bury their own dead!'[44] Theology therefore presumes the faith that arises from the knowledge of truth as a whole because it 'does not concern the functioning of this or particular thing, but the truth of our being itself.'[45] The dynamism of history rests upon the existence of faith.

Ratzinger credited his teacher for leading theology 'out of the grid of a mere restorationist Neo-Scholasticism'.[46]

42 The intellectual affinity between Söhngen and Henry Newman is evident; see also Söhngen's monograph on Newman, *Kardinal Newman. Sein Gottesgedanke und seine Denkergestalt* (Bonn: G. Schwippert, 1946); earlier Söhngen interpreted Newman as a reformer of Augustinian thought; see 'Kardinal Newman, ein Neugestalter augustinischer Religionsphilosophie', in *Wissenschaft und Weisheit* 4 (1937), 23–35.
43 As Verweyen has pointed out, philosophy has here a preparatory role. And yet, theology can benefit more from philosophy, if the former acknowledges the latter's automony. In this context, Verweyen referred to the encyclical *Fides et Ratio* which emphasizes the autonomy of philosophy; see Verweyen, *Entwicklung*, 33.147.
44 Söhngen, *Philosophische Einführung* (München, 1955), 137.
45 *NTM*, 56.
46 *Einsicht und Glaube. Gottlieb Söhngen zum 70. Geburtstag am 21. Mai 1962*, edited by Joseph Ratzinger – Heinrich Fries (Freiburg: Herder, 1962), 7: 'aus dem Gitter einer bloß restaurativen Neuscholastik.'

2.2 Ratzinger's Methodological Approach to Augustine's Writings

When his professor assigned to him the task to investigate the ecclesiology of Augustine, Ratzinger was facing the difficulty of a beginner, namely, whether he can still offer something new to a field already covered by many great minds.[47] Because there were already good historical monographs on Augustine's ecclesiology, Ratzinger decided to interpret Augustine from a systematic angle. By 'systematic', Ratzinger meant the method which opens up the historical context and relates it to the present experience. Thus the systematic approach can lead to deeper insights into the historical context. A systematic approach involves a move beyond the letter in order to discover the spirit of a particular time which the author could not have seen in the past. In this way, the old can still shed light on the new. But one can discover the spirit of history only through a systematic questioning which is based upon a new systematic experience (*"systematische Erfahrung"*). This occurs in the way the Church awakes in the souls of the faithful, for the Church as a living organism, led and enlivened by the Holy Spirit.

The aim of Ratzinger's dissertation was to confront the historical Augustinian context with this new systematic experience. At the same time, the present situation is also challenged by the historical context. In this sense, systematic experience illustrates the limitation of the historical efforts, just as the historical context can reveal the narrowness of the systematic experience. Thus, the systematic experience provides a new set of questions for historical research, just as such experience continually poses questions to historical research.[48] In this dialogue between the past and the present, new answers and new questions emerge in a progression that enables the truth to shine forth.

---

47   *JRGS* 1, 43. Ratzinger named in particular the works of Herman Reuter, *Augustinische Studien* (Gotha, 1887); and Fritz Hoffmann, *Der Kirchenbegriff des hl. Augustinus in seinen Grundlagen und seiner Entwicklung* (München, 1933).

48   *JRGS* 1, 43: 'so kann er doch Antwort nur erhalten, wo er zuerst gefragt hat. Fragen aber kann er nur aus seiner eigenen vorbestehenden systematischen Erkenntnis heraus.'

In applying this "open system" in his doctoral dissertation, Ratzinger was convinced that the expositions of Augustine's ecclesiology by Reuter and in particular by Hofmann were not yet exhausted. Thus Augustine can still provide new answers and fresh questions, thereby challenging and widening contemporary experience.

Hence, Ratzinger was grateful for his teacher's methodology. And as we shall see, his new answers pose questions for the systematic experience of his teacher:

> In the topic "People and House of God in the Doctrine of the Church", chosen by Professor Söhngen, a new systematic experience is connected with a new question, which also gives a new possibility for a new answer.[49]

3. The Awakening of the Ecclesiology in the Post-War Germany: *Corpus Christi mysticum* vs. People of God

At the time of Ratzinger's doctoral project in 1950, the reflection on the Church was prominent in the post-war theological debates in Germany.[50] In the aftermath of the Second World War, there was a common thirst for community and visible unity among the people who were fatigued and dismayed by their wartime experience. And so, the Church naturally became the focus of attention. Ratzinger often recalled Romano Guardini's famous remark, 'A process of incalculable importance has begun: the Church is awakened in the

---

49   *JRGS* 1, 44.
50   *Mi*, 57: 'All of us lived with a feeling of radical change that had already arisen in the 1920s, the sense of a theology that had the courage to ask new questions and a spirituality that was doing away with what was dusty and obsolete and leading to a new joy in the redemption. Dogma was conceived, not as an external shackle, but as a living source that made knowledge of the truth possible in the first place. The Church came to life for us above all in the liturgy and in the great richness of the theological tradition...we were convinced that we did well to trust the Church's experience of many centuries...'.

souls.'[51] However, it was also evident that a simple return to the narrow concept of the ecclesiology of Vatican I was not possible because the Church was now conceived to be much more than an institutional-hierarchical organization.[52] As the phrase of Guardini suggests, the Church, led by the Holy Spirit, was experienced as a living organism – a living reality experienced in the liturgical celebration.[53] From this yearning for community emerged the Body-of-Christ ecclesiology which underscores the mystical nature of the Church. The climax of this ecclesiological movement was the Papal encyclical *"Mystici corporis"* in which Pope Pius XII equated the Church with the Mystical Body of Christ.[54] According to the Pope, the membership in the Church is a necessary condition for salvation.[55] However, the membership is subjected to three conditions: a) the baptism; b) the true faith; and c) the incorporation into the unity of the true Church.[56] As a consequence, Non-Catholics were excluded

---

51 Romano Guardini, *Vom Sinn der Kirche. Fünf Vorträge* (Mainz: Matthias Grünewald, 1923), 1; also *JRGS* 1, 5.
52 The emphasis on the institutional and juridical dimension of the Church is particularly expressed in the encyclical letter *Satis Cognitum* (1896) by Leo XIII, who based his teaching on the ecclesiology developed by Robert Bellarmine; see *The Christian Faith*, edited by J. Neuner – J. Dupuis (Dublin: Cork, 1973), 228–230.
53 Guardini, 43.
54 *Mystici Corporis*, no. 1: 'The doctrine of the Mystical Body of Christ, which is the Church;' also Heinrich Denzinger, *Enchiridion*, 3809: 'Christi Corpus, quod est Ecclesia, mysticum esse appllandum.'
55 See Gerald Vann, '*Mystici Corporis*: The Fullness of Catholic Life', in *New Blackfriars* 25.290 (1944), 163–172.
56 *Mystici Corporis*, no. 22: 'Actually only those are to be included as members of the Church who have been baptized and profess the true faith, and who have not been so unfortunate as to separate themselves from the unity of the Body, or been excluded by legitimate authority for grave faults committed… As therefore in the true Christian community there is only one Body, one Spirit, one Lord, and one Baptism, so there can be only one faith. And therefore, if a man refuse to hear the Church, let him be considered – so the Lord commands – as a heathen and a publican. It follows that those who are divided in faith or government cannot be living in the unity of such a Body, nor can they be living the life of its one Divine Spirit.'

from the membership.⁵⁷ Thus, this image of the Church may be too narrow and unsuited for ecumenical dialogue. Theological criticism followed. As Ratzinger wrote,

> Various theologians criticized that with the idea of the Church being the mystical body of Christ, the relationship between visible and invisible dimensions of the Church, the law and grace, or the order and life is still not clarified yet.⁵⁸

Within the chorus of critical voices directed against the Mystical-Body-of Christ ecclesiology, the Dominican friar Mannes Dominikus Koster (1901–1981) refused the adjective "mystical", maintaining that the word *"mysticum"* was too broad in its meaning, and therefore it was 'useless for scientific theology'.⁵⁹ The designation of the Church as 'mystical' risks undermining the collective visible dimension of the Church. Further, it can lead to a "Heilspersonalismus" (subjective personalist view of salvation) wherein salvation is seen as a matter between God and the individual. Citing the work by Ludwig Deimel,⁶⁰ Koster listed four biblical and theological reasons against the usage of the image *"corpus mysticum"*: a) the concept of the Church as Body of Christ is alien to the New Testament. It is only attested in the Pauline literature and there it is treated as part of the theology of Grace; b) one cannot assume that Paul advocated the same idea of the Body of Christ as it is commonly used by modern Christians; c) the presumption, deriving from the studies of religions, that the idea of the Body of Christ is rooted in the *Gnosis* must be considered as erroneous; d) It is likewise inaccurate to construe a living community only from a single metaphor which is not com-

---

57   *JRGS* 8.1, 270.
58   *JRGS* 8.1, 269.
59   Piotr Napiwodzki, *Eine Ekklesiologie im Werden. Mannes Dominikus Koster und sein Beitrag zum Verständnis der Kirche*, PhD Dissertation University of Fribourg/Switzerland, 2005, 52; thesis is published as e-thesis; see <ethesis.unifr.ch/theses/downloads.php?file=NapiwodzkiP.pdf>.
60   Ludwig Deimel, *Leib Christi. Sinn und Grenzen einer Deutung des innerkirchlichen Lebens* (Freiburg i. Breisgau: Herder, 1940).

monly used in the New Testament.[61] Koster sought to find a better image to serve, not as an absolute definition of the nature of the Church, but rather as a comprehensive theological symbol of the Church.[62] For Koster, this was found in the image of the "people of God": it can better mediate between the sociological and juridical categories of the Church. It underscores more the collective, continual and open nature of the Church. It highlights both the visible unity of the salvation history, which includes Israel and the Church together in their journey, and emphasizes the eschatological nature of the Church.[63]

Ratzinger learned from Koster's work on the Church[64] through his teacher, Söhngen who had asked whether this ecclesiological concept could open up a new understanding of the Church. If it turned out, however, that the ecclesiology of Augustine was not centred on the idea of Church as the Body of Christ, but in the people of God, then there would be a new turning point.[65] Would the people-of-God ecclesiology not lead logically to a communion ecclesiology? If so, the theological ramifications for the ecumenical dialogue would be substantial.

Söhngen, therefore commissioned his favourite student Joseph Ratzinger to investigate the ecclesiology of Augustine.

---

61 Napiwodzki, 52–53.
62 Ibid., 46: 'deutliche und bildlose Sachbezeichnung der Kirche;' see also *JRGS* 1, 48–49.
63 Ernst Käsemann, *Das wandernde Gottesvolk. Eine Untersuchung zum Hebräerbrief* (Göttingen: Vandenhoeck & Ruprecht, 1939); Berhard Oestreich, 'Volk Gottes im Hebräerbrief', in *Spes Christiana* 21 (2005), 25–42.
64 Mannes Dominikus Koster, *Ekklesiologie im Werden* (Paderborn: Schöningh, 1940).
65 *JRGS* 1, 7.

4. Ratzinger and Empathy for the Faith of the Church

Before discussing Ratzinger's approach to Augustine, let me point to another pre-condition which is important for his interpretation of Augustinian ecclesiology. I have mentioned that systematic experience broadens the horizon of history. New answers to new questions serve to broaden the scope of systematic experience. Ratzinger later added a crucial third psychological element, namely, the role of empathy in hermeneutics.

The notion of empathy is notably present in the works of Edith Stein. For this convert and Carmelite nun, empathy was the missing link between subjective and inter-subjective experience that her teacher Edmund Husserl had overlooked, although Stein had alerted him to this gap. Stein perceives therefore empathy as an act,

> which ... allows us to constitute not only the world but also ourselves as objective for others, as it allows us to constitute the I as different from other I's, and as experienced by these ... Stein had thus contended that empathy is crucial for understanding the constitution of ourselves not only as psycho-physical individuals but also as human persons.[66]

But empathy is also a condition for solidarity and compassion which are the foundations for the establishment of a community. While Stein recognized various levels of empathy, its highest form is the solidarity arising from the 'value response involving our very personalities when we are motivated by the same thing.'[67] It is through this sharing of 'motivational energy stemming from the values with others', that an empathetic community is established.[68] Accordingly, it engenders a strong simple sense of community because it involves the whole person in the integrity of both of will and psyche in a personal response

---

66   Mette Lebech, 'Why Do We Need the Philosophy of Edith Stein?', in *Communio* 38.4 (2011), 692.
67   Ibid., 702.
68   Ibid., 704.

to others, and without instrumentalizing them. Thus, divine empathy, concretized in the sufferings of Jesus Christ on the Cross, expresses the essence of this self-involvement. As the core meaning of community, it makes possible mutual comprehension and transforms the members into a "we" without prejudice to each individual freedom.[69] Such an understanding of community necessarily respects the principle of unity in diversity.[70]

But was Ratzinger aware of Stein's theory of empathy? Given the fact that Ratzinger's earlier assessment of Stein's conversion to Catholicism had provoked criticism by the Jewish authorities,[71] it would seem that Ratzinger was not conscious of her work on empathy. Nonetheless, he comes close to this notion through Buber, who conceived dialogue as a personal process between the "I" and "you", and not between the "I" and the "it".[72] By including suffering as a core element of empathy, Ratzinger and Stein stand on the same ground. His spiritual Christology is a good example of the result.

In a collection of essays on Christological themes, published in 1986 under the title *"Behold the Pierced One"*, Ratzinger presented seven theses as 'fundamental characteristics of the indivisible inner unity of Jesus and Christ, Church and history.'[73] For instance, he emphasised that one must show a 'certain degree of empathy', if one wishes to know who Jesus Christ really is.' By empathy Ratzinger meant that one must

---

69 See Frances Horner, *Sufferings and Its End: Edith Stein's Empathic Community*; <http://carmelstream.com/CarmelStream/Short%20Articles/Edith%20Stein%20Empathy.pdf> – (access on October 17th 2012).
70 Ibid.: 'The only means to move the concluding experience of diversity away from fragmentation and towards unity is through a community where every action is informed by empathic understanding among the individual members – empathic community. Stein's genius, balancing the tension between the two poles of individualism and absolute community, is characteristic of the Carmelitist charism: she found a middle way that is life-giving.'
71 See John Allen, *Cardinal Ratzinger: The Vatican Enforcer of Faith* (London: Continuum, 2005), 250–252.
72 See Pierpaolo Donati, *Relational Sociology. A New Paradigm for Social Sciences* (New York: Routledge, 2011), 85.
73 *PO*, 15.

'enter, so to speak, into the person or intellectual reality concerned, become one with him or it, and thus become able to understand.'[74]

To penetrate the Christological mystery, prayer is of its very nature an 'act of self-surrender by which we enter the Body of Christ,'[75] and so become the Body of Christ from within. The Eucharist is paradigmatic in that it fuses together the Last Supper and the death of Jesus Christ:

> His dying words fuse with his words at the Supper, the reality of his death fuses with the Supper. For the event of the Supper consists in Jesus sharing his body and his blood, i.e. his earthy existence; he gives and communicates himself. In other words, the event of the Supper is an anticipation of death, the transformation of death into an act of love.[76]

Empathy with Christ is therefore an ecclesial event. It takes place within a community in which the Spirit of Christ is present, and whose tradition 'is the transcendental subject in whose memory the past is present.'[77] Only by becoming the Church can we enter the reality of Christ whose sufferings manifest the empathy of his Father for humankind. The Church and Christ are united in a bond of love. For its part, the Church is not merely an idea or a symbol, but a real body,[78] a living reality enlivened by the thoughts and feelings of the faithful as they participate in the life and self-surrender of Jesus Christ. Participation in Christ's life and death is mediated through the Church, and becomes the condition for the identification of each person with other persons. In this fundamental identification ("Grundidentifikation") with Jesus Christ, alienation is overcome, and reconciliation is enabled.[79] The Christocentric nature of the Church is evident, leading to an ecclesiology centred on the Eucharist. Augustine is hereby seen as the champion of the Eucharistic ecclesiology.

74 Ibid., 25.
75 Ibid., 26.
76 Ibid., 24.
77 Ibid., 31.
78 *EV* 64–65.
79 *JRGS* 8,1, 188; also Heim, 147–150.

5. Ratzinger and Augustine's Concept of the Church

Ratzinger's choice for the Augustinian ecclesiology was a result of his love for the African bishop. His study of the writings of Augustine not only confirmed the Eucharistic ecclesiology that is characteristic of Augustine, but also led Ratzinger to a lifelong attachment to Augustine which also impacted Ratzinger's theological work at Vatican II:

> In retrospect I can only feel a deep gratitude because the task [assigned by Söhngen] not only opened the door to a lifelong friendship with St. Augustine, but has put me also on the track of an Eucharistic ecclesiology, which has introduced me to an understanding of the Church's reality, which matches with the deepest intentions of Vatican II and which leads me to the spiritual Centre of Christian existence.[80]

Surprisingly, Ratzinger's findings did not fulfil the expectations of his teacher. Here, Verweyen notes an oddity in the assessment of Ratzinger's thesis. His own theological faculty awarded Ratzinger a *summa cum laude*, despite not meeting the expectations of his teacher.[81] Söhngen indicated three theological areas needing further discussion: a) the ecclesiology, focussed particularly on the Body of Christ, might be the result of a narrow perspective of patristic scholars. He had hoped that a study of Augustine's ecclesiology would correct this narrowness; b) there was a second topic to be investigated, namely, the "House of God". Söhngen suspected that this image arose from the early experience of the domestic church. While "people" suggest the extended clan or tribe, "house" suggests a family within the network of the tribe, and so confirm "the people of God" ecclesiology; c) a further consideration of the house of God is its association with worship as in a temple – the Church then would be more than an institutional body. The Church is first and foremost a spiritual dwelling

---

80 *JRGS* 1, 9.
81 Verweyen, *Unbekannter Ratzinger*, 23: 'Damit ergibt sich eine zweite Merkwürdigkeit. Die Fakultät hatte Ratzingers unter dem Titel "Volk und Haus Gottes..." verfaßte Arbeit mit der Höchstnote ausgezeichnet. Dem eigenen Lehrer erteilte er darin aber im Grunde die Note "Themen*stellung* verfehlt".'

inhabited by God and gathered in Christ. Söhngen anticipated that his student's investigation would also provide a new approach to the theology of liturgy. Overall, Ratzinger summarizes the main expectation of his teacher with these words: 'The main task, set out by my teacher, was clearly "the people of God" as the new hermeneutic key for the patristic understanding of the Church.'[82] Söhngen had secretly hoped that his student's study of Augustine would confirm the thesis of the Koster.

But Söhngen's expectations were disappointed. This student's liberty was a consequence of his teacher's own method of posing radical questions designed to open up the narrowness of contemporary pre-conceptions. In this respect, Söhngen was a victim of his own method. In any case Läpple recalled in an interview, published in the magazine *30Days* 1.2 (2006), the humility with which Söhngen accepted the findings of his student:

> He [Söhngen] said: now my student knows more than me who am the teacher! Söhngen had great esteem for the man he considered his best student. He once said that he felt like Saint Albert Magnus, when in the Middle Ages he declared that his student would make more noise than him. And the student was Saint Thomas! He was glad that somebody was capable of developing in an original and not pre-planned manner his suggestions.[83]

Söhngen accepted the theological "corrections"of his student with both humility and enthusiasm, clearly faithful to his own method.

5.1 Augustine and the People of God

Ratzinger disagreed with his teacher for two reasons. Firstly, he became increasingly aware that at the time of his doctoral project, a few theologians had endeavoured to correct the confrontational views on the nature of the Church as developed during the years 1920–1940.

---

82   *JRGS* 1, 50–51.
83   <http://www.30giorni.it/articoli_id_10125_13.htm>.

During this time, the ecclesiological debate was often dominated by the dichotomy of the institutional-hierarchical vs. the mystical-idealistic Church. It was in particular the Jesuit French theologian, Henri de Lubac, whose "Catholicism"[84] impressed the young Ratzinger.[85] In this work, de Lubac accepted the ecclesiological definition *"corpus mysticum"*, but he clarified the mystical aspect of the Church. Following patristic theology, he maintained that the Church is mystical because she is sacramental.[86] De Lubac also observed in the patristic theology a close link between the Body of Christ and the Eucharist. Accordingly, the true Body of Christ is visible only where the Eucharist is celebrated in mutual love:

> And just as the body of Christ was signified more exactly by the bread and his blood by the vine, so the Church, which is also the body of Christ, seemed signified by the consecrated bread, whilst the wine changed into the blood of Christ was naturally the symbol of love which is like the blood wherein is the life of this great Body.[87]

It follows that the Eucharist as the real symbol of the unity always presupposes a concrete community. It is only through Christ' sacrifice that the people of Israel are transfigured into the Body of Christ: 'Where Christ is, and there alone, can be found the true Israel, and it is only through incorporation in Christ that participation in the blessings of Abraham may be obtained.'[88] The people of God become the Body of Christ only in relation to Christ. The Church as *"corpus mysticum"* is, therefore, not only an inward-looking spiritual reality, but also a socially constituted body. The interpenetration of the inner-spiritual and the public-social realities of the Church is visible in the

84 Henri de Lubac, *Catholicism. A Study of Dogma in Relation to the Corporate Destiny of Mankind*, translated by Lancelot C. Sheppard (London: Burns, Oates & Washbourne, 1950). This work was originally published in French in 1943; see also *Mi*, 98: 'This book was for me a key reading event.'
85 *JRGS* 1, 7.
86 *JRGS* 1, 7: 'In der Väterzeit bedeutet das Adjektiv "mysticum" soviel wie sacramental, dem Sakrament – dem "Mysterium" – zugehörig.'
87 de Lubac, 43.
88 Ibid., 22.

Eucharistic celebration. Secondly, Ratzinger's own studies of Augustine's ecclesiology only reinforced de Lubac's view on the patristic ecclesiology.

Augustine too considered Christology as indispensable for the sacramental concept of the Church. Thus, Ratzinger wrote: 'The twin elements of Augustine's vision of the Church are the Christological re-reading of the Old Testament and the sacramental life centred in the Eucharist.'[89] This Christological re-reading of the Old Testament transforms also the concept of the people of God. In his reading of the patristic texts, particularly the writings of Augustine, Ratzinger discovered that the early Fathers consistently associated the image of the people of God with the children of Abraham. Thus, people of God are related to the people of the Old Testament. However, in Ratzinger's view, Augustine never employed this image to designate the Church. The *ecclesia*, for Augustine, is the Body of Christ. The characteristic of the people of God is its historic-eschatological nature as the Body of Christ on the way towards its fulfilment. Nonetheless, Augustine considered neither the children of Israel nor the Gentiles members of the Church. This was more evident for the Gentiles who were not even the children of Abraham. Gentiles were not the people of God no more than the children of Abraham were members of the Body of Christ. Gentiles can become the Body of Christ only through the Christological-pneumatological transformation. And so, Ratzinger concluded that the membership of the Church is not the product of human decision, but the work of Christ in us, who, in sending his Spirit, transforms us, who are non-people, into his Body.[90] Thus, the Church is an outcome of grace. For this reason, the Church is Catholic because she is essentially the Body of Christ gathering all nations into the celebration of the Eucharist.[91]

---

89   *JRGS* 1, 53.
90   *JRGS* 1, 52: 'das Handeln Christ an uns, der uns aus Nicht-Volk zu Volk werden lässt.' It is not difficult to see that this Christological-pneumatological action serves as a theological pre-condition for Ratzinger's interpretation of the divine revelation.
91   *JRGS* 1, 52: 'Kirche ist Volk Gottes nur im und durch den Leib Christi.'

Ratzinger, of course, admitted that Augustine had come to his theological conclusion only through a lengthy intellectual discernment which involved two major controversies.[92] As a young adult, Augustine was attracted to Manichaeism which claimed to be the true religion based on pure reason. For nine years, Augustine was exposed to this esoteric cult, as *auditor*.[93] Shortly after his baptism in Milan (387), Augustine turned against his former Manichaean associates by emphasizing the efficacy of an authoritative faith as the only viable path to truth.[94] Against the Manichaean *"Winkelreligion"* (arcane and secretive religion),[95] Augustine drew attention to the objective public dimension of the Catholic Church.

A decade later as Catholic bishop, he took aim at the Donatists who represented a true threat for the Catholic Church in North Africa. In his anti-Donatist polemic, Augustine campaigned for the unity of the Church deriving from the charity of Christ. The catholicity of the Church is not only extensive and visible, as he once had argued against the Manichaeans, but it is also lived in the form of mutual charity. In this case, Augustine accentuated in countering the Donatists the inner spiritual bond between Christ and the Church. He was focussed on the spiritual dimension of the Church because the Donatists possessed the same sacramental and hierarchical structure as the Catholic Church. What the Donatists lacked was the charity, and this made them not only schismatic, but also heretical.[96]

---

92   Ratzinger skipped over the Pelagian controversy. He believed that the nature of this debate did not contribute much to the progress of ecclesiological discourse. Recently publications, however, showed a great concern for the Church by the Pelagians; see Sebastian Thier, *Kirche bei Pelagius* (Göttigen: Vandenhoeck, 1999).
93   Leo C. Ferrari, 'Augustine's "Nine Years" as a Manichae', in *Augustiniana* 25 (1975), 210–216; Kevin J. Cole, 'What Did Augustine Know about Manichaeism When He Wrote His Two Treatises De moribus', in *Augustine and Manichaeism in the Latin West. Proceedings of the Fribourg-Utrecht Symposium of the International Association of Manichaean Studies (IAMS)*, edited by Johannes van Oort – Otto Wermelinger – Gregor Wurst (Leiden/Boston/Köln: Brill 2001), 43–56.
94   *JRGS* 1, 82–87.
95   *JRGS* 1, 88.
96   *Cresc* 2,15: 'Si schismatici sunt, si haeretici sunt…'; see also *JRGS* 1, 207–208.

5.2 Against the Manicheans: The Visible Catholicity of the Church

In joining the Manichean religion Augustine encountered dualism within the one sensible world.[97] The graphic below illustrates the Manichean concept of a dualism:

```
  Sphere: Light / Good
  ─────────────────────
  Sphere: Darkness / Evil
```

According to the Manicheans, the world reality is static because the two opposite forces are absolutely separated from each other. In Manichean cosmology the physical sphere is subordinated to the spiritual. The two forces can never be united, although they were the two sides of the one world. If unity is impossible, so too is catholicity. Two concrete examples illustrate this separation: a) the Manichaean Church consists of two groups, namely the saints *(electi)* and the ordinary people *(auditores)*. The saints *(electi)* were set apart from the rest of the people who can be seen as sinners. In this context, Manichean ritual visibly illustrates the separation between the *electi* and the *auditores*. While the *electi* progress in knowing the truth through the performance of the secretive rituals, the *auditores* gather outside the temple, waiting for the revelation of the truth by the *electi*; and b) the Manicheans also reject the Old Testament because it portrays God in an anthropomorphic manner. Ordinary people can be saved only through the teaching of the few saints.

Since his reading of Cicero's "Hortensius" (372), in which the Roman philosopher called for a philosophical-intellectual life dedicated to the pursuit of truth, Augustine was aware that ordinary people were not able to live such a life. For that reason, according to Ratzinger, Augustine's thought was focused on the question of

---

97   *JRGS* 1, 74: 'die eine Welt konkreter Greifbarkeit, die uns allen vor Augen steht.'

how the vast majority of people can, nevertheless, gain truth and achieve salvation. What is the best and suitable way for the ordinary people?

Against the Manichaean esoteric cult Augustine set the public objective faith of the Catholic Church. Through this public faith, which is shared by the all Christians (extensive catholicity), all people participate in the same knowledge so that the truth is popularized and not restricted to a limited circle. The theological necessity of a public authoritative faith lies in the clemency *(clementia)* with which the divine wisdom assumes human flesh so that humanity can ascend to the divine truth. In Ratzinger's interpretation of Augustine's writings, incarnational Christology is clearly pivotal in Augustine's departure from the Manichean religion. Augustine was impressed with the importance of faith as a vehicle for the search of truth. In this context, Ratzinger spoke of the salutary benefit of the obedience of faith. He writes,

> So there is indeed no other path except through the humility of faith, by which we become disciples of the Word of God, who deigned to take upon himself the infirmity of our human flesh.[98]

Because of the incarnation, the Church is now truly inclusive of all since the truth of God is now universally known to all through the visible faith which is a gracious divine gift.[99] This authoritative faith is more certain because it is shared by all believers. Thus Ratzinger concluded with Augustine that the Church's nature lies in the fact that she communicates in visible manner the presence of the invisible.[100]

In short, Augustine's anti-Manichaean concept of the Church assumes that the people of God are incorporated in the Catholic Church

---

98 *JRGS* 1, 69: 'So gibt es keinen anderen Weg zur Weisheit als den, in der Nachfolger des in unsre Fleschesniedrigkeit herabgestiegenen Gotteswortes in die Niedrigkeit des Glaubens einzugehen.'
99 *JRGS* 1, 90.
100 *JRGS* 1, 94.

because of her faith. Through it the divine truth is universally communicated and shared:

> The Church appears in this anti-Manichaean period as the *Catholica*, as the multitude of the believers spreading over the whole earth. Therefore, the Church as a visible divine miracle transcends herself to the invisible.[101]

5.3 The Discovery of Neo-platonism and the Anti-Donatist Controversy

Theological debate naturally changed with the arrival of the Donatists. While Manichaeism was a religion in its own right, the Donatist controversy was an intra-Christian debate. Thus, it was more or less an ecumenical problem. Donatists and Catholics not only share visibly the same ecclesial structure, but also both have the same sacraments. At the time of Augustine, the Donatists were widespread in North Africa. Many cities often hosted two episcopal seas, one for the Catholics and one for the Donatists. Hippo Regius was not an exception in this regard. The political-ecclesial strength of the Donatists can concretely be shown at the Council of Carthage in 411, at which 285 Donatist bishops faced the 286 Catholic bishops.[102] The Donatist presence in North Africa was a real threat to the Catholic Church in Africa. Thus the anti-Donatist controversy must be regarded as one of the most important theological debates in the life of Augustine.

From the outset, it is clear that Augustine could not debate the Donatists in terms of the anti-Manichaean concept of extensive but still external catholicity. He realized that the Donatists shared this too. He had to dig deeper and expand his understanding of catholicity –

---

101 *JRGS* 1, 95.
102 Alexander Evers, 'Augustine in the Church (Against the Donatists)', in *A Companion to Augustine*, edited by Mark Vessey (Malden, MA: Willey-Blackwell, 2012), 375–385; Serge Lancel, *Saint Augustin* (Paris: Fayard, 1999), 404–429.

especially, as Ratzinger suggests, of its inner dimension. Peace and charity were now the focus.

A consideration of the inner dimension of catholicity must include the importance of the transitional stage from Manichaeism to Neo-Platonism. It helps us to understand the logic in Augustine's decision to leave the Manichaeism. But on his departure, he did not join Neo-platonic philosophy immediately, but first turned for a short time to the Academics. In Ratzinger's view, this encounter was critical.[103] The very scepticism of the Academics became the weapon used by Augustine to overcome the sceptical void he felt after leaving the Manichaeans. Augustine discovered in the academic argument a philosophical inconsistency. The Academics wanted to be seen as wise people – but they argued that there is no truth as such. However, Augustine saw it differently. If one claims to be wise, then it is evident that the wise one also possesses the truth; otherwise no one could be regarded as wise. The problem is whether there exists one wise person. That there is wisdom is now certain for Augustine. However, the answer to the question of the existence of one wise person cannot be expected from the Academics because of their philosophical contradiction. Augustine solved this problem by pointing to the incarnation of the divine wisdom which is manifested in faith. This means that the humble acceptance of faith was at this stage for Augustine the only certain way to truth.[104]

However, the next difficulty Augustine had to deal with was the question of how the visible is related to the invisible. Manichaean dualism was of no help because it denied the possibility of one reality. The turning point for Augustine came with the Neo-platonic philosophy. Ratzinger spoke here of a breakthrough of Augustine's cosmology.[105] Neo-Platonism still taught a dualism; but this dualism is now located between two worlds and not within one world of two mutually

103   *JRGS* 1, 72: 'Es war eine folgenschwere Begegnung…'
104   *JRGS* 1, 73: 'Es gibt Weisheit, die echte Einsicht vermittelt, aber es gibt zugleich diese Einsicht nur über die Demut des Glaubens.'
105   *JRGS* 1, 75: 'die Entdeckung des Neuplatonismus… als das große Durchbrucherlebenis Augustins.'

opposing realities, as the Manicheans claimed. The graphic below illustrates this modification:

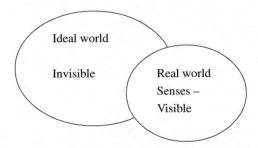

More importantly, Augustine now discovered that the two worlds are not absolutely separate. The sensible world can be seen as "doxa" (radiance) of the transcendent world of ideals. Moreover, in so far the visible world exists, it contains seeds of goodness. Neo-platonic dualism was therefore porous and dynamic, despite the fact that both worlds are not absolutely identical. This dynamism allowed Augustine to perceive the visible reality as a mixed reality consisting of both good and evil.

Neo-platonic cosmology gave Augustine the necessary intellectual equipment to interpret the twofold realities of holiness and sinfulness within the one Church as *"corpus mixtum"*. Furthermore, Neo-platonic dynamism helped Augustine to formulate the unity existing between the Old and New Testament. He saw the Old Testament as the figurative preview of the New Testament, so that Ambrose's Christocentric allegorical-figurative exegesis of the Old Testament became freshly meaningful.[106]

Ratzinger observes several consequences for Augustine's theology deriving from his controversy with the Academics and his Neo-

---

106 This Christocentric allegorical exegesis of the Old Testament is exemplified in Ambrose's commentary on the Psalms *"Explanatio XII psalmorum"* written in 387–389. In this commentary, Ambrose interpreted the psalm as expression of joy and expectation for the future beatitudes, which are inaugurated by Christ. Augustine was surely aware of this Ambrosian allegorical exegesis because he stayed in Milan from 384–388.

platonic discoveries. He could now coherently reject the two foundations of the Manichaean exegesis: 1) the Manichean "solum Novum Testamentum"; and 2) likewise, exegesis "sola ratione".[107] This anti-Manichaean criticism will later serve as a basis for Ratzinger's rejection of the historical critical approach to the Bible.

Clearly, too, Neo-platonic philosophy provides the intellectual framework for Augustine's anti-Donatist interventions.[108] Because the controversy was theological, Augustine had to include the role of Christ. Here, the Bishop of Hippo stressed particularly the *"caritas Christi"*.[109] This Christocentric charity adds an inner spiritual dimension to the understanding of catholicity. Such an emphasis was of great importance for Augustine because the Donatists shared with the Catholics many external similarities, such as sacraments and hierarchical structure.

Ratzinger draws from Augustine's anti-Donatist concept of *"caritas"* the following consequence: The Catholics truly practise catholicity because of mutual charity, while the Donatists only claimed it. In reality they refused communion with Catholics. For them Donatists and Catholics were separated peoples *(populi)*.[110] In effect, the Donatists were betraying the peace of Christ, for charity and communion can be visibly realised only in the Catholic Church. In fact, Augustine did not hesitate to equate *ecclesia* with *caritas*, so that the Catholic Church is the objective representation of charity. One can participate in *caritas* only through membership in the Catholic Church. Of course, one can partake externally in this Church without feeling

---

107 *JRGS* 1, 81: 'War es ihm also mithilfe der neuplatonischen Schriften gelungen, die materialen Gehalte des manichäischen Systems endgültig abzutun, so fand er durch die Akademiker die Mittel, das verlockende manichäische Formalprinzip des "sola ratione" zurückzuweisen.'

108 Here we encounter already Ratzinger's criticism of historical theology; see *JRGS* 1, 198: 'Das Historische, das aus seinem eigenen Bereich heraus nicht mehr entschieden werden konnte, sollte gleichsam vom Theologischen her präjudiziert werden.'

109 Here Ratzinger pointed to Augustine's anti-Donatist work *Cresc* II, 12, 15.

110 *JRGS* 1, 234.

the need to change one's own life. One can be a member of the visible Church, albeit one still commits sins. Augustine therefore moved to a deeper exploration of Church membership by focussing on charity as the effect of the redemptive grace: in the ecclesial communion redemptive grace is visible in the form of mutual charity brought about by the working of the Holy Spirit. Mutual charity as practised in the Catholic Church derives from Trinitarian love, the invisible centre of the Church's visible communion.[111] The refusal of charity by the Donatists was, therefore, a concrete sign of disobedience to God's command. It is a direct offence against the Holy Spirit.

The fact that the Catholic Church possesses and practises mutual charity is for Augustine a sign that the Church is not only a juridical-hierarchical institution. She is the bride of Christ *(sponsa Christi)* who gave up his life for her. In this Christological connection, the Church is truly the new people of God, because in her the promise is fulfilled. It is only here that the Church is truly the Body of Christ. But this Church is at the same time eschatological in that she is fully revealed only at the time determined by God himself. And yet, Augustine admonished his opponents not to refuse the visible communion with the Catholics because such a refusal would contradict the charity and peace given by the Holy Spirit. The Donatist refusal of communion therefore must be taken as a transgression against God's love.

As a conclusion, we can now say that Augustine discovered in the anti-Donatist controversy the mystical-sacramental dimension of the Church. Yet, this is not a hidden dimension since it is made visible in the Eucharistic communion. Ratzinger summarises the ecclesiology of Augustine: 'Communion with the *catholica* includes therefore the idea of standing in sacramental unity and participating in Eucharistic peace.'[112] Such a sacramental ecclesiology sees the *ecclesia catholica* as one people of God *(populus)* made up of peoples

---

111 *JRGS* 1, 207–217.
112 *JRGS* 1, 229: 'Gemeinschaft mit der *catholica* ist daher In-Sein in ihrer sakramentalen *unitas*, Teilhabe an ihrer eucharistischen *pax*.'

(populi) who are united visibly through the sacrament of the Eucharist. It is now clear that the one *"populus"* of God is not a mere image or analogy, but is a concrete-pneumatological reality.

6. The House or Temple of God

Augustine's discovery of the mystical-sacramental dimension of the Church is basic to his understanding of the House of God. As we have seen, Söhngen, Ratzinger's teacher, had assumed that this image designates, in the early Church, only the domestic church. "House of God" therefore was part of the people of God. But Ratzinger's interpretation of Augustine's ecclesiology did not endorse Söhngen's hypothesis.

Characteristically, the house or temple of God in Augustine's theology has two dimensions as well, gradually taking shape in Augustine's refutations of paganism and Donatism. In contrast to the pagan cult, Augustine interpreted the house of God not as a building in which sacred rituals are performed, but as the temple of God in Christian terms of the interiority of the human person. Ratzinger considered that Augustine used the temple of God as a figurative image for a spiritual person in whom the Holy Spirit dwells. As the heart *(cor)* is the centre of the human person, it is there that the true worship takes place. Thus the whole human life, including conscience, should be described as the *habitaculum verum Dei* ("the true dwelling of God").[113] As a consequence, the worship of God involves moral and spiritual conversion to God. In short, the house of God is the image for oneness with the spirit of Christ.[114] Sacrifice, therefore, moves beyond ritualism. Augustine spiritualized the meaning of sacrifice. He considered prayers and good moral life as adequate forms of sacrificial practices. The house or temple of God is not the static building in which sacrifice is per-

---

113 *JRGS* 1, 248–249.
114 *JRGS* 1, 260.

formed, but rather the entire living community united in worship and praise directed to God in imitation of Jesus Christ. The living community rests on its sacramental foundation. On this point, Augustine followed Pauline ecclesiology which sees the body as the temple of God because of the indwelling of the Holy Spirit (1 *Cor* 3:16; 6:19). Christians are not individuals, but bound together to form a collective "we" because 'none of us lives to himself alone and none of us dies to himself alone.'[115] So understood, the house or the temple of God was for both Paul and Augustine the Body of Christ (1 *Cor* 6:15; *John* 2:21). Augustine confirmed it by saying: 'The living temple of God as a community receives is further characterized as the "Body of Christ".'[116] This Body of Christ, which is the Church, is concretized as a visible Eucharistic assembly gathered in the love of God and its members. The Augustinian anti-Manichaean and anti-Donatist positions reach here their theological climax. First, Augustine dismissed the Manichaean concept of arcane Gnosis separating the *electi* from the *auditores*. The convert now emphasized the visibility of the Christian truth accessible through faith. However, this emphasis on the visibility of faith would not be sufficient to counter the Donatist claim which precisely grounds its unshaken faith and holiness of its Church in the visible sainthood of its bishops. Thus the Donatist faith visibly excels that of the Catholic Church. Consequently, Augustine in his anti-Donatist response cannot refer to faith alone. He must now delve into the inner foundation of the Church's faith not found in the Donatist Church. Though the Donatists have faith, they lack love. They have sacraments, but not love. The fullness of all these elements lies in the practice of charity in communion with the Body of Christ in which all are transformed into an organism built upon charity *(compages caritatis)*:

> To belong to the *compages caritatis* therefore means nothing else than to belong to the Body of Christ. This again means nothing else than to receive in a real sense the Eucharist.[117]

115 *Rm* 14:7.
116 *JRGS* 1, 249.
117 *JRGS* 1, 258.

In summing up Augustine's ecclesiology, Ratzinger claims that the Church as the Body of Christ is not a profane sociological or political institution, but a *theological-sacramental* reality.[118] This reality has Christ as its foundation (*fundamentum*), built upon faith and held together through charity.[119] In short, Ratzinger only partially lived up to the expectations of his doctoral supervisor. Although the student agreed with the teacher that the Church is more than an institutional-juridical body, the people of God can become the *ecclesia* only in relation to Christ and the Spirit. On the one hand, the unity between the people of God and the Church is brought about by the sacrifice of Christ. And on the other hand, the Church is the Body of Christ because of the indwelling of Christ's spirit. Thus, the Church is house of God for she is united by the Spirit.[120] For this reason, the Church is a visible manifestation of the invisible divine communion. Theologically considered, salvation of Christ is mediated through the Church. This sets Christianity apart from the Roman cult. The refusal of the early Christians to attend the pagan cult has its basis in this ecclesial self-confidence.

6.1 The New Cult

Augustine in particular demonstrated this new Christian self-assurance by rejecting the accusation made by the pagan elite against Christians. Given the catastrophic consequences in the aftermath of the invasion of Rome by the Goths in 410, the Roman elite blamed Christians for this disaster, for abandoning the cult of the gods. Instead, they called for the re-installation of the sacrificial cult.

Augustine responded to the accusation in his monumental work "On the City of God" (412–426). He declared the Roman pagan cult

---

118 *JRGS* 1, 252.
119 *JRGS* 1, 287–297.
120 *JRGS* 1, 260: 'Das Volk Gottes ist die Gemeinde, die die Einheit mit der mit Christus Opfernden darstellt, Haus Gottes meint dies innere Einssein im Christusgeiste, das freilich nicht wird ohne das Einssein um Christusleibe.'

void in contrast to the Christian conception of worship. His argument was based upon his understanding of Roman ritual. According to Ratzinger, Augustine saw in Roman ritualistic practice a reduction of religion to a mere visible reality. A strict observance of the rituals was demanded, regardless of individual faith and opinions concerning truth. Ritualism is indifferent to faith and truth which is regarded as a private concern. The Roman elite considered public ritual objectively, as an expression of unity above all individual religious and cultural worldviews. It therefore intends to enforce political-social unity in contrast to unity in faith.[121] Ratzinger wrote:

> The pagan religion is built completely upon the visible cult. This means that it leaves the reflection on supernatural matters to private sphere. What it concerns with is only the concrete visible. In this sense rituals obtain the character of finality. Rituals therefore are closed up in themselves.[122]

Thus Christians can uphold their specific faith as long as they observe the rituals which are due to the gods. Here, Ratzinger believed that, in the West, ritualism might have led to the neglect of intelligible-spiritual reality.[123] This may also explain Augustine's difficulty prior to his conversion in failing to penetrate the intelligible-spiritual reality of the Christian faith. As a result, Augustine's discovery amounted to a great conversion.

In his response to the pagan accusation against Christians, Augustine proposed a new cult which involves the entire human life. The worth of sacrifice is inseparable from a life that conforms to the divine truth *("gottförmig")*: 'Only a person, who lives according to God's will, is a real sacrifice for God.'[124] Here, Augustine has clearly cut with his past. Sacrifice requires the personal willingness to sur-

---

121 See also George Heyman, *The Power of Sacrifice: Roman and Christian Discourses in Conflict* (Washington D.C: Catholic University of America, 2007), 12.
122 *JRGS* 1, 300.
123 *JRGS* 1, 301.
124 *JRGS* 1, 283; here Augustine followed Paul's letter to the *Romans* 12:1: 'Therefore I urge you, brethren, by the mercies of God, to present your bodies a living and holy sacrifice, acceptable to God, which is your spiritual service of worship.'

render oneself to God. This implies the humility of faith. He often referred to this personal adherence to God in the phrase, *"sursum cor"* (the heart elevated to God) to designate both the new altar of sacrifice and the binding of the heart to the concrete visible bond of love.[125] Love for God is therefore the first requisite of a true sacrifice: 'The only cult, which exists in truth, is love.'[126] There is no single person, however, who has ever lived in absolute conformity with God's commandments. Consequently, there is no human being who can ever offer sacrifices that were worthy of God. Can anybody then offer sacrifices that are commendable to God? That becomes now the crucial question. In this situation, humanity needs a true mediator. In this respect, the only person who has ever lived in complete conformity to God's will is Christ whose entire life consisted in love of his Father. Ratzinger termed this "filial pro-existence", exemplified in 'Christ's obedience, his final "yes" to the Father' which is 'accomplished on the Mount of Olives ... this act of self-giving ... to God.'[127] In this filial self-surrender, Christ becomes the perfect priest who offers himself as a sacrifice pleasing to God.

The crucial question for Augustine now became how can the sinful person participate in the immaculate sacrifice of Christ? It is only through the incorporation into Christ that participation in his sacrifice becomes possible. Through the incarnation, Christ, by assuming our humanity, sacrifices on our behalf. The goal of the incarnation is to transform earthly human beings into spiritual beings by endowing them with the spirit of Christ. The sign of the presence of Christ's spirit is faith through which one remains united to Christ. Here Ratzinger observed a clear shift in the Augustinian thought. Instead of the ontological unity through *gnosis*, Augustine now considered the act of will, directed by faith, as the source of spiritual unity.[128]

---

125 *JRGS* 1, 293.
126 *JRGS* 1, 266.
127 *JoN*, vol. 2, 164.
128 *JRGS* 1, 286. This voluntary aspect can be seen as an essential element of his later understanding of revelation.

This unity of wills binds together Christians and Christ stronger because faith is the result of a free and conscious affirmation of love. With his emphasis on charity, Augustine in effect acknowledged the limitation of knowledge. Truth alone does not lead automatically to conversion because truth without love remains an external affair. Only through love is truth internalized and lived.

It seems that Augustine now promoted a subjective-personal unity to the point of neglecting its objective dimension. According to Ratzinger, Augustine designated only the Church as Body of Christ, and not the single person. If he would identify an individual as the Body of Christ, it would affect negatively the individual freedom because a direct identification with the divinity would diminish human freewill. For this reason, Augustine maintained that the union between God and humanity is never direct, but always mediated through the Body of Christ which is the Church.[129] The Church mediates the spirit of Christ because she, as his Body, lives from the spirit of charity. And where the Body is, there is also the Head. As a result, one cannot offer the adequate sacrifice of love, except within the visible Body of Christ. Sacrifice, therefore, has also its objective concrete social form.

Hence, the essence of Christian liturgy is about truth and life. On the relationship between liturgy and life, Ratzinger, in his book on the "Spirit of the Liturgy", comments:

> Cult, liturgy in the proper sense, is part of this worship, but so too is life according to the will of God; such a life is an indispensable part of true worship... Ultimately, it is the very life of man, man himself as living righteously, that is true worship of God, but life only becomes real life when it receives its form from looking toward God.[130]

Accordingly, the nature of Christian liturgy is to give structure to human life by orientating it towards the divine life. This orientation is made concrete in the sacramental celebration. Human ethics there-

---

129 *JRGS* 1, 287–288.
130 *SL*, translated by John Saward (San Francisco: Ignatius, 2000), 17–18.

fore is given a sacramental structure which reaches even beyond everyday life. In this sense,

> Worship, that is, the right kind of cult, of relationship with God, is essential for the right kind of human existence in the world. It is so precisely because it reaches beyond everyday life.[131]

Ratzinger's interpretation of the Augustinian concept of liturgy can be summed up in three points: firstly, Augustine opposed the ritualistic cult of the pagans by presenting the Christian liturgy as an imitation of Christ's charity. The house of God is not made out of stones, but out of living sacrifices which are worthy of God. Secondly, the imitation of Christ's charity is only possible if one participates in the spirit of Christ. It is through faith that one is incorporated into Christ's spirit. This requires, thirdly, that one must stand in communion with the Body of Christ, which lives from Christ's spirit.[132]

The most visible expression of the communion with the Church is the Eucharist:

> The sacrament of charity, the Holy Eucharist, is the gift that Jesus Christ makes of himself, thus revealing to us God's infinite love for every man and woman. This wondrous sacrament makes manifest that "greater" love which led him to "lay down his life for his friends" (*Jn* 15:13). In those words, the Evangelist introduces Christ's act of immense humility: before dying for us on the Cross, he tied a towel around himself and washed the feet of his disciples.[133]

Here, the Eucharist is a sacrament of unity in a double sense. It looks both towards a vertical unity with God and establishes a horizontal community among the believers. In this twofold dimension the Eucharist is therefore the fulfilled anticipation of the Jewish Passover.

---

131 Ibid., 21.
132 *JRGS* 8. 1, 174.
133 *SCar* no. 1.

6.2 The Eucharist as Sacrament of the Body of Christ

Reflection on the Eucharist, the 'source and summit of all Christian existence'[134], occupies a great part of Ratzinger's writings. Its earliest appearance is found in his doctoral dissertation on the ecclesiology of Augustine. There, Ratzinger observed a close relationship between the Eucharist and the Church. For Augustine, Church membership is tied to participation in the Eucharist, the "sacramentum corporis Christi".[135] Consequently, the Eucharist is the sacramental foundation of the Church gathered in charity. The Eucharist therefore is the most intense sign of charity which is the centre the Church:

> The Eucharist is not just some social ritual where people meet in an amicable way; rather, it is the expression of being in the centre of the Church. It therefore cannot be detached from this condition of belonging – for the very simple reason that the Eucharist is the act of belonging itself.[136]

Augustinian Eucharistic ecclesiology represents the theological nucleus of Ratzinger's ecclesiology. It is for him the source of constancy and renewal. The Eucharist means further the anticipatory transformation of the entire human journey, from the creation *(exitus)* to the return *(reditus)* in God. Thus, Ratzinger perceives the goal of worship and the goal of creation as a whole aiming at the divinization of the world, and leading to freedom and love. Here, he refers to Teilhard de Chardin who saw in the 'transubstantiated Host ... the anticipation of the transformation and divinization of matter in the Christological fullness.'[137] All this is achieved through the sacrifice of Christ:

> Such sacrifice has nothing to do with destruction. It is an act of new creation, the restoration of creation to its true identity. All worship is now a participation in this "Pasch" of Christ, in his "passing over" from divine to human, from death to life, to the unity of God and man.[138]

---

134 *CCC* no. 274.
135 *JRGS* 1, 296.
136 *LW*, 148.
137 *SL*, 29.
138 *LW*, 34.

Hence, sacrifice is not destruction of life (slaughtering of animals), as was required in the pagan rituals. Contrary, the sacrifice of Christ transforms life in the sense that through Christ's sacrifice people are empowered to live a godly life.[139] Here, Ratzinger is dependent on Augustine's concept of sacrificial Eucharist:

> That is why St. Augustine could say that the true "sacrifice" in the *civitas Dei*, that is, mankind transformed in love, is the divinization of creation and the surrender of all things to God: God all in all (cf. 1 *Cor* 15:28). That is the essence of sacrifice and worship.[140]

As we have said earlier, sacrifice is not a solitary act, but the common act of a community. In his meditation of the incarnation of Christ, Ratzinger wrote: 'God gives himself so that we might give.'[141] Already in 1958, Ratzinger stated that the aim of the liturgy is to introduce all people to Christ through the Church: 'The Meaning of liturgy is to lead the people into the temple of the human race, to Christ who is present in his Body which is the Church, the new temple of the human race.'[142] In this way, Christian community has its visible form in the Eucharist.

6.2.1 Eucharist as Sacrifice

Sacrifice is an essential element of the Eucharist. Depending on individual religious, philosophical or social backgrounds, sacrifice can be understood differently. Ratzinger considers the philosophical-cultural individualism as the greatest challenge for the Catholic understanding of Eucharist.[143] Perhaps, Luther's rejection of the Catholic

---

139 *JRGS* 11, 649: 'But destruction does not honour God. Hecatombs of animals or whatever it may be, cannot honour God ... Not in destruction, not in these or those things, but in the transformation of mankind, in the sense that it lives a godly life.'
140 *SL*, 28.
141 *GnU*, 45.
142 *JRGS* 8.1, 159.
143 *JRGS* 11, 648: 'It is unimaginable to think that human guilt can hurt God; and still less, that it necessitates an atonement, such as the cross of Christ represents.'

understanding of the Mass as sacrifice may still echo in the ears of some Catholic liturgists.[144] In separating the Eucharist from its sacrificial character, they grossly misinterpreted the true nature of the Eucharist.[145] The Christian concept of sacrifice can be fully comprehended only against its Jewish background and in contrast to Roman cult. Here, Ratzinger's view on the sacrifice is influenced by Augustine's reaction against the pagan cult, as outlined in the *City of God*. Like the Bishop of Hippo, Ratzinger does not see in the achievement of social unity or control the only goal of Christian worship. For him, sacrifice has its meaning within the dialogue between God and the believer. Sacrifice is therefore a movement towards the communion with the Holy God. This, as Augustine maintained, can be achieved only through love. Sacrifice is therefore not perceived as an external concrete response to God. But sacrifice is not an individual matter. The nature of sacrifice points to communion because sacrifice aims to establish the unity between God and humanity, and between humans themselves.[146] Therefore, it is an ecclesiastical event:

> The Church is formed and consists in that sense that the Lord continues to communicate with us. In communicating with us, he also facilitates communion among the people. For this reason, the Church is shaped around the altar.[147]

Clearly, the meaning of the sacrificial Eucharist is to promote the vertical and horizontal dimension of dialogue in which the partners exchange more than words. Dialogue – in contrast to Roman cult – is based upon truth which gives meaning to sacrifice and it this surren-

---

144 *JRGS* 11, 642–644.
145 Bartholomew Ugochukwu, 'Postmodern Understanding of the Eucharist as Community Celebration: An African Perspective', in *East Asian Pastoral Review* 46.4 (2009); see <http://eapi.admu.edu.ph/content/postmodern-understanding-eucharist-community-celebration-african perspective> [access 22/11/2012]. This article is very indicative for contemporary perspective on the Eucharist. The author in his discussion of the Eucharist avoided the sacrifice, although he considered love as the foundation of the community celebration.
146 *JRGS* 11, 649.
147 *JRGS* 1, 548–549.

der to truth which distinguishes Israel from other nations. As Ratzinger saw it, Israel's exodus out of Egypt is completed only in the worship of the true God. Accordingly, God's promise, worship and love are closely linked:

> The land is given to the people to be a place for the worship of the true God. Mere possession of the land, mere national autonomy, would reduce Israel to the level of all the other nations. The pursuit of such a goal would be a misunderstanding of what is distinctive about Israel's election ... It only becomes ... a promise fulfilled, when it is the place where God reigns. Then it will not be just some independent state or other, but the realm of obedience, where God's will is done and the right kind of human existence developed.[148]

The worship is right in that it involves the renunciation of the false gods and with them, their false promises. Sacrifice involves now a new form of life in accordance with God's will and law: 'It is only, therefore, when man's relationship with God is right that all of his other relationships ... can be in good order.'[149]

Christianity retains the double dimensions of Jewish worship, love of God and love for the neighbour. Furthermore, it sees in the offering of sacrifice an act of truth which is accessible only through faith. However, Christian liturgy is also in discontinuity with Jewish worship.[150] From its Christological perspective, Christianity sees in the Eucharist not only a memorial of the exodus, but also its fulfil-

---

148 *SL*, 17.
149 Ibid., 21.
150 *JoN*, vol. 2, 106–115. According to Pope Benedict, Jesus died before the time of the Passover. This would mean that Jesus could not have possibly celebrated the Passover. And yet, Jesus, who was aware of his own death, anticipated the Passover by making himself the Paschal Lamb. Instead of the Jewish Passover, Jesus 'instituted *his* Passover' (113). Here, the Pope agrees with Peter J. Meier, *A Marginal Jew: Rethinking the Historical Jesus*, vol. 1 (New York: Doubleday, 1991), 372–433. Recently, Colin Humphreys in his book *The Mystery of the Last Supper: Reconstructing the Final Days of Jesus* (Cambridge: Cambridge University, 2011) suggested that Jesus' calendar usage differed from John who relied on the official Jewish calendar. Therefore, Humphrey concluded that Jesus probably celebrated the Passover on Wednesday, instead of a Thursday. Pope Benedict has taken over the theological perspective of John.

ment. Ratzinger drew attention to passages in the New Testament concerning the fulfilment of the promise in Jesus Christ. In particular, the high-priest prayer in *John* 17 confirms the consummation of the Jewish worship and therefore 'the "newness" of the figure of Jesus Christ – made visible in the outward discontinuity with the Temple and its sacrifices.'[151]

Relying on André Feuillet's work[152], Pope Benedict argues that the key to understand the newness of Jesus Christ is the Jewish feast of atonement, as explained in *Leviticus* 16 and 23:26–32. The aim of this sacrificial ritual is to restore to Israel 'its character as a holy people.'[153] This is achieved when the high priest 'pronounces in God's presence the otherwise unutterable holy name that God had revealed at the burning bush.'[154] In this symbolic action, God becomes accessible and is placed within the Israel's reach. It is through the sacrifices, performed by the high priest for himself and for others, that reconciliation is achieved and the covenant restored. When Christ repeats this prayer during his farewell discourse, he not only reproduces the prayer of the Old Testament high priest, but also he presents himself as its fulfilment because 'he sanctifies himself, and he obtains the sanctification of those who are his.'[155] In a rather spiritual interpretation of this high priestly prayer, the Pope sees a close tie with the Eucharist. But it is not anymore in the context of the sacrifice of animals in which the Eucharist takes place; rather, the sacrifice is now transformed into the words (prayers) of Jesus Christ. In Christ, the Word *(Logos)* of the Father, all forms of sacrifices are consummated and perfected. Christ therefore perfects and sanctifies sacrifice through the truth of which he is the *Logos*.[156] Accordingly,

---

151 *JoN*, vol. 2, 81,
152 *The Priesthood of Christ and His Ministers*, (New York: Doubleday, 1975).
153 Ibid., 78.
154 Ibid., 77.
155 Ibid., 78.
156 See *Jn* 17:17–19: 'Sanctify them in the truth; thy word is truth. As thou didst send me into the world, so I have sent them into the world. And for their sake I consecrate myself, that they also may be consecrated in truth.'

the act of consecration is inseparable from the act of sanctification. However, this truth is not an external consecration, but involves also an act of inner freedom by which one accepts and surrenders to Christ's consecration. For this reason, Pope Benedict emphasises the inseparable link between the Word and love which represent the reality of the Eucharistic celebration:

> Admittedly, this "word" that supplants the sacrificial offerings is no ordinary word. To begin with, it is no mere human speech, but rather the word of him who is *"the* Word", and so it draws all human words into God's inner dialogue, into his reason and his love ... The Word is now flesh, not only that: it is his body offered up, his blood poured out. With the institution of the Eucharist, Jesus transforms his cruel death into "word", into the radical expression of his love, his self-giving to the point of death.[157]

In this act of self-giving, Christ points to his mission for which he consecrates and sanctifies his disciples. The mission, as existence for others (pro-existence), is an essential element of the Eucharist through which one shares in Jesus priestly mission as a service to the truth.[158]

If we were to examine the genesis of the Pope's idea of spiritual sacrifice which is offered 'after the manner of the word' *(thysía logikē)*[159], then Augustine may be a good starting point. The influence of Augustine on Ratzinger is undisputed.[160] In one of his early articles in 1957, he investigated the theological and liturgical meanings of Augustine's confession,[161] and observed that the Bishop of Hippo had embedded his *confessio* within the context of the sacrificial Eucharist – the *'logikē thysía* of the Church of God.'[162] However, this Eucharistic sacrifice has less to do with sacrificial asceticism – an idea which

---

157 *JoN*, vol. 2, 80.
158 Ibid., 90.
159 Ibid., 81.
160 See my own book *Theologische Verwandtschaft: Augustinus von Hippo und Joseph Ratzinger/Papst Benedikt XVI.* (Würzburg: Echter, 2009).
161 This article, originally published as 'Originalität und Überlieferung in Augustins Begriff der confessio', in *Revue des Études Augustiniennes*, is now re-edited in *JRGS* 1, 457–479.
162 *JRGS* 1, 476.

is alien to Augustine, as Ratzinger admitted.[163] Rather, Augustine's confession took the shape of *"sacrificium laudis"* or *"hostia iubilationis"*. Through this act of confession, the faithful offer themselves as a living sacrifice to be consecrated and sanctified by God. Such a confession is a personal offering to God because it aims at reconciliation with God. As evidence, Ratzinger cited from *de civitate Dei* 10, 6:

> There is, then, a true sacrifice in every work which unites us in a holy communion with God ... For this reason, a man himself who is consecrated in the name of God is a sacrifice, inasmuch as he dies to the world that he may live for God. For, this is a part of that mercy which each one has on himself, according to the text: "Have pity on thy own soul, pleasing God".[164]

Thus, the confession of faith is integral to worthy sacrifice. United in God, believers live no more for themselves, but for God who is the truth. Life and worship are therefore inseparable.[165] Confession of faith now becomes a sacrifice of praise to God in a transformation intelligible only because it is "doing the truth" *(facere veritatem)* and therefore "coming to the light" *(venire ad lucem)*. Ratzinger cites the *Confessions* 10, 1: 'For behold Thou hast loved truth, since he who does the truth, comes to the light. I desire to do this in my heart, before Thee in confession; and in my writing, before many witnesses.' However, Augustine considered the act of confession to be inspired by God because the light of truth precedes and enables every act of confession.[166] Only in the light of truth can the act of confession be seen as sacrifice which is worthy of God:

> 'I shall know Thee, o Knower of mine, I shall know Thee even as I have been known. Virtue of that Thou mayst have and possess it without spot or wrinkle. This is my hope and that is why I speak.'[167]

---

163 Ibid., 477.
164 *JRGS* 11, 651–652.
165 Ibid., 478: 'We ourselves are the sacrifices, in so far we orient our lives towards God.'
166 *Conf.* 10, 6: 'A sacrifice, even though it is done or offered by man, is something divine.'
167 *Conf.* 10,1.

In this sense, Augustinian *confessio* is truly *thysía logikē* – true worship according to the word *(Logos)*.

This early Augustinian study provides Ratzinger with the foundational notion of the Eucharist to be further worked out in the course of his theological career, as we have seen above. From the Christological perspective, sacrifice is always an act of the living worship in accordance with the truth *(Logos)*. This truth is the essence of liturgy in its proclamation of the saving mystery of the death, resurrection and ascension of Christ.[168] The primary actor in the liturgy is God in whose name the faithful gather to praise and glorify the living God.[169]

If worship is *actio divina*, what is then the role of people? Should the faithful remain in a state of passivity while the celebration is conducted by the priest? If liturgy is a divine initiative, how can people be part of the celebration? Finally, if worship has its foundation in the divine, can liturgical forms change, or are they immutable? Cardinal Ratzinger endeavoured to address these questions particularly in his work *The Spirit of the Liturgy*. In the preface of his book, Ratzinger revealed his intentions and the reason for choosing the book's title:

> One of the first books I read after starting my theological studies at the beginning of 1946 was Romano Guardini's first little book, *The Spirit of the Liturgy* ... My purpose in writing this little book ... its basic intentions coincide with what Guardini wanted to achieve in his own time with *The Spirit of the liturgy*. That is why I deliberately chose a title that would immediately reminiscent of that classic of liturgical theology. The only difference is that I have had to translate what Guardini did at the end of the First World War, in a totally different historical situation, into the context of our present-day questions, hopes and dangers.[170]

---

168 *JRGS* 11, 639. Here, Ratzinger also quoted *Sacrosanctum concilium* no. 5: 'God who "wills that all men be saved and come to the knowledge of the truth ... He achieved His task principally by the paschal mystery of His blessed passion, resurrection from the dead, and the glorious ascension, whereby dying, he destroyed our death and, rising, he restored our life.'
169 *JRGS* 11, 632.
170 *SL*, 7–8.

6.3 Active, Full and Fruitful Participation in the Eucharistic Celebration

Since the publication of his book, *The Spirit of the Liturgy*, Ratzinger has been severely criticised for his "conservative" approach on the liturgy. Particularly, the Dominican liturgist Pierre-Marie Gy († 2004)[171] went so far to question Ratzinger's faithfulness to Vatican II.[172] Furthermore, Ratzinger provoked harsh criticism because of the 'reappearance of many elements used in older papal liturgies ... but also ... the virtual liberation of the Old Latin Mass.'[173] Predictably, some critiques were of a polemical nature in playing off the young promising progressive theologian at Vatican II against the conservative Churchman after Vatican II. However, John F. Baldovin in his non-polemical evaluation of Ratzinger's theological critique concluded that Ratzinger's critiques against certain aspects of the Post-Vatican II liturgical reform were in line with his theology as a whole. Baldovin criticised Ratzinger, not for his theological criticism, but rather for his very selective approach to historical and exegetical sources.[174] Agreeing with Baldovin, Gribbin writes,

> When comparing Pope Benedict's liturgical theology with his Magisterium, we have seen how the former has been extremely important for understanding the latter, while being conscious of the distinction which must also be made between them. We cannot understand what happened with the liturgy during Pope Ben-

---

171 Anselm J. Gribbin, Pope *Benedict XVI and the Liturgy. Understanding recent liturgical developments* (Herefordshire: Gracewing, 2011), 48: 'Given Gy's prominence and background, he is representative of the viewpoint of many liturgists after the council,'
172 'L'esprit de la liturgie du Cardinal Ratzinger est-il fidèle au Concile ou en réaction contre?', in *La Maison-Dieu 229.1 (2002)*, 171–178. His main criticism is directed against Ratzinger's lack of reference to *Sacrosanctum Concilium* and other ecclesiastic documents.
173 Gribbin, vi.
174 John F. Baldovin, *Reforming the Liturgy. A Response to the Critics* (Collegeville/Minn.: Liturgical Press, 2008), 89.

edict's pontificate without reference to his liturgical theology, which has also directly influenced his Magisterium.[175]

Ratzinger's critics considered that his metaphysical theology preferred 'being over doing,'[176] as the main reason for his liturgical conservatism. It cemented the ontological nature of liturgy and supported a static concept of liturgy in contradiction to the liturgical reform of Vatican II, which called for "active participation" of the faithful in the liturgical celebration.[177] Relying on the findings of the social history of religion, the proponents of an anthropologically centred worship assessed the value of liturgy relative to aesthetic and psychological functionality. Psychological criteria would favour constant change and constant cultural adaptation.[178] Therein lies its relevance.

Pope Benedict, of course, was not against an authentic liturgical celebration involving an 'active, full and fruitful participation of the entire people of God in the Eucharistic celebration.'[179] However, his reservations were directed against certain aspects of the Post-Vatican II liturgical reform,[180] in particular in German speaking countries. This he described as an 'activist participation,'[181] too focussed on the external-practical aspects of liturgy. Worship becomes merely a human production adaptable to the needs of the moments. This

---

175 Ibid., 180.
176 Allen, 35 sq.
177 *SC* no. 14.
178 *JRGS* 11, 613.
179 *SCar* no. 52.
180 With regard to the Father's view on liturgy, Ratzinger stated in *Mi*, 122: 'The reform of the liturgy in the spirit of the liturgical movement was not a priority for the majority of the Fathers, and for many not even a consideration ... The fact that this text [schema on the sacred liturgy] became the first subject for the Council's discussions really had nothing to do with the majority of the Fathers having an intense interest in the liturgical question.'
181 Denis Crouan, *The History And The Future Of The Roman Liturgy* (San Francisco: Ignatius, 2005), 156; see also *Mi*, 134: 'When I came home after the Council's first session, I had been filled with joyful feeling, dominant everywhere, of an important new beginning. Now I became deeply troubled by the change in ecclesial climate that was becoming ever evident.'

type of celebration was comparable with the idolatry of the golden calf in the Old Testament. This problem derived from the philosophical heritage of the Enlightenment in its advocacy of critical creativity. Liturgy is now seen as a 'show, a piece of theatre, a spectacle ... of self-production' in which the "self" is reproduced and reinvented.[182]

For Ratzinger, liturgy 'is not about our doing something, about our demonstrating our creativity, in other words, about displaying everything we can do.'[183] That would be a gross misinterpretation of the call of Vatican II.[184] Pope Benedict reminds Catholics that 'the active participation called for by the Council must be understood in more substantial terms, on the basis of a greater awareness of the mystery being celebrated and its relationship to daily life.'[185] What does the Pope mean by the expression "more substantial"? We should note here that the Pope refers to Romano Guardini's own language,[186] according to whom the essence of the liturgy is not

> the expression of individual's reverence and worship for God ... Nor does the onus of liturgical action and prayer rest with the individual ... not even rest with the collective groups, composed of numerous individuals, who periodically achieve a limited and intermittent unity in their capacity as the congregation of a church.'[187]

Rather, the "I" of the liturgy is the whole community of the faithful, more than the mere total number of individuals. This community is the Church, called and gathered through the Holy Spirit in the faith of Christ. Worship is not a mere action from below, but primarily an initiation from above which is a divine action. Hence, the participation

---

182 *LW*, 156.
183 Ibid., 156; also *SL*, 174: 'external actions – reading, singing, the bringing up of the gifts ... are quite secondary here.'
184 *SL*, 175: 'If the various external actions ... become the essential in the liturgy, if the liturgy degenerates into general activity, then we have radically misunderstood the "the-drama" of the liturgy and lapsed almost into parody.'
185 *SCar* no. 52.
186 *SL*, 7: 'It led a striving for a celebration of the liturgy that would be "more substantial" (*wesentlicher*, one of Guardini's favourite words).'
187 Guardini, *Spirit of the Liturgy*, 19.

'in more substantial terms' would therefore mean to 'rediscover the liturgy in all its beauty, hidden wealth, and time-transcending grandeur, to see it as the animating centre of the Church, the very centre of Christian life.'[188]

Clearly, the liturgy refers to God, the Church's true life: 'Worship gives us a share in heaven's mode of existence, in the world of God, and allows light to fall from that divine world into ours.'[189] This light is the divine truth which animates the Church.

As we have said earlier, the participation in the knowledge of the divine truth *(Logos)* occurs through prayer. Ratzinger continues to write:

> We were now willing to see the liturgy – in its inner demands and form – as the prayer of the Church, a prayer moved and guided by the Holy Spirit himself, a prayer in which Christ unceasingly becomes contemporary with us, enters into our lives.[190]

Hence, the most intense form of a conscious awareness of the divine mystery is prayer. The faithful are not 'strangers or silent spectators, but ... participants in the sacred action, conscious of what they are doing, actively and devoutly.'[191] But what is this sacred action in which the faithful partakes actively and devoutly? In studying the biblical, patristic and liturgical sources, Ratzinger surprises us with his answer. For him, this sacred action refers primarily to the Eucharistic prayer:

> Calling the Eucharist *oratio* was, then, a quite standard response to the pagans and the questioning intellectuals in general. What the Fathers were saying was this: The sacrificial animals and all those things that you had and have, and which ultimately satisfy no one, are now abolished. In their place has come the Sacrifice of the Word.[192]

As a spiritual religion, Christian worship is therefore a "Word-based worship." But this Word becomes flesh and assumes human existence.

---

188 Ibid., 7.
189 *SL*, 21.
190 Ibid., 7.
191 *SCar* no. 52; also *SC* no. 48.
192 *SL*, 172.

The incarnation has a twofold effect in human beings. Firstly, it is a gracious act transforming sinners into addressees of the divine truth. Through the incarnation, Christ draws the faithful into cooperation with himself. Secondly, it therefore enables humans to speak and to do the truth, for it is always Christ who, as the Word of the Father, is always praying inwardly with us.[193] Consequently, the faithful can now offer sacrifice according to the truth and so be an active part of Christ's Eucharistic oration. Thus, Christ's sacrifice becomes also the sacrifice of the congregation:

> But we must still pray for it to become our sacrifice, that we ourselves ... may be transformed into the Logos, conformed to the Logos, and so be made the true Body of Christ.[194]

Nowhere is the influence of Augustine more evident than at this point. In his commentary on the Psalm 26, the Bishop of Hippo explained the effects of Christ's sacrifice for the life of the faithful. Christ, by his sacrifice, incorporates us into himself because he has anointed us through his death.[195] Being baptised into Christ's death, the faithful now desire to imitate Christ by living a life in accordance with Christ's spirit.[196] Consequently, the sacrificial offerings in the form of bread and wine displayed on the altar are not only Christ's sacrifice, but also the offering of the congregation. In a catechesis to the newly baptized, Augustine explained the exchange between Christ and the recipients of the Eucharistic gifts:

> You ought to know what you have received, what you are going to receive, and what you ought to receive daily. That Bread which you see on the altar, consecrated

---

193 *JRGS* 11, 418. Once again Ratzinger may be under the influence of Augustine who often stated that Christ prays in us *(ex persona nostra)* and with the Church *(ex persona corporis, ex membris)*; see en. Ps. 39, 5; 30. 2, 4; 140, 3.7; see also Michael Fiedrowicz, *Psalmus vox totius Christi. Studien zu Augustins "Enarrationes in Psalmos"* (Freiburg: Herder, 1997), 298–325.

194 *JRGS* 11, 173.

195 *en. Ps.* 26, 2, 2; 94, 6; 132, 7.

196 *Io. eu. tr.* 26, 13: 'fiant corpus Christi, si uolunt uiuere de spiritu Christi.'

by the word of God, is the Body of Christ. That chalice, or rather, what the chalice holds, consecrated by the word of God, is the Blood of Christ. Though those accidents the Lord wished to entrust us His Body and the Blood which He poured out for the remission of sins. If you have received worthily, you are what you have received, for the Apostle says: The bread is one, we though many, are one body.[197]

Through the reception of the Eucharistic gifts, the faithful are consecrated with Christ.

Referring to Augustine, Ratzinger also saw in the reception of the Eucharist gifts an act of consecration to God – including an act of adoration and faith in the true presence of Christ in the gifts (transubstantiation).[198] Overall, it is an act of cosmological significance:

> The elements of earth are transubstantiated, pulled, so to speak, from their creaturely anchorage, grasped at the deepest ground of their being, and changed into the Body and Blood of the Lord.[199]

Clearly, the congregation is not passive, but participates very much and in "a more substantial" way in the divine action. They join in Christ's prayer in order to present themselves as offerings on the altar. In the act of common prayers, the difference between Christ's action and 'our own action is done away with. There is only *one* action, which is at the time his and ours – ours because we have become one "body and one spirit" with him.'[200]

Liturgy is not concerned only with our contemporary experience; but rather with the whole depth of human existence.[201] The Eucharistic prayer exactly expresses our innermost longing: With Christ, we pray that we become with Him the Eucharist offered to God.[202]

---

197 *S.* 227, 1.
198 *JRGS* 11, 624–625.
199 *SL*, 173. Here Ratzinger relied very much on Teilhard de Chardin's concept of *Christo-genesis*.
200 *SL*, 174.
201 *JRGS* 11, 630.
202 Ibid., 418: 'We ask therefore that the Logos, Christ, who is the real sacrifice, incorporates us into his sacrifice so that his sacrifice becomes ours and be accepted by God as ours.'

Ratzinger intended to convey the message that the Church, whose existence is based upon the Eucharist, is a sacramental community. Accordingly, participation in the Eucharistic celebration is conditional. It is tied to the willingness to repent and to convert; even more so, because the Eucharist is not a mere ritual, but finds its salvific efficacy in divine power by far transcending all human capability.[203] The awareness of God's saving action will inspire the faithful to praise and to give thanks to God. Ratzinger's spiritual Christology finds here its concretization.

Consequently, a liturgy which is focussed more on external reform would surely miss the very nature of liturgy. Liturgical celebration aims mainly at the construction of the relationship between God and the faithful. And yet, this relationship is not a human production but a gift received from above, an *actio divina*, for which the Church gives thanks through worship. As a consequence, the essence of liturgy is not primarily about mission, but the celebration the beauty and splendour of the truth of God's love:

> There is no mere aestheticism, but the concrete way in which the truth of God's love in Christ encounters us, attracts us and delights us, enabling us to emerge from ourselves and drawing us towards our true vocation, which is love ... The beauty of the liturgy is part of this mystery; it is a sublime expression of God's glory and, in certain sense, a glimpse of heaven on earth ... Beauty, then, is not mere decoration, but rather an essential element of the liturgical action, since it is an attribute of God himself and his revelation.[204]

6.4 Eucharist and Mission

The liturgy is an invitation to contemplate the beauty of God and to glorify his name. Nonetheless, the Eucharist includes a missionary dimension. But the mission as human action aiming to attract or to recruit "outsiders", is secondary to the liturgy. If mission were the

---

203   Ibid., 402.626.
204   *SCar* no. 35.

essence of the liturgy, then liturgy would exist only for anthropological-social purpose. Worship would be reduced to mere social rituals to facilitate the gathering of the people and establishing closer bonds between them. When rituals function as incentives for the construction of social-moral identity, the Church is seen as one of the many profane institutions or political-social organizations commending a particular "Weltanschauung" (worldview).[205] As a consequence, faith in God as a prerequisite for liturgical participation is not necessary. But the Church is not an institution or organization like others, for she is the living organism of Christ, because Christians

> believe that the Eucharist we really receive Christ, the Risen One. And if every member receives the same Christ, then we are all really gathered in this new, risen body as the locus of a new humanity.[206]

Against this anthropological model of liturgy and in referring to the Byzantine liturgy, Ratzinger argued for a non-politico-social dimension of the Christian liturgy. For him, the liturgy does not fulfil a practical purpose, but is meant to lift up human hearts to encounter with the heavenly mystery (*"sursum cor"*). Thus, the main purpose of liturgical celebration is the 'divinization of creation and the surrender of all things to God: God all in all.'[207] In an article, originally published in 1997 in the German journal *Forum Katholische Theologie*, Ratzinger wrote about the non-missionary essence of liturgy:

> The essence of the Byzantine liturgy was ... not missionary. It did not aim to be attractive to outsiders. Rather it was located in the inner dimension of faith ...

---

205 The similarity with Emile Durkheim's psychological sociology is obvious; see James Hitchcock, 'Continuity and disruption in the liturgy: a cultural approach', in *Benedict XVI and the Sacred Liturgy. Proceedings of the First Fota International Liturgy Conference 2008*, edited by Neil J. Roy and Janet E. Rutherfords (Dublin – New York: Four Courts, 2011), 93: 'Participants in self-consciously "modern" liturgy want to hear only echoes of themselves, there it seeming to confirm the claim by another pioneer sociologist, Emile Durkheim, that religion is really the community objectifying and worshipping itself.'
206 *LW*, 137.
207 *SL*, 28; see also 1 *Cor* 15:28.

> The Eucharist does not serve the missionary task of awakening faith. The Eucharist rather is the inner essence of faith. As such it nourishes faith.[208]

As Ratzinger saw it, the Eucharistic liturgy is inseparable from faith. Hence the Eucharist is not directed at the "outsiders"; but rather as a mystery it presupposes faith:

> The Eucharistic liturgy as such is not addressing the unbelievers; but rather as mystery it requires "initiation": Only those, who enter the mystery with their own lives, that is who know Christ not from outside ... can take part in the Eucharist ... The communication with Christ through the sacrament is only open to those who through the communion of faith has arrived at an inner accord and comprehension of Him.[209]

Though the Eucharist is not celebrated with a missionary agenda, it remains the inner wellspring of mission, in that it nourishes faith, the pre-requisite for participation in God's mission. From this liturgical perspective, one should not mistakenly regard the mission exclusively as a human task. Rather, it is primarily the *"missio Dei"* which is the foundation of all human missionary activities. In this context, the Church is missionary because she believes in a God who is himself missionary by sending his Son into the world so that it can have life.[210] If the *"missio Dei"* is the basis, then all human and ecclesial missionary efforts must obediently and creatively correspond with the paths that God has drawn and mapped out.[211] The direction is given by Jesus Christ who serves humanity with his sacrificial death on the cross. In receiving of the Eucharist the faithful become servants of God and humanity. The empathy expressed through faith in Christ demands solidarity with one's fellow humans. The theology of the cross and the Eucharist therefore interpenetrate each other.

208 *JRGS* 11, 398.400.
209 Ibid., 398.
210 *John* 6:51: 'I am the living bread that came down out of heaven; if anyone eats of this bread, he will live forever; and the bread also which I will give for the life of the world is my flesh.'
211 Wolfgang Ratzmann, 'Missionarische Liturgie? Überlegungen zu einem umstrittenen Phänomen', in *Jahrbuch für Liturgik und Hymnologie* 42 (2003), 57.

However, in the Eucharistic celebration, the horrifying nature of the death on the cross is transformed into the gift of *agape*. For Ratzinger and Augustine,[212] the cross is the real expression the humble descent of God into this world in order to bind humanity to himself.[213] This means that through the incarnation God is present in the "little ones", so that service to them is also a service to God. In this, God is all in all. Ratzinger strikingly expresses this interconnection:

> To receive the Eucharist means ... to merge two existences together ... divinity and humanity ... This union has become possible because God in Christ is descended from above. In accepting and identifying fully with the limitations of the human condition the door to the infinite was pushed open through the infinite love of the cross.[214]

Thus, mission always has as its basis in union with Christ, because the mission of the Church is to proclaim and to transmit faith in Christ. The *instrumentum laboris* of the recent synod of bishops in on the new evangelization unmistakably portrays Jesus Christ as the true evangelizer:

> Jesus himself, the Good News of God, was the very first and the greatest evangelizer. He revealed himself as being sent to proclaim the fulfilment of the Gospel of God, foretold in the history of Israel, primarily through the prophets, and promised in Sacred Scripture.[215]

212 Lam Cong Quy, 'Incarnatio', in *AL*, vol. 3, 566: 'Die tiefste Bedeutung der *incarnatio* in Jesus Christus liegt für Augustin in der gnadenhaft-freiwilligen "humilatio" Gottes im Dienste der Erlösung.'
213 *DC*, no.12–13: 'His death on the Cross is the culmination of that turning of God against himself in which he gives himself in order to raise man up and save him. This is love in its most radical form. By contemplating the pierced side of Christ (cf. 19:37), we can understand the starting-point of this Encyclical Letter: "God is love" (*1 Jn* 4:8) ... God's condescension towards us, operates at a radically different level and lifts us to far greater heights than anything that any human mystical elevation could ever accomplish.'
214 *JRGS*, 11, 406.
215 *Synod of Bishops. XIII Ordinary General Assembly. The New Evangelization For the Transmission of the Christian Faith. Instrumentum laboris*, Vatican, 2012, no. 21.

With regard to the goal of this evangelization, the document continues to say: 'For Jesus, the purpose of evangelization is drawing people into his intimate relationship with the Father and the Spirit.'[216]

Mission therefore derives from faith in the incarnate Word.[217] There is a social component because faith has its origin in the promise of salvation given to all by God. It is precisely this divine promise which made Paul the slave to the gentiles:

> Paul, a bond-servant of Christ Jesus, called as an apostle, set apart for the gospel of God, which He promised beforehand through His prophets in the holy Scriptures, concerning His Son, who was born of a descendant of David according to the flesh, who was declared the Son of God with power by the resurrection from the dead, according to the Spirit of holiness, Jesus Christ our Lord, through whom we have received grace and apostleship to bring about the obedience of faith among all the Gentiles for His name's sake, among whom you also are the called of Jesus Christ. (*Rm* 1:1–6)

Moreover, the social dimension of faith derives from the communal nature of God who is self-giving love. Therefore, the mission cannot be separated from faith. However, this faith is nourished by the Eucharist in which the violent death on the cross is transformed into an *agape* to God. And this *agape* is the very source of faith which also calls for a peaceful mission *"ad gentes"*.[218] But the mission, originated from the Eucharistic faith, at the same time exceeds all forms of human union:

> The union with Christ brought about by the Eucharist also brings a newness to our social relations: this sacramental "mysticism" is social in character. Indeed, union with Christ is also a union with all those to whom he gives himself. I cannot possess Christ just for myself; I can belong to him only in union with all those who have become, or who will become, his own.[219]

---

216 Ibid., no. 23.
217 Augustine was the first Father of the Church in the West who emphatically used the together the words *"fides incarnationis"*; see Lam, *Incarnatio*, 566.
218 *JRGS* 8.2, 1049: 'Mission does exist, not in spite of the promise, but *because of* the promise, as its non-violent fashion.'
219 *SCar* no. 89.

From this quotation, it is obvious that the Church's universal mission is based upon the universal quality of the Eucharist in which she partakes through faith and prayers.

6.5 "Dominus Iesus" and the Universality of the Church

And yet, the Pope is aware that in the current relativistic ideological climate the profession of the Church's universality is met with suspicion:

> It is obvious that the concept of truth has become suspect ... it has been much abused. Intolerance and cruelty have occurred in the name of the truth. To that extent people are afraid when someone says, 'This is the truth', or even 'I have the truth'.[220]

Naturally, a Church document such as the declaration of *Dominus Iesus*, which explicitly claims the universality of Christ's truth and his Church, provokes protest from various quarters.[221] In a postmodern culture which lacks a metaphysical concept of truth, it is often affirmed that no one can know or have the truth because the truth is ultimately unattainable. Critics thus saw in the declaration *"Dominus Iesus"* nothing else than the Church's presumption

> to speak about the truth in matters of religion, much less to claim that one knows the truth, the one truth, which does not invalidate the knowledge that others have of truth but gathers the broken pieces together into one.[222]

The declaration is therefore regarded as a further obstacle to ecumenical and interreligious dialogue.

Reacting to this criticism, Ratzinger agreed with the opposition that no one has truth because no one can possess truth. At the same time he also disagreed with the critics. While truth is not a personal

---

220 *LW*, 50.
221 It is often criticised for its lack of sensitivity, for its narrowness and for its polemical nature.
222 *OWC*, 68.

possession because it is not a human invention, it can be found as a gift given by the Holy Spirit. In referring to 1 *Cor* 12:3: 'Therefore I want you to understand that no one speaking by the Spirit of God ever says "Jesus be cursed!", and no one can say "Jesus is Lord" except by the Holy Spirit', Ratzinger states that

> this affirmation is the expression of a truth that we do not invent but merely find, a truth that we can only receive as a gift from him who is himself the light and the interior foundation of all seeing and knowing.[223]

The Christian understanding is that humans are clearly capable of truth. If it were otherwise, human nature would be degraded, because without truth, human life would be meaningless:

> Thinking and living are no longer separable when man confronts the ultimate questions. The decision for God is simultaneously an intellectual and an existential decision – each determines the other reciprocally.[224]

Ratzinger portrayed the unity of thinking and living with the duality of "seeing and knowing". From here he makes the connection to prayer and the *Credo*. Once again, the liturgical dimension of the truth is underlined. As we have said earlier, it is through prayer that the faithful come to know Christ in his 'inner totality and unity'.[225] It is the activity of understanding from within because of the intimacy involved.[226] The disciple sees who Christ truly is! As an example of this seeing

---

[223] Ibid., 55.
[224] Ibid., 67.
[225] *PO*, 13. Prayer would therefore prevent the tendency of contemporary Christology to split the divinity from the humanity of Jesus Christ; see Ilia Delio, 'Christology From Within', in *Heythrop Journal* 48.3 (2007), 438–457.
[226] A similar approach can be detected in the spiritual Christology of Hans Urs von Balthasar; see Mark A. McIntosh, *Christology from within: spirituality and the Incarnation in Hans Urs von Balthasar* (Notre Dame: Notre Dame University, 2000); on the impact of Balthasar's theology on Ratzinger see further the article by Rudolf Vorderholzer, *"Glaubhaft ist nur die Liebe" – "Deus caritas est"*. *Hans Urs von Balthasar als Inspirator der Theologie Joseph Ratzinger/Papst Benedikt XVI*, published on <http://www.balthasar-stiftung.org/images/1_JG_07_Voderholzer_20070607.pdf> (accessed November 4th 2012).

from within, Ratzinger mentioned the confession of St. Peter who had replied to Jesus: 'You are the Christ' (Mk 8:29). Ratzinger interpreted this Petrine profession of faith as a form of prayer: 'The Petrine formula is addressed to Jesus and is a "prayer".'[227] The prayer arises from illumination which gives insight into the mystery of Christ's suffering and humiliation. Of course this initial profession of faith is further reflected upon. In so doing, one would gain a deeper insight into the faith in Jesus Christ. And as a model of knowing, Ratzinger pointed to the Pauline *credo* in which the term "Messiah" is replaced with "Kyrios", and 'thus the identification of Jesus with God, his true divinity.'[228] To Peter's existential act of faith, Paul added an intellectual element. The Word of God is the universal Logos. Both cases, however, emphasise the

> revelatory character of the profession ... in which a kind of knowledge unfolds that is more than human experience and the explanation thereof, that is to say, a new insight, inaccessible to the unaided human mind, but granted to mankind from above, namely, "revelation".[229]

If prayer and the *Credo* are the essential elements of the worship, then the liturgy also possesses a revelatory quality. It urges worshippers to speak and live according to the truth, so that mission is service in accordance with the truth and love. Mission is not presumption; but an intrinsic aspect of faith in Jesus Christ, the *Logos* of God and truth incarnate. Presumption consists in withholding this truth because, without it, religions would

> degenerate into habit ... Religion then ends up in the field of psychology (subjective experience and notions) and sociology (communal directives in ritualized form), but it does not unlock the mystery of man.[230]

It is precisely here that the uniqueness of Christian faith emerges. Uniqueness, however, is not absolutist in the sense that Christian

---

227 *OWC*, 56.
228 Ibid., 57.
229 Ibid., 56.
230 Ibid., 75.

faith suffices in itself and exists only for itself. Such an understanding is clearly incompatible with Christian faith which exists from the other (God), and for the other (humanity). Christian faith consists in an exchange with the other. Uniqueness is neither exclusive nor antisocial. Ratzinger argues, relying on phenomenology, that Christian faith does not fall under a common generic concept of religion of which individual religions are merely the different types. Ratzinger took his definition of religion from Jacques Albert Cuttat[231] who had reasoned that the Christian faith can best be summarized under the paradoxical pair of "separation" and "unity". This paradox emerges from the nature of God. Though God is universal, and Yahweh is the God uniting all peoples, it is this universality that is specific to Judaeo-Christian faith:

> He is not the God of fertility or fertile powers of the earth, but the God of the Universe, who also makes the earth fertile ... And that means finally and above all: He is not only the God of Israel, but the one only God of the world, who elects and discards nations.[232]

In his universality, God is inclusive of all; but at the same time, such inclusivity is the outcome of exclusion. Faith in Jesus Christ is required because God is not an unknown power, but a personal God who can be invoked, and there lies the uniqueness of Christian faith. To call upon the almighty name of God involves logically the renunciation of the gods. Thus, the truth which appears in Jesus Christ is the only criterion of measurement:

> The truth can and must have no other weapon but itself. Someone who believes has found in the truth the pearl for which he is ready to give everything, even himself ... Someone who can both believe and say, "We have found love", has to pass this gift on. He knows that in doing so he does no violence, does not disrupt cultures, but rather sets them free to realize their own great potential.[233]

---

231 *Begegnung der Religion* (Zürich: Johannes Einsiedeln, 1956); see also *JRGS* 8/2, 1037–1038.
232 *JRGS* 8.2, 1039.
233 *OWC*, 71.

Truth sets religions free with the result that Christian faith is not primarily a realm of religion and does not consider as one religion among many:

> The Church Fathers found the seeds of the Word, not in the religions of the world, but rather in philosophy, that is, in the process of critical reason directed against the [pagan] religions, in the history of progressive reason, and not in the history of religion.[234]

The Christian identity therefore evolved from its critical reasoning against religions. This is nowhere clearer than in the rejection of the Roman Imperial cult. At the same time, Ratzinger argues that Christianity is not pure reason for Christian worship is fully intelligible only from its Jewish heritage. And yet, this continuity is also a discontinuity, because the Christian faith also challenges it and all other religions to live according to the claims of the truth.

Thus, Ratzinger rejects a relativistic attitude:

> That is why a Christian can never simply say, "Everyone should just live in the religion that historical circumstances have allotted to him, since all of them are paths to salvation, each in its own way."[235]

This would amount to a sort of indifferentism which

> does not bring people together but instead immures them in their respective tradition concerning the essential questions of humanity and hence separates them from one another.[236]

The abolition of truth in favour of pragmatism is not helpful for an interreligious dialogue. Scepticism and pragmatism can lead to a false concept of tolerance. What is more, indifference to truth can open the doors to pragmatic intolerance. In his assessment of the contemporary culture, the Pope observes a kind of intolerance spreading across the Western culture:

---

234 Ibid., 72.
235 Ibid., 75.
236 Ibid.

> A new intolerance is spreading ... There are well-established standards of thinking that are supposed to be imposed on everyone. These are then announced in terms so-called "negative tolerance", e.g. when people say that for the sake of negative tolerance [i.e. "not offending anyone"] there must be no crucifix in public buildings. With that we are basically experiencing the abolition of tolerance, for it means, after all, that religion, that the Christian faith is no longer allowed to express itself visibly.[237]

Clearly, indifference to truth would ultimately narrow one's own view, and end in ideology. Religion therefore needs truth lest it become destructive. It follows that interreligious dialogue must listen to the *Logos*.[238] When this is so, mission is not obsolete, but contributes to the search for truth.

7. Summary

Ratzinger's ecclesiology is not only an outflow of his spiritual Christology, but also shaped by the Bonaventurian concept of revelation behind his spiritual Christology. This lies in the fact that both his study of Augustine's ecclesiology and of Bonaventure's theology of revelation precede chronologically his Christology.

From Augustine's reaction against the pagan cult and his ecclesiological controversy with the Donatists, which took place at the same time, there emerges his notion of the spiritual-sacramental nature of the Church. The Body of Christ is the true sacrament of unity because it lives by charity. It is love that represents the "motivational synergy" which is foundational for our identification with Christ and the Church. Because of its sacramental nature, the Church is not a mere institution with socio-political ambition. Because of its sacramentality, the Church transcends it social structure, and is truly inclusive.

---

237 *LW*, 52.
238 *JRGS* 8.2, 1134–1135.

Two things follow: firstly, worship is not merely the execution of external rituals, but involves the "cor", the "heart", the symbol of the entire human being. It is the temple where God is worshipped and praised. Worship is therefore inclusive as it demands the whole human being. Secondly, the sacramental nature of the Church also reflects the social structure of the Church. It is social because of its Eucharistic foundation. The Eucharist is the expression of "Dasein für andere" (pro-existence). It is existence for God and for the neighbour. Thus, the Church, in the celebration of the Eucharist, imitates Christ's sacrifice. This is the foundation of the Church's mission. Of course, the participation in the Eucharist is preceded by the act of the incorporation into the Church – which makes membership in the Church conditional. Here, the ethical preparation of the catechumen is completed by sacramental incorporation. But reception of sacraments is based upon faith. Augustine's anti-Manichaean polemics made plain that the faith of the Church is known to all because it is preached and transmitted by the Church. Here lies the evidence of the Church being the work of God who alone is the source of faith. As a consequence, liturgy is the not a human product, for through the liturgical celebration, one encounters God in Christ. This encounter is the foundation of faith flowing from the divine revelation of God sending his Word-Son into the world in *agape*. This "missio Dei" reveals God as love, giving himself for the life of the world. In Christian terms, salvation is uniquely found in Christ, the wisdom and love of God for the world.

Conclusion

The goal of our investigation of Ratzinger's writings is to review the development of his theological thought. This project is legitimate because Ratzinger himself admits that there have been changes and development in his life and thought. In fact, such a change of mind in Ratzinger already occurred during the final phase of the Second Vatican Council. At the Annual Gathering of German Catholics in Bamberg 1966, he voiced his reservations about a mentality which aimed more at pleasing the *"Zeitgeist"* than it was concerned with theological "Tiefgang" (depth). Some commentators considered this move as a first evidence of Ratzinger's transition from a progressive to a conservative theologian who seeks to defend the teaching of the Catholic Church. There is no doubt that the faith of the Church is a guiding principle for Ratzinger's theological reflection. Heim has made this point very clear in his study of Ratzinger's ecclesiology. However, our study shows also that Ratzinger's theological basis is much more complex and comprehensive. In fact, it always sees the Church as recipient of divine revelation, mediated through Jesus Christ. It is Revelation that also defines the nature of the Church. Thus, Ratzinger's theological reflection is always embedded in the Trinitarian foundation of faith: Revelation, Christology and ecclesiology. According to Ratzinger, Revelation in its strictest sense is not a neutral concept. Rather, it is theological because it originates in God. Revelation is an invitation and granting of participation in fullness of divine life. The appropriate answer to Revelation is faith which aims at the participation in the divine communion. Ratzinger reacts here perhaps against the rational tendency within Catholic theology which interprets Revelation as instructive manifestation of divine truths. This tendency towards an intellectual perception of Revelation has always been part of the history of theology; but it was reinforced with the reception of Aristotelism into the medieval theology for which Thomas Aquinas was also co-responsible.¹ In rejecting this theological trend, Ratzinger brought back the communicative-personal dimension of Revelation and thereby opens the door to an ecumenical understanding of Revelation. This achievement was revolutionary because it paves the path to *Dei Verbum* which is considered by many commentators as one of the significant theological document of Vatican II. It is *Dei Verbum* that gives the ecclesiology of Vatican II a healthy outlook. The Church lives from and serves the Word of God. Thus, the Church is truly ecumenical-pastoral. Furthermore, Ratzinger's understanding of Revelation also contributes very much to a healthy understanding of the dynamic relationship between Scriptures and Tradition. They are not sources, but mediations *(ordo cognoscendi)* of the one revelatory reality which is the Word of God which appears in human form. Neither Scriptures is *per se* nor is Tradition without Scriptures sufficient. The faith of the Church is then the key to Scriptural understanding: 'Saint Bonaventure states that without fait there is no key to throw open the sacred text.'²

Seen from this theological perspective, the origin of the Church is therefore also theological. It is God who calls and gathers his people. This call has reached its climax and newness in the incarnation, death and resurrection of Jesus Christ. These Christological events complete on the one side the expectation of Israel because in Jesus Christ the Messiah has appeared and the time is therefore fulfilled. On the other side the fulfilment of God's promise in Jesus Christ is visible in a concrete new reality: the Church. For Ratzinger, the Church is formed not after the resurrection, but is already theologically established at the Last Supper when Jesus institutes the Eucharist whereby he not only completes the hope of Israel, but also inaugurates a new form of communion. In the celebration of the Eucharist, the Church is united in Christ's sacrifice and in this sense, she also participates in the salvation of Jesus Christ. The Church is the theo-

1   *JRGS* 2, 100.
2   *Verbum Domini*, 2010, 54.

logical extension of the *"missio dei"*. The missionary character of the Church is grounded in the Eucharist. For this reason, the Church is not essentially a social institution, although she is by nature socially oriented. The Church is not a political democracy, although freedom is one constituent of hers. In fact, Ratzinger's difficulty with the liberation theology has its root in this social-political reduction of the Church. The Church is constituted by the will of God. She serves God alone! Because of this divine service, the Church cannot act as a political institution which lobbies for a certain policy or ideology. Pope Benedict XVI made this point very clear in Encyclical "Spe salvi".[3] The Church must therefore act universally because God in Jesus Christ has taken up the entire humanity. Thus, the Church is truly Catholic because she exists for the entire humanity. Christology and ecclesiology are therefore inseparable. Christ' presence gives the Church her dual provenance. As Christ's body, she is the instrument and sacrament for the salvation of the world. It is only through the baptism in Christ that the people of Israel (through the faith of Abraham) and the non-believers (pagans) can become members of the body of Christ. Here, the universality of the Church is christologically endorsed. Thus, baptism is the beginning of a life journey with Christ *("vademecum")*. For this reason, the Church is bound to Christ whose words are normative for her existence. In this point, Ratzinger was able to correct the people of God ecclesiology advocated by Koster in the 1950s. Already in his doctoral thesis on Augustine, Ratzinger had argued for a Christological definition of the Church which he repeated in his latter assessment of the ecclesiology of Vatican II. The same foundational argument can also be discovered in the document *"Dominus Iesus"*.

It is obvious that a pure historical-critical exegesis cannot establish this connection between Revelation, Christ and the Church. For

---

3 *Spe salvi*, no. 4: 'Christianity did not bring a message of social revolution like that of the ill-fated Spartacus, whose struggle led to so much bloodshed. Jesus was not Spartacus, he was not engaged in a fight for political liberation like Barabbas or Bar- Kochba.'

Ratzinger, only a spiritual Christology can fulfil this task. It was in the year 1981 that he became aware of the strength of this type of Christology, although certain seeds were planted already in his earlier writings. But it was because of the crisis caused by historical-criticism that the spiritual Christology emerged gradually. This process reaches its completion in the three volumes on *Jesus of Nazareth*. Ratzinger was not the first to have discovered this idea. Already Ambrose, Augustine in the West and Origen in the East have practiced an allegorical exegesis which saw in Christ, the *Logos* its spiritual centre. However, Ratzinger's theological creativity lies in his capability to apply it to our time thereby adding to it a theological-spiritual freshness which the early Fathers could not have achieved in their time. Furthermore, the discovery of the spiritual Christology has also a retrospective consequence for the interpretation of Vatican II. The Constitution *Lumen Gentium* is now interpreted form the background of communion which is facilitated by Christ. The communion ecclesiology was clearly a theological development out of spiritual Christology. This communion ecclesiology, which emerged from the extraordinary Synod in 1985 as its main theological synthesis, emphasises both the vertical and horizontal dimensions of the Church. On the one side, it highlights the growth of the Church from within because of God's presence in her. On the other side, it transcends the notion of community *(Gemeinde)* as it underscores the fellowship of humankind which merges into the fellowship with the One and Triune God. Commenting on 1 *John* 1:3: 'That which we have seen and heard we proclaim also to you, so that you also may have fellowship with us; and our fellowship is with the Father and with his Son Jesus Christ. And we are writing this that our joy may be complete', Ratzinger wrote in 2001:

> Here the starting point of *communio* is brought to the fore: the encounter with the Son of God, Jesus Christ, who comes to men and women through the Church's proclamation. So there arises communion among human beings, which in turn is based on *communio* with the Triune God. We have access to communion with God through the realization of the communion of God with man which is Christ in person; the encounter with Christ creates communion with him and thus with

the Father in the Holy Spirit; and from this point unites human beings with one another.[4]

The hinge between the Church and Revelation is therefore a spiritual Christology. It respects the historical continuity between the Old Testament and the New Testament. At the same time it also confirms the discontinuity because the Church is now seen as the sole recipient of the divine revelation. For this reason, the faith tradition of the Church goes also beyond the contents of the Old Testament. This is the result of the continuing revelation.

Ratzinger's studies of Augustine's ecclesiology and Bonaventure's concept of revelation were not only crucial for Ratzinger's later theological reflection on the Church. While he observed in the Augustinian ecclesiology a continuity in discontinuity with the people of God, which Augustine used to designate Israel only, the dynamic characteristic of the Church comes fully to the fore in his study of Bonaventure's concept of Revelation. This dynamism also determined Ratzinger's hermeneutics of Vatican II. In an address to the collaborators of the Roman Curia on December 22nd 2005 the Pope, in opposing to a hermeneutic of discontinuity, proposed a 'hermeneutic of reform' which clearly echoes the mutual relationship between change and constancy. In this speech the Pope spoke of a commitment,

> to expressing a specific truth in a new way demands new thinking on this truth and a new and vital relationship with it; it is also clear that new words can only develop if they come from an informed understanding of the truth expressed, and on the other hand, that a reflection on faith also requires that this faith be lived.[5]

For Ratzinger, this specific truth does not encompass the Church alone, but must also include Revelation and Christology. They are theological correlates and cannot be taken in separation. The three express the totality of this truth. The faith in God, who lovingly com-

---

4 'The Ecclesiology of the Constitution on the Church, Vatican II, *Lumen Gentium*', in *Osservatore Romano* (2001) September 19th, 5.
5 <http://www.vatican.va/holy_father/benedict_xvi/speeches/2005/december/documents/hf_ben_xvi_spe_20051222_roman-curia_en.html>.

municates himself to us, is lived in the Church which represents the Body of Christ. This totality of truth is the paradigm for the interpretation of Ratzinger's writings. This totality of truth is the paradigm for the interpretation of Ratzinger's writings. Indeed, the "canonical" exegesis also applies here to the study of Ratzinger's writings. This is true even for those passages in which one believes that Ratzinger contradicts himself. Isolating them from the whole, these passages appear indeed to reverse earlier positions. But when evaluating them from the whole truth, they may in fact highlight further insights of which Ratzinger possibly could not have previously seen because of epistemological limitations. As life progresses earlier positions manifest their limitations. Within a new context, they require revision and perhaps further adaptation. In matter of truth which is pre-given, the process of adaption is not to re-invent it, but to renew or to develop our positions in conformity with it. It is all about a spiritual growth into the truth.

Regarding the development of his theological thought, Joseph Ratzinger has himself said that he has not – consciously or unconsciously – changed the fundamentals of his theological reflection, and that any observed "changes" are more in the nature of different nuances of his thought that have developed over time. Possibly, therefore, we should accept as an initial premise that he has really meant what he said.

Selective Bibliography

A. Documents of the Church

The Christian Faith in the Doctrinal Documents of the Catholic Church, edited by Joseph Neuner – Jacques Dupuis (Dublin: Mercier, 1973).
Decrees of the Ecumenical Councils, vol. 2, edited by Norman Tanner (London: Scheed & Ward, 1990).
Enchiridion symbolorum definitionum et declarationum de rebus fidei et morum – Kompendium der Glaubensbekenntnisse und kirchlichen Lehrentscheidungen, Lat.-Dt., edited by Peter Hünermann (Freiburg: Herder, 1991).
Austin Flannery (ed.), *Vatican Council II, More Postconciliar Documents*, revised ed. (Northport, New York: Costello, 1998).
Acta Apostolicae Sedis, vol. XCVIII (Vatican: Libreria Editrice Vaticana, 2006).

B. Works by Joseph Ratzinger / Pope Benedict XVI

German

Joseph Ratzinger Gesammelte Schriften, (Freiburg: Herder, 2009–2011).
—, vol. 1: Volk und Haus Gottes in Augustins Lehre von der Kirche Die Dissertation und weitere Studien zu Augustinus und zur Theologie der Kirchenväter, 2011.
—, vol. 2: Offenbarungsverständnis und Geschichtstheologie Bonaventuras Habilitationsschrift und Bonaventura-Studien, 2009.
—, vol. 8/1-2: Kirche – Zeichen unter den Völkern Schriften zur Ekklesiologie und Ökumene, 2010.
—, vol. 11: Theologie der Liturgie. Die sakramentale Begründung christlicher Existenz, 2010.
Volk und Haus Gottes in Augustins Lehre von der Kirche (München: Karl Zink, 1954).
Einsicht und Glaube. Gottlieb Söhngen zum 70. Geburtstag am 21. Mai 1962, edited by Joseph Ratzinger – Heinrich Fries (Freiburg: Herder, 1962).
'Kardinal Frings und das II. Vatikanische Konzil', in *Kardinal Frings: Leben und Werk*, edited by D. Froitzheim (Cologne: Bachem, 1980), 191–205.
'Kirche als Tempel des Heiligen Geistes', in *Vom Wiederauffinden der Mitte – Grundorientierungen: Texte aus vier Jahrzehnten*, edited by Stephan O. Horn, Vinzenz Pfnür and others (Freiburg: Herder, 1997), 148–157.
Unterwegs zu Jesus Christus (Augsburg: Sankt Ulrich, 2005).

Licht der Welt. Der Papst, die Kirche und die Zeichen der Zeit. Ein Gespräch mit Peter Seewald (Freiburg: Herder, 2011).

English

Revelation and Tradition, edited by Karl Rahner and Joseph Ratzinger (New York: Herder and Herder, 1966).
Introduction to Christianity (London: Burns & Oates, 1968).
'Dogmatic Constitution on Divine Revelation', in *Commentary on the Documents of Vatican II*, edited by Herbert Vorgrimler, vol. 3 (London: Burns & Oates, 1969).
The Theology of history in St. Bonaventure, translated by Zachary Hayes (Chicago: Franciscan Herald, 1971).
The God of Jesus Christ. Meditations on God in the Trinity (Chicago: Franciscan Herald, 1979).
The Ratzinger Report: An Exclusive Interview of the State of the Church, by Joseph Ratzinger and Vittorino Messori (San Francisco: Ignatius, 1985).
The Pierced One. An Approach to a Spiritual Christology (San Francisco: Ignatius, 1986).
Principles of Catholic Theology: Building Stones for a Fundamental (San Francisco: Ignatius, 1987).
To Look on Christ. Exercises in Faith, Hope, and Love (Slough: St. Pauls, 1991).
The Nature and Mission of Theology. Approaches to Understanding its Role in the Light of the Present Controversy (San Francisco: Ignatius, 1995).
Milestones. Memoirs 1927–1977 (San Francisco: Ignatius, 1997).
Salt of the Earth: Christianity and the Catholic Church at the end of the Millennium. An Interview with Peter Seewald, (San Francisco: 1997).
Spirit of Liturgy, translated by John Saward, (San Francisco: Ignatius, 2000).
Dominus Iesus, 2000. <http://www.vatican.va/roman_curia/congregations/cfaith/documents/rc_con_cfaith_doc_20000806_dominus-iesus_en.html>.
God and the World. Believing and Living in Our Time. A Conversation with Peter Seewald (San Francisco: Ignatius, 2002).
God is near us (San Francisco: Ignatius, 2003).
The End of Time? The Provocation of Talking about God: Proceedings of a Meeting of Joseph Cardinal Ratzinger, Johann Baptist Metz, Jürgen Moltmann, and Eveline Goodman-Thau in Ahaus, edited by Tiemo Rainer Peters and Claus Urban (Mahwah, N.J.: Paulist, 2004).
On the Way to Jesus Christ (San Francisco: Ignatius, 2004).
Pilgrim Fellowship of Faith, edited by Stephan O. Horn and Vinzenz Pfnür (San Francisco: Ignatius, 2005).
Deus Caritas est, 2005
Spe salvi, 2007

Caritas in veritate, 2009; <http://www.vatican.va/holy_father/benedict_xvi/encyclicals/index_en.htm>.
'The Power and the Grace. The presentation of the book by 30Days on the actuality of Saint Augustine, with Cardinal Joseph Ratzinger, in the "Sala del Cenacolo" of the Chamber of Deputies', in *30Days* (2005) 5; see <http://www.30giorni.it/articoli_id_8926_l3.htm>.
Jürgen Habermas – Joseph Ratzinger, *Dialectics of Secularization. One Reason and Religion*, edited with a Foreword by Florian Schuller (San Francisco: Ignatius Press, 2006).
A New Song for the Lord (New York: Crossroad, 2006).
Fathers of the Church. From Clement of Rome to Augustine (San Francisco: Ignatius, 2008).
Theological Highlights of Vatican II (New York: Paulist, 2009).
Jesus of Nazareth, vol. 1: From the Baptism in the Jordan to the Transfiguration (New York: Doubleday, 2007).
'Cardinal's Frings's Speeches During the Second Vatican Council: Some Reflections Apropos of Muggeridge's The Desolate City', in *Pope Benedict XVI – Joseph Ratzinger in Communio*, vol. 1: The Unity of the Church, Introduction by David L. Schindler, translated by Peter Verhalen (Grand Rapids, Michigan: Eerdmans, 2010).
'The Ecclesiology of the Second Vatican Council', in *Pope Benedict XVI – Joseph Ratzinger in Communio*, vol. 1: The Unity of the Church, Introduction by David L. Schindler, translated by Peter Verhalen (Grand Rapids, Michigan: Eerdmans, 2010).
Light of the World: the Pope, the Church, and the Signs of the Times / Pope Benedict XVI: A Conversation with Peter Seewald (San Francisco: Ignatius, 2010).
Verbum Domini. The Word of God in the Life and Mission of the Church. Post-synodal apostolic exhortation (Strathfield: St. Pauls, 2010).
Jesus of Nazareth, vol. 2: Holy Week: From the Entrance into Jerusalem to the Resurrection (San Francisco: Ignatius, 2011).
Jesus of Nazareth, vol. 3: The Infancy Narratives (New York: Image, 2012).

C. Secondary Literature

Hans Albert, 'Joseph Ratzingers Apologie des Christentums: Bibeldeutung auf der Basis einer spiritualistischen Metaphysik', in *Zeitschrift für Religions- und Geistesgeschichte* 59.1 (2007), 14–35.
John Allen, *Cardinal Ratzinger: The Vatican Enforcer of Faith* (London: Continuum, 2005).
Dale C. Allison, *Constructing Jesus: Memory, Imagination and History* (Grand Rapids: Baker Academic, 2010).

Karen Armstrong, *The Case For God* (New York: Anchor, 2010).
Jan Assmann, *Religion and Cultural Memory* (Stanford: Stanford University, 2000).
Grzegorz Bachanek, 'St. Thomas Aquinas in the Reflections of J. Ratzinger (Benedict XVI)', in *Logos-Vilnius* (2010) 65, 29–40.
John F. Baldovin, *Reforming the Liturgy. A Response to the Critics* (Collegeville/Minn.: Liturgical Press, 2008).
Umberto Betti, *La trasmissione della divina rivelazione* (Roma: Pont. Athenaeum Antonianum, 1985).
Hubert Blaumeister, *Martin Luthers Kreuzestheologie. Schüssel zu seiner Deutung von Mensch und Wirklichkeit. Eine Untersuchung anhand der Operationes in Psalmos (1519–1521)*, (Paderborn: Bonifatius, 1995).
Hans Boersma, 'History and Faith in Pope's Benedict XVI *Jesus of Nazareth*', in *Nova et Vetera* 10.4 (2012), 985–991.
Lieven Boeve, 'Revelation, Scripture and Tradition: Lessons from Vatican II Constitution *Dei verbum* for Contemporary Theology', in *International Journal of Systematic Theology* 13 (2011) 3, 416–433.
—, '"La vraie reception de Vatican II n'a pas encore commence". Joseph Ratzinger, Révelation et autorité de Vatican II', in *Ephmerides Theologicae Lovaniensis* 85.4 (2009), 305–339.
Walter Brueggemann, *Great Prayers of the Old Testament* (Louisville: Westminster John Knox, 2008).
Emil Brunner, *Truth as Encounter* (London: SCM, 1964).
Riccardo Burigana, *La biblia nel concilio. La redazione della costituizione "Dei verbum" del Vaticano II* (Bologna: Il Mulino, 1998).
Brendan Cahill, *The Renewal of Revelation Theology (1960–1962). The Development and Responses to the Fourth Chapter of the Preparatory Schema De deposito Fidei* (Roma: Gregorian University, 1999).
Christopher S. Celenza, 'Marsilio Ficino', in *The Stanford Encyclopedia of Philosophy (Summer 2011 Edition)*, Edward N. Zalta (ed.), URL = <http://plato.stanford.edu/archives/sum2011/entries/ficino/>.
Denis Crouan, *The History And The Future Of The Roman Liturgy* (San Francisco: Ignatius, 2005).
Christopher M. Cullen, *Bonaventure* (Oxford: Oxford Scholarship online, 2007).
Geoff Deegan, 'On the Goodness of Being According to Thomas Aquinas', in *Universitas* 12 (2005) retrieved from the website of the Centre for Thomistic Studies Australia <http://www.cts.org.au/articles.htm on Dec 7th 2011>.
Ludwig Deimel, *Leib Christi. Sinn und Grenzen einer Deutung des innerkirchlichen Lebens* (Freiburg i. Breisgau: Herder, 1940).
Ilia Delio, *Simply Bonaventure. An Introduction to His Life, Thought, and Writings* (New York: New City, 2006).
—, 'Bonaventure's Metaphysics of Good', in *Theological Studies* 60.2 (1999), 228–246.

Pierpaolo Donati, *Relational Sociology. A New Paradigm for Social Sciences* (New York: Routledge, 2011).
John P. Donnelly, *Calvinism and Scholasticism in Vermigli's Doctrine of Man and Grace* (Leiden: Brill, 1976).
Brett Doyle, 'Ratzinger on Prayer', in *Australian Catholic Record* 86.3 (2009), 328–346.
Avery Dulles, *Revelation Theology. A History* (New York: Herder and Herder, 1969).
James D. G. Dunn, *A New Perspective on Jesus. What the Quest for the Historical Jesus Missed* (Grand Rapids: Baker Academic, 2005).
André Feuillet, *The Priesthood of Christ and His Ministers* (New York: Doubleday, 1975).
Michael Fiedrowicz, *Psalmus vox totius Christi. Studien zu Augustins "Enarrationes in Psalmos"* (Freiburg: Herder, 1997).
Heinrich Fries, *Revelation* (New York: Herder and Herder, 1969).
Emery De Gáal, *The Theology of Pope Benedict XVI. The Christocentric Shift* (New York: Palgrave Macmillan, 2010).
Robert Gascoigne, *The Church and Secularity. Two Stories of Liberal Society* (Washington D. C.: Georgetown University Press, 2009).
Josef R. Geiselmann, *The Meaning of Tradition* (*Questiones disputate* 15, London: Burns & Oates, 1966).
—, 'Das Konzil von Trient über das Verhältnis der Heiligen Schriften und der nicht geschriebenen Traditionen', in *Die mündliche Überlieferung. Beiträge zum Begriff der Tradition*, edited by Michael Schmaus (Munich, 1957), 123–206.
Moshe Greenberg, *Biblical Prose as Prayer as a Window to the Popular Religion of Ancient Israel* (Berkeley: University of California, 1983).
Anselm J. Gribbin, *Pope Benedict XVI and the Liturgy. Understanding recent liturgical developments* (Herefordshire: Gracewing, 2011).
Romano Guardini, *Vom Sinn der Kirche. Fünf Vorträge* (Mainz: Matthias Grünewald, 1923).
—, *The Spirit of the Liturgy* (New York: Crossroad, 1998).
Maurice Halbwachs, *On Collective Memory*, edited, translated and with an Introduction by Lewis A. Coser (Chicago: Chicago University, 1992).
Adolf von Harnack, *History of Dogma*, trans. by Neil Buchanan (New York: Dover, 1961).
Maximilian H. Heim, *Joseph Ratzinger – Kirchliche Existenz und existentielle Theologie unter dem Einspruch von Lumen Gentium* (Frankfurt: Peter Lang, 2005).
Martin Hengel, *The Four Gospels and One Gospel of Jesus Christ. An Investigation of the Collection and Origin of the Canonical Gospels* (London: SCM Press, 2010).
George Heyman, *The Power of Sacrifice: Roman and Christian Discourses in Conflict* (Washington D.C: Catholic University of America, 2007).
Fritz Hoffmann, *Der Kirchenbegriff des hl. Augustinus in seinen Grundlagen und seiner Entwicklung* (München, 1933).

Kurt Hübner, *Das Christentum im Wettstreit der Religionen* (Tübingen, 2003).
Collin Humphreys, *The Mystery of the Last Supper: Reconstructing the Final Days of Jesus* (Cambridge: Cambridge University, 2011).
Joachim Jeremias, *Abba: The Prayers of Jesus* (London: SCM, 1967).
Ernst Käsemann, *Das wandernde Gottesvolk. Eine Untersuchung zum Hebräerbrief* (Göttigen: Vandenhoeck & Ruprecht, 1939).
Alan Kirk – Thomas Thatcher (eds.), *Memory, Tradition, and Text. Uses of the Past in Early Christianity* (Atlanta: Society of Biblical Literature, 2005).
Joseph A. Komonchack, 'A Postmodern Augustinian Thomism?' in *Augustine and Postmodern Thought: A New Alliance against Modernity?*, edited by Lieven Boeve, Matthijs Lamberigts, and Martin Wisse (Bibliotheca Ephemeridum Theologicarum Lovaniensium, 219; Leuven: Peeters, 2009), 123–146.
Mannes Dominikus Koster, *Ekklesiologie im Werden* (Paderborn: Schöningh, 1940).
Robert Krieg, 'Cardinal Ratzinger, Max Scheler and Christology', in *Irish Theological Quarterly* 47.3 (1980), 205–219.
Joseph Lam Cong Quy, *Theologische Verwandtschaft: Augustinus von Hippo and Joseph Ratzinger / Papst Benedikt XVI* (Würzburg: Echter Verlag, 2009).
Alfred Läpple, *Benedikt XVI. Und seine Wurzeln. Was sein Leben und seinen Glauben prägte* (Augsburg: Pustet, 2006).
Rene Latourelle, *Theology of Revelation, including a Commentary on the Constitution "dei verbum" of Vatican II* (New York: Alba House, 1966).
Jorg Lauster, 'Marsilio Ficino as Christian Thinker', in *Marsilio Ficino: His Theology, His Philosophy, His Legacy*, edited by Michael J.B. Allen, Valery Rees, Martin Davies (Leiden: Brill, 2001).
Gerardus van der Leeuw, *Phänomenologie der Religion*, 2nd edition (Tübingen: 1956).
Claudio Leonardi, 'Christ', in *Encyclopedia of the Middle Ages*, vol. 2, edited by A. Vauchez in association with R.B. Dobson (Cambridge: James Clark & Co, 2000).
Henri de Lubac, *Catholicism. A Study of Dogma in Relation to the Corporate Destiny of Mankind*, translated by Lancelot C. Sheppard (London: Burns, Oates & Washbourne, 1950).
Jesús Martínez Gordo, 'The Christology of J. Ratzinger – Benedict XVI in the Light of His Biography', in *Edition Cristianisme y Justicía*, 1–31; see <www.fespinal.com> (accessed on 14 April 2012).
Mark A. McIntosh, *Christology From Within: Spirituality and the Incarnation in Hans Urs von Balthasar* (Notre Dame: Notre Dame University, 2000).
Peter J. Meier, *A Marginal Jew: Rethinking the Historical Jesus*, vol. 1 (New York: Doubleday, 1991).
Daniel L. Migliore, *Faith Seeking Understanding* (Grand Rapids, Mich.: Eerdman, 2004).
John Montag, 'Revelation: The False Legacy of Suárez', in J. Milbank, C. Pickstock and G. Ward (eds.), *Radical Orthodoxy* (London: Routledge, 1999).

Piotr Napiwodzki, *Eine Ekklesiologie im Werden. Mannes Dominikus Koster und sein Beitrag zum Verständnis der Kirche*, PhD Dissertation University of Fribourg / Switzerland, 2005.

Antonio Negri – Michael Hardt, *Empire* (Boston / MA: Harvard University, 2000).

Gerald O'Collins, *Jesus Our Redeemer. A Christian Approach to Salvation* (Oxford: Oxford University, 2007).

Neil Ormerod, 'Vatican II – Continuity or Discontinuity? Toward an Ontology of Meaning', in *Theological Studies* 71 (2010), 609–636.

Karl Rahner, 'The Development of Dogma', in *Theological Investigations*, vol. 1 (New York: Herder and Herder, 1961).

—, 'De Trinitate', in Id., *Schriften zur Theologie*, vol. 4 (Freiburg: Herder, 1964).

—, 'Observation on the Concept of Revelation', in Karl Rahner – Joseph Ratzinger, *Revelation and Tradition* (New York: Herder and Herder, 1968).

Marius Reiser, *Bibelkritik und Auslegung der Heiligen Schrift: Beiträge zur Geschichte der biblischen Exegese und Hermeneutik* (Tübingen: Mohr Siebeck, 2007).

Herman Reuter, *Augustinische Studien* (Gotha, 1887).

Gerhard Ring, 'Initium fidei', in *Augustinus-Lexikon*, edited by Cornelius Mayer, vol. 3, fasc. 3/4 (Basel: Schwabe, 2006), 205–210.

Tracey Rowland, *Ratzinger's Faith. The Theology of Pope Benedict XVI* (Oxford: University, 2008).

Neil J. Roy and Janet E. Rutherfords (eds), *Benedict XVI and the Sacred Liturgy. Proceedings of the First Fota International Liturgy Conference 2008* (Dublin – New York: Four Courts, 2011).

Markus Rutsche, *Die Relationalität Gottes bei Martin Buber und Joseph Ratzinger* (München: Grin, 2007).

Pablo B. Sarto, 'Joseph Ratzinger, pertito del Concilio Vaticano II (1962–1965)', in *Anuario de Historia de la Iglesia* 15 (2006) 43–66.

Karim Schelkens, *Catholic Theology on the Eve of Second Vatican Council (1958–1962). A Redaction History of the Schema de Fontibus Revelationis* (Leiden / Boston: Brill, 2010).

Marianne Schlosser – Franz-Xaver Heibl (eds.), *Gegenwart der Offenbarung. Zu den Bonaventura-Forschungen Joseph Ratzingers* (Regensburg: Friedrich Pustet, 2011).

Michael Schmaus, *Die psychologische Trinitätslehre des hl. Augustinus* (Tübingen, 1927).

—, *Dogma*, vol. 1: God in Revelation (New York: Sheed and Ward, 1968).

Mark Smith, *The Memoirs of God: History, Memory and the Experience of the Divine in Ancient Israel* (Minneapolis: Fortress, 2004).

Gottlieb Söhngen, *Kardinal Newman. Sein Gottesgedanke und seine Denkergestalt*, (Bonn: G. Schwippert, 1946).

—, *Philosophische Einführung in die Theologie*, (München, 1955).

Theodor Steinbüchel, *Der Umbruch des Denkens. Die Frage nach der christlichen Existenz erläutert an Ferdinand Ebners Menschdeutung* (Darmstadt: Wissenschaftliche Buchgesellschaft, 1966).

Basil Studer, *Augustinus: De Trinitate. Eine Einführung* (Paderborn: Ferdinand Schöningh, 2005).

Sebastian Thier, *Kirche bei Pelagius* (Göttigen: Vandenhoeck, 1999).

Terrence W. Tilley, *History, Theology and Faith: Dissolving the Modern Problematic* (New York: Orbis, 2004).

Florian Trenner (ed.), *Joseph Ratzinger – Benedickt XVI* (Vatican: Libreria Editrice Vaticana, 2007).

Norbert Trippen, *Josef Kardinal Frings (1877–1978)* (Paderborn: Schöningh, 2005).

Hansjürgen Verweyen, *Joseph Ratzinger – Benedikt XVI. Die Entwicklung seines Denkens* (Darmstadt: Primus, 2007).

—, *Ein unbekannter Ratzinger. Die Habilitationsschrift von 1955 als Schlüssel zu seiner Theologie* (Regensburg: Friedrich Pustet, 2010).

Rudolf Vorderholzer (ed.), *Der Logos-gemäße Gottesdienst – Theologie der Liturgie bei Joseph Ratzinger* (Regensburg: Pustet, 2009).

Thomas Weiler, *Volk Gottes – Leib Christ. Die Ekklesiologie Joseph Ratzinger und ihr Einfluß auf das Zweite Vatikanische Konzil* (Mainz: Grünwald, 1997).

Jared Wicks, 'Dei Verbum Developping: Vatican II's Revelation Doctrine 1963–1964', in *The Convergence of Theology. A Festschrift Honoring Gerald O'Collins*, edited by Daniel Kendall and Stephen T. Davis (New York: Paulist Press, 2001), 109–125.

—, 'Pieter Smulders and Dei Verbum', in *Gregorianum* 82 (2001), 241–297.

—, 'Six texts by Prof. Joseph Ratzinger as *peritus* before and during Vatican Council II', in *Gregorianum* 89.2 (2008), 233–311.

—, 'Vatican II on Revelation – From Behind The Scenes', in *Theological Studies* 71 (2010), 637–650.

Wolfgang Wieland, *Offenbarung bei Augustinus* (Mainz: Grünewald, 1978).

Index of Names

Albert, H. 92, 110
Allen, J. 165
Allison, D.C. 93
Aquinas, T. 20, 27, 30–34, 48, 155, 214
Aristotle 48
Armstrong, K. 101
Assmann, J. 93
Augustine of Hippo 11, 15, 18, 34, 38–42, 66–67, 123–126, 147–193, 211
Bachanek, G. 31
Baldovin, J. 194
Balthasar, H.U. von 206
Barth, K. 26, 51
Bellarmine, R. 161
Betti, U. 55
Blaumeister, H. 26, 47
Boersma, H. 136
Boeve, L. 78–87, 133
Bonaventure 9, 17, 19–20, 23–49, 143, 210, 214
Brueggemann, W. 115, 119, 144
Brunner, E. 26–27, 51, 86
Buber, M. 105, 165
Burigana, R. 55
Cahill, B. 133
Celenza, C.S. 40
Chardin de, T. 186
Cole, K. 171
Crouan, D. 195
Cuttat, J.A. 208
Deegan, G. 38
Deimel, L. 162–163
Delio, I. 34–41, 206
Donati, P. 165
Donelly, J.P. 32
Doyle, B. 116

Dulles, A. 23, 26, 77
Dunn, J.D.G. 70, 86, 93
Ebner, F. 105
Ferrari, L. 171
Ficino, M. 40
Fiedrowicz, M. 198
Fiore, J. of 47–49
Francis of Assisi 20, 45–57
Fries, H. 26
Frings, J. 9, 56–58, 63, 148–149
Gaál de, E. 16, 90
Gascoigne, R. 48
Geiselmann, J. 60–62
Gordo, J.M. 96
Greenberg, M. 115
Greshake, G. 106
Gribbin, A. 16, 126, 194
Guardini, R. 160–161, 196, 196
Gy, P.-M. 194
Hahn, S. 95–100
Halbwachs, M. 93–94
Harnack, A. von 28
Hegel, F. 105
Heim, M. 15, 54, 81, 83, 112
Hengel, M. 60, 70, 95, 110
Heyman, G. 182
Hitchcock, J. 201
Hoffmann, F. 159–160
Honorius II 46
Hoping, H. 15
Horner, F. 165
Husserl, E. 164
Humphreys, C. 189
Hübner, K. 79
Jeremias, J. 117
John XXIII 63, 147

Kasper, W. 109
Käsemann, E. 163
Koch, K. 15
Komonchack, J. A. 31, 74
Koster, M. 162–163, 215
Krieg, R. 92, 109
Lam, J. 11–12, 15, 31, 95, 191, 203–204
Lancel, S. 174
Lauster, J. 40–41
Läpple, A. 31–32, 73, 168
Lebeck, M. 165
Leeuw, G. v. de 99
Leo the Great 11
Leo XIII 27, 161
Leonardi, C. 46
Lubac de, M. 169
Luther, M. 25–26, 46, 187
Mackay, H. 84
Marga, A. 15
McIntosh, M. A. 206
Meier, J. 174
Migliore, D. 23
Milbank, J. 73–74
Montag, J. 74
Murphy, J. 16
Musser, F. 110
Müller, G. L. 10, 17
Napiwodzki, P. 162
Negri, A. 101
Newman, H. 158
Nichols, A. 16
O'Collins, G. 42–43, 100–101
Oestreich, B. 163
Ormerod, N. 71
Paul VI 64
Philips, G. 147–148
Pius IX 147
Pius XII 161

Rahner, K. 9, 36, 42, 54, 69, 75–76, 92, 133
Ratzmann, W. 202
Reiser, M. 136
Reuter, H. 159–160
Ring, G. 77
Rowland, T. 16, 31–32, 73–73
Rutsche, M. 105
Sarto, P. 16, 54
Schaller, C. 15
Scheler, M. 109–110
Schelkens, K. 55–58
Schlosser, M. 15, 111
Schmaus, M. 31–34, 39, 51
Siebenrock, R. 90
Smith, M. 93
Smulders, P. 55
Söhngen, G. 19, 31–35, 51, 57, 86–87, 154–158, 160, 163, 167–168
Stein, E. 164–165
Steinbüchel, T. 35
Studer, B. 42
Stuhlmacher, P. 110
Suárez, F. 31–32
Tanner, N. 65–67, 86
Their, S. 171
Tilley, T. 42
Trenner, F. 73
Trippen, N. 56
Ugochukwu, B. 188
Vann, G. 161
Verweyen, H. 15, 73, 106, 132, 158, 167
Vorderholzer, R. 15, 148, 206
Wainwright, G. 143
Weiler, T. 54, 73
Wicks, J. 54–59, 61–64, 133
Wieland, W. 76
William, T. D. 105
Wilmsen, A. 30